essential plants for
SMALL GARDENS

essential plants for
SMALL GARDENS

SUE FISHER

CASSELL ILLUSTRATED

First published in paperback in 2003 by Cassell Illustrated
A Member of the Octopus Publishing Group Ltd
2-4 Heron Quays
London
E14 4JP

Distributed in the United States of America by
Sterling Publishing Co., Inc.,
387 Park Avenue South, New York, NY 10016-8810

A CIP catalogue record for this book is available from the British Library.

1 84403 033 4

Colour Separation by Tenon & Polert Colour Scanning Ltd.
Printed in Spain by Bookprint S.L., Barcelona

Contents

Introduction

G ARDENING IN A SMALL SPACE is a modern-day challenge. A hundred or so years ago a plot of several acres was considered 'small', but nowadays the tiniest gardens can be little more than the size of the tablecloths which would have graced the house accompanying such a plot.

Paradoxically, today's gardeners have access to a far greater range of plants than our great-grandparents' generation could ever have dreamed of. Faced with a vast selection of plants at the garden centre or in a pile of catalogues, choosing the right handful to grace your small site can appear a near-impossible challenge. But, having spent many years getting the proverbial quart out of the pint pot that is my own small garden, as well as helping others to do the same, I can assure you that the tiniest plot can look magnificent and provide reward and satisfaction out of all proportion to its size.

Where space is limited, choosing the right plants is all-important. Apart from personal choice and experience of the plants detailed in this book, two main factors have influenced my selection. The first, and most important, is eventual size, for there are few things more disheartening than wageing constant battle with

Small-space gardens need plants that are hard-working and provide long-lasting interest, often from foliage. Flowers are very much in the minority here.

a plant that is grimly determined to outgrow its allotted portion of ground. Second is ornamental value, for when the number of plants in a garden has to be limited, those select few must really sing for their supper and look good for the maximum possible time.

This book contains lots of information for both new and experienced gardeners. Those who are taking on a garden for the first time will find guidance on how to get to grips with your site in the first instance and on planning your planting, plus practical information on ground preparation, weeding, planting and aftercare. More experienced gardeners can go straight to the sections on how to get the most from your garden in terms of planting styles, border layout, plant combinations and colour schemes. A host of useful tips and handy plant lists are also provided throughout the book.

All-year interest tends to be of supreme importance, as most small gardens are on full view all year round – choosing plants for this purpose has been made straightforward by means of the Plant Directory (see page 126). Each group of plants has been subdivided with ease of choice in mind: for example, the major plant groups such as shrubs and perennials are divided according to their flowering season or foliage interest, while climbers are listed under flowering or foliage varieties. So, to achieve a

varied mix of plants that will look good over a long period of time, simply choose a few from each section.

Some groups of plants are not included at all, due to the fact that virtually all are suitable for a small garden and so there is no need to be selective. On this basis, alpines and herbs are the chief absentees, while seasonal plants like annuals, tender perennials and bulbs are given just a brief mention for the same reason.

Finally, a brief word on plant names. Where there is one, I have used the common name for a plant (except in plant lists), although these are accompanied by their botanical (Latin) titles. These names can be off-putting, but they are immensely useful as a universal way of tracking down and identifying the particular plants that are required, from garden centres and growers anywhere in the world. Common names are pretty and easy to remember, but they can vary from one region to another and cause immense confusion.

But, regardless of whether the plants featured in this book have simple names or tongue-twisting Latin tags, they are here because of their excellence for a small space. So, whether you have a city courtyard, a suburban plot or a pocket-handkerchief patch in the country, there will be plenty of plants here to grace and beautify your garden the whole year round.

Walls festooned with climbers and wide borders ensure maximum planting space, turning an overlooked town garden into a lush oasis.

Assessing your Site

TAKING ON A NEW GARDEN is an exciting time. There is enormous temptation to leap into action straightaway – to get out and start digging, rush down to the garden centre on a buying spree and start planting immediately. Don't. Instead, take some time to become familiar with your garden: look at its size and shape, the influence of its surroundings, check which areas are sunny or shady, and study your soil. The advantages and disadvantages of your garden rarely reveal themselves all at once. As the seasons change, so will the character of the garden as well as the plants themselves, and there may be hidden horticultural gems that will only reveal their beauty at a given season. Time spent getting to know your plot is an excellent investment that will save you money on wasted plants and pay huge dividends later. During this period of grace you can amass the basic yet vital information that will form the foundation of the future success of your garden.

Keen gardeners will, of course, be bursting with frustration at this advice. However, patience in starting on the permanent planting certainly need not mean lack of activity. Undoubtedly there will be weeds and rubbish to be cleared, and the garden can be furnished temporarily with annuals to provide bursts of ephemeral colour, along with plants in containers that can be moved easily to fit in with your new design.

The importance of environment

The influence of a small garden's surroundings is of supreme importance, as the more limited the area of garden, the greater the effects upon it of the immediate environment. Regardless of whether your surroundings are good or bad, they need to be taken into account right at the very start, before you begin to plan your planting.

Adjacent buildings are likely to wield a considerable influence. They cast long shadows, particularly in winter, and, depending on the direction of the prevailing wind, may prevent a good proportion of rain from reaching your soil. Wind strength is often intensified by tall buildings that can create a wind funnel (see page 13).

Mature trees can have an even greater effect on the small plot. Bear in mind that although in winter the branches of deciduous trees form a delicate tracery against the sky and let through plenty of light, when cloaked with summer foliage they can darken your plot considerably. Trees are no respecters of boundaries either and will make your soil drier and poorer, taking up nutrients and many litres of water from networks of roots that have an underground spread roughly equivalent to the tree's height. Tall boundary hedges have a similar effect, particularly in the case of a ravenous plant like green privet, which spreads its roots over a wide area and absorbs the nourishment put down for your own plants.

ASSESSING YOUR GARDEN ENVIRONMENT

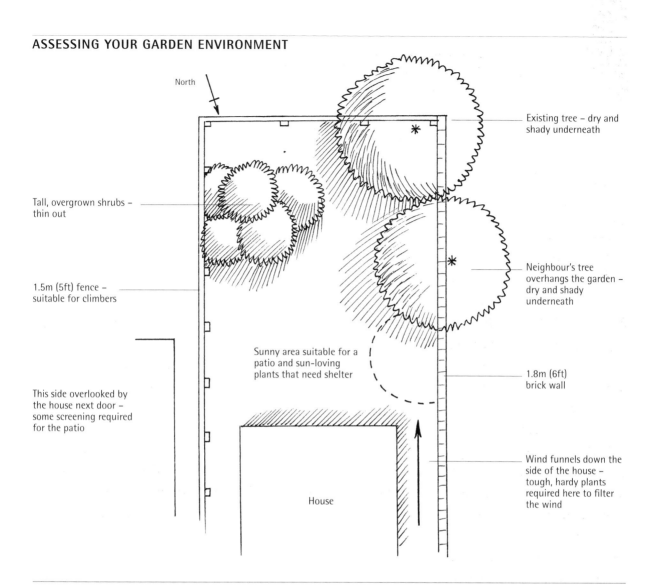

North

Existing tree – dry and shady underneath

Tall, overgrown shrubs – thin out

Neighbour's tree overhangs the garden – dry and shady underneath

1.5m (5ft) fence – suitable for climbers

Sunny area suitable for a patio and sun-loving plants that need shelter

1.8m (6ft) brick wall

This side overlooked by the house next door – some screening required for the patio

Wind funnels down the side of the house – tough, hardy plants required here to filter the wind

House

However, neighbouring plants can also become a considerable asset. If next door's garden has handsome trees or large shrubs that peer over the boundary, they can be 'borrowed' to fit into your planting scheme by the careful placing of plants on your side to make a balanced group. For example, two crab-apple trees next door can be joined by a third on your side; add a couple of climbers or some shrubs to disguise the boundary wall or fence, and it will look as though all the plants belong in your own garden.

Attractive surroundings can obviously be a great asset and the planting of the garden can be

ROOT SPREAD OF A MATURE TREE

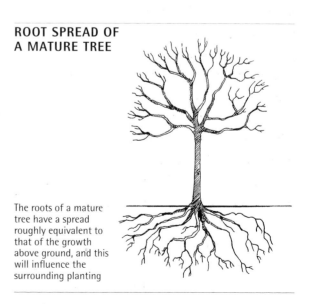

The roots of a mature tree have a spread roughly equivalent to that of the growth above ground, and this will influence the surrounding planting

A broadleaved tree and a conifer can be seen over the boundary fence

By planting a tree and one or two shrubs, and concealing the fence with climbers, this corner now appears larger than it actually is and the planting gives the impression of a balanced whole

planned to make the most of them. A pleasant view, a glimpse of an attractive building or a church spire, for example, could be emphasized by framing it with a pair of trees or large shrubs to create a vista in miniature. If the garden borders a field or park, the dividing boundary could consist of an informal grouping of shrubs or a low fence that is completely covered with plants, so that your garden seems to merge with the area beyond and thereby appears much larger. Should the layout of your garden allow, the planting could also be designed in sympathy with its surroundings, with similar results. For example, a garden that backs on to a field could begin with a more formal style of planting near the house, changing to wild flowers and informal perennials at the end to blend in with the adjacent countryside.

Alas, in most cases our surroundings are not attractive or at best are mediocre, and in the majority of cases the aim has to be to create a small, private oasis of verdant greenery and colourful flowers. Providing privacy by screening out nearby houses and roads, and blocking the views from overlooking windows with hedges, tall shrubs, or strategically placed trees, is dealt with in detail on pages 93–6.

Climate and location

In order to choose the plants that will do best in your garden, it is important to consider the effects of climatic conditions in your area and any particular implications of your location. The main points to consider are frost, water and wind, and whether your garden is in a town or in the country, situated inland or near the coast.

In colder climates, frost can wreak havoc if your garden is in a dip, because cold air sinks downhill and gathers at the bottom while warm air rises. Such an area is known as a frost pocket. In this situation there is little that can be done apart from choosing tough, hardy plants to cope with the conditions. If your garden is on a slope, beware of actually *creating* a frost pocket by putting a solid fence or dense hedge on the lower side that will hamper the progress of cold air down the slope. If such a situation already exists, make the barrier less solid by replacing a fence with trellis or by thinning out a thick hedge, so that cold air can readily drain through.

GROUND LAYOUT THAT CREATES A FROST POCKET

Cold air flows downhill and is trapped by the fence, creating a frost pocket

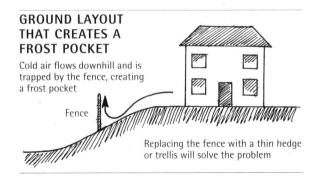

Fence

Replacing the fence with a thin hedge or trellis will solve the problem

Intrusive buildings are tackled with a two-pronged attack: tall plants provide screening while dramatic foreground planting distracts the eye.

Waterlogging may also be a problem in a low-lying site. Soil that is naturally moist is no cause for concern – in fact, it provides a magnificent opportunity for growing those large-leaved, architectural perennials that need a constant supply of moisture to keep their lush leaves in prime condition. But if water is lying on the ground for long periods or the soil is sodden and stagnant, nothing will thrive, as the water deprives the plant roots of vital air. Artificial drainage is the only solution. For a small garden a soakaway should be adequate. This can be made by digging a pit at the lowest point of the garden and filling it with rubble. A land drain can be incorporated to take water away quickly if the surroundings allow.

Drought, by contrast, can be a real summer problem if the garden is on a hill and exposed to drying winds. The effects will be exacerbated further if the soil is an open and free-draining type such as sand or chalk. Improving the soil and creating shelter will mitigate the situation to a certain extent, although again the best course of action is to choose only plants that are tolerant of these conditions.

Strong winds, the other main environmental consideration, can cause a lot of damage – breaking and bruising plant growth, killing and disfiguring plants in winter and intensifying the effects of drought in summer. The risk of wind damage may not be immediately obvious. A garden perched on a hill is a prime candidate for protection – less apparent is the danger posed by nearby tall buildings that may channel the air to create a wind funnel. If wind is likely to be a problem, don't put up a solid barrier such as a fence or wall to try to block its progress. Turbulence will actually build up on the leeward side, and such a barrier is also likely to blow down under the sheer force of a strong wind. Instead, put up an open screen such as one made of bamboo or hessian, trellis clothed with plants, or a hedge, that will filter out the worst of the wind without trying to block it completely.

The geographical location of your garden will have a strong influence on which plants can be grown successfully. Obviously, in milder areas it is possible to grow potentially tender plants that would keel over and die in colder parts, where it is necessary to select tough varieties with absolute hardiness guaranteed. Less obvious, though, is the difference between town and country. The human activity and industry in towns actually make the temperature a degree or two warmer than in the surrounding countryside, and that, coupled with the shelter and storage-heater effect of house walls, makes it possible in cold areas to grow a range of plants on the borderline of hardiness.

The climate is kinder near the sea and, as with town gardens, it is possible to grow plants here that could die of cold further inland. This bonus, however, may be tempered by the adverse effects of salt-laden onshore winds, which can cause a lot of damage to plants. In such a situation, create shelter by putting in hedges of plants that are tolerant of salt. Once these are well established, your garden will provide a warm and wonderful microclimate in which a wide range of plants will flourish.

Whatever your location, a bit of local research will pay dividends. Chat to neighbours who are keen gardeners and find out what plants do best in their gardens, take a stroll around the locality to look at the sorts of plants that thrive nearby and visit gardens that are open to the public. The

A trellis clothed with the vigorous climber *Clematis montana* 'Rubens' creates privacy and also helps to filter out the wind.

local nursery or garden centre can be a mine of information, too, and staff are usually more than happy to advise, particularly if you avoid the busy weekends and go in midweek when trade is likely to be slow.

Assessing your garden

Once you have a feel for your immediate surroundings and the area in which you are living, attention can be focused on the garden itself. At this point, it is a good idea to make a very rough sketch plan of the site in order to jot down your thoughts and ideas as they occur, as well as the influences of any of the points discussed above. Start building up a dossier on your site from day one, by making notes and taking photographs from all angles and at different times of the day and year, particularly if you are likely to be living with your garden for a while before starting to plan your planting. Do *not* rely on memory to provide all the details you will need. Such a record will be a tremendous source of interest in later years too, as well as a great morale-booster when you look back to see how far you've come and how your plot has been transformed.

Orientation and soil

Assessing your garden's orientation, soil type and soil pH (its level of acidity or alkalinity) is crucial in selecting which plants will do well there. Different plants have different preferences, and although some are go-anywhere creatures that tolerate a wide range of conditions, others are very selective – needing full sun to thrive, for example, or disliking lime in the soil. Given the wrong situation, a plant's response can vary from just performing poorly, to sickening and eventually dying. So, to achieve the best results and to avoid wasting money on unsuitable plants, check out these factors right at the start. There is a wide variety of plants available to suit every situation that a garden can offer, and it is far, far easier and much more rewarding to work with nature rather than against it.

SUN OR SHADE?

The direction in which your garden faces determines the amount of sun or shade that it receives. The most accurate way of assessing the orientation is to use a compass. Remember, though, that in addition to this a small garden will be greatly affected by buildings and trees that can block out light. Observe the garden at different times of the day, and bear in mind the time of year when doing so: in winter the sun is low on the horizon and its rays are likely to be blocked by any surrounding structures, while its higher position in summer means that in most cases it should clear the neighbouring rooftops.

The house itself is the greatest influence on how much sun or shade the garden receives. Shade is often more pleasant to sit in than sun.

SOIL TYPE

Soil type relates to the size of the particles that make up the fertile top layer of soil. A clay soil is composed of tiny particles that stick together and readily retain moisture, making it sticky and difficult to cultivate when wet. It is slow to warm up in spring, which means that any plants to be raised from seed are best sown late in the season, but it does hold warmth well into the autumn. Clay is also good at retaining nutrients. By contrast, sandy soil is very coarse in texture and consists of large particles through which water drains quickly. As such, it is easy to work soon after rain and warms up fast in the spring, although nutrients are soon washed through so fertilizers will need to be applied regularly. The gardener's ideal soil type is a good loam, which is a combination of these two, with a balanced mixture of small and large particles – it has most of their good features and few of their disadvantages. Nevertheless, however poor a soil may be, it can be improved by cultivation and the addition of organic matter (see pages 112–14).

There are several ways of establishing which soil type you have. First, take a handful of soil, moisten it and work it between your palms to form a sausage shape. Then, try to form it into a ring – clay will hold its shape, while sand will quickly crumble. Again, some local research at the garden centre and among near neighbours should turn up useful information.

The soil of a garden belonging to an older house has a good chance of being in good condition. Hopefully it will have been well worked over the years and enriched with compost or manure, to result in fertile, humus-rich topsoil. On the other hand, the gardens of brand-new houses tend to be a breed apart. Often there is little or no good quality topsoil, and the subsoil may be very near or at the surface.

Builders' rubble may litter the ground and cultivation can throw up all sorts of unpleasant debris. In severe cases, it may be necessary to buy in some good quality topsoil to provide an adequate growing environment for plants. If signs of waterlogging are visible, you will probably need to cultivate deeply to break up the subsoil – which may have been compacted to form an impenetrable layer – to allow water to drain through.

ACID OR ALKALINE?

The soil pH – its level of acidity or alkalinity – is an important fact to determine. A simple soil test kit, which is readily available from garden centres, can be used for this. The pH is measured on a sliding scale that for most soils ranges from pH 5.0 (acid) to pH 8.0 (alkaline). The majority of plants grow best on a slightly acid soil with a pH of around 6.5, although certain plants, including rhododendrons and azaleas, prefer an acid soil and will sicken and die if grown in soil that is alkaline (limy). A sample of soil for testing should be taken from a few centimetres below the surface. It is perfectly possible for soil to vary from one part of the garden to another, so to be on the safe side take several separate samples for testing.

An acid soil can be made more alkaline by adding lime. However, it is a waste of effort trying to make a limy soil suitable for acid-lovers. In these conditions, by far the best approach is to confine lime-hating plants to containers and raised beds that can be filled with ericaceous (lime-free) potting compost.

Looking at layout

Your garden's location and its orientation will begin to suggest the type and layout of the planting, but it is a close assessment of the plot itself that will reveal its finer possibilities. If you look at the garden piece by piece, the potentially bewildering task of getting to grips with your site will begin to fall into place.

Size and shape

The overall size of a garden will obviously have an enormous influence on the plants that can be grown – in fact, the discipline imposed by a limited area of ground can be a great help in whittling down the range of plants from which to choose. Garden shapes can vary tremendously and in virtually every case can be turned to positive advantage, even though this may not be immediately obvious at first glance. A long, thin plot, for example, can be divided into a series of 'rooms', an L-shaped garden could have an arbour in the hidden portion, while odd, awkward corners are perfect for concealing nitty-gritty basic features such as a shed or dustbins. By contrast, the straightforward square or rectangle may look boring, but it offers the chance to adopt some exciting ideas that can be lifted readily from the pages of garden design books and magazine articles.

Internal factors

Next, you will need to take a look at factors within the garden. Starting at ground level – is the site flat or is there any change in level? A flat site can benefit enormously from even a small variation in level, such as that created by the introduction of a raised bed, which would also allow for the possibility of growing plants that need a different soil to that of your garden. Good candidates for a raised bed are alpines, those small-scale charmers with fine features that are much more readily appreciated at close quarters, and, if your soil is limy, acid-loving plants can be grown here in lime-free soil (see page 110).

Raised beds are also a real boon for gardeners of restricted mobility, as they dispense with the need for constant bending.

A sloping site could be terraced into two or more separate areas by building walls of timber or brick to retain the soil, with trailing plants tumbling from one level to the next. If you have very young children, however, bear in mind that terraces and their attendant steps can be a real hazard and it may be best to keep to a simple slope for the time being. A sloping site that faces the sun is a great bonus in colder areas, as it can absorb up to twice as much of the sun's heat as it could if it were level.

The existing 'flooring' of the garden also needs to be considered. Grass is nearly always present in a garden, however small a patch it may be, even though a tiny lawn may be scuffed and balding from too much concentrated wear and tear. Depending on your preference, you could decide on what many see as the ultimate heresy – getting rid of grass altogether. In a small garden,

A sloping site can be a real asset as the change in levels creates much more interest than a flat area.

it can be a downright nuisance to keep a tiny lawn in good condition and an alternative surface such as gravel, paving or chipped bark may be much more suitable – and a good deal less work, too. For the enthusiast, doing away with grass means much more space for plants, which can be incorporated into all these alternative surfaces.

The vertical elements of a small garden – the walls and boundaries – offer enormous potential to increase the planting area and enhance the character of the garden. A house without any foliage covering looks bleak and almost indecently naked, but takes on a friendly, welcoming air when clothed with plants (see page 84). If paved or hard surfaces surround the house, it may be possible to lift a couple of slabs in order to put in plants. An alternative to planting directly in the ground is to use large containers such as wooden half-barrels, which provide plenty of root space for permanent climbers. Fences can be tackled in a similar fashion, with the added bonus that a well covered fence or wall makes the garden appear larger as the boundaries blend in with their surroundings.

The view from inside

As often as not, the greater part of a small plot will be visible from inside the house, which makes

PLANNING PLANTING TO BE SEEN FROM INDOORS

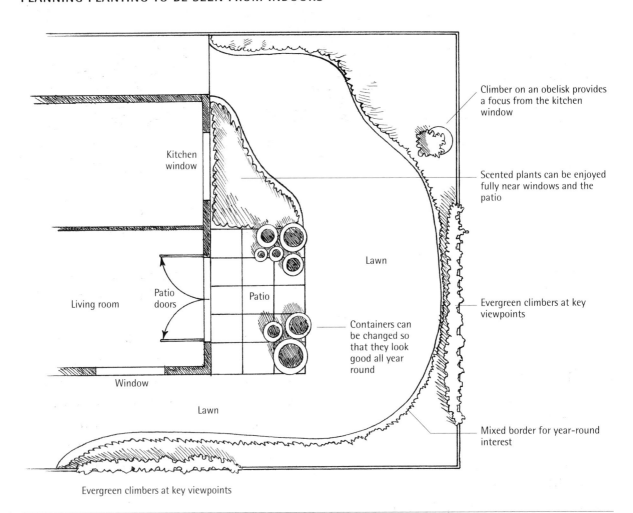

Kitchen window

Climber on an obelisk provides a focus from the kitchen window

Scented plants can be enjoyed fully near windows and the patio

Lawn

Patio doors

Patio

Living room

Evergreen climbers at key viewpoints

Containers can be changed so that they look good all year round

Window

Lawn

Mixed border for year-round interest

Evergreen climbers at key viewpoints

the view out an important aspect of planning the planting. It is all too easy to concentrate on planting a garden purely for enjoyment whilst out of doors, and forget that for some of the year at least – maybe a good part of it, depending on your location – the garden will mostly be seen from the warmth and comfort of the house.

So, at this early stage, go round your house and check out the main viewpoints. The living room is an obvious choice for a good view out, but don't forget other much-used vantage points such as the kitchen window, where the sight of attractive flowers and plants can go a long way towards mitigating the tedium of washing up and cooking. Mark key viewpoints exactly by

Often forgotten, the view from the house is tremendously important as most of a small garden is seen from indoors.

working in pairs – one person indoors, and the other outside with a handful of canes to 'plant' in the right spots.

Within a border, a mixed planting will give year-round colour and interest, using a good proportion of evergreens and plants with long-lasting attractive foliage as well as flowers (see page 65). Where hard areas such as paving make containers the only option, as is so often the case close to the house, include some plants for winter interest as well as seasonal plants for summer display (see page 108).

Practical features

A garden is a space for living in every sense of the word, and therefore has to be a compromise between aesthetic and practical considerations. In order to conceal these businesslike facilities to the greatest degree while still creating a garden that works successfully, it is best to consider them right at the very start.

Storage of some sort is usually essential for garden tools and other items such as bicycles, unless you are fortunate enough to have an outbuilding or two that can be used for this

Small gardens have to be practical as well as beautiful. Here a shed and storage area have been cleverly integrated into the overall design.

purpose. Depending on the amount of equipment to be housed, it may not be necessary to have a full-sized shed: a lean-to shelter may be perfectly adequate and will be a lot less obtrusive. Dustbins and compost bins can be hidden from view behind a screen such as trellis, hazel hurdles or bamboo panels.

A washing line must be situated in an open

spot, in full sun if possible, although it need not be in a lawn: an area of low-growing plants would be a more than acceptable alternative if conditions allow. Water will be required by the dense, sheltered planting in a small plot, so an outdoor tap would be extremely useful, along with a water butt in which to save rainwater.

Frequently used routes to places such as the garage, back gate or washing line are best surfaced with some kind of hard material. Paving is the obvious choice, although it can be in the form of stepping stones rather than a solid path. Alternatively, you could use gravel, perhaps interplanted with ground-cover plants.

Once you have sited all the features that you *must* have, look at those which you would *like* to include. A patio for sitting out and relaxing is the ideal choice for a sheltered, sunny spot, and if space permits it is very pleasant to have an additional place to sit – either just a tucked-away bench, or something more elaborate such as an arbour draped with climbing plants. A small water feature such as a pebble fountain is excellent alongside a patio, where the splash of moving water intensifies the feeling of relaxation. Many plant enthusiasts like to include a greenhouse, and as with a shed, a lean-to model is surprisingly capacious where space is really limited. Another exceptionally useful area for the keen gardener is a tiny, hidden-away nursery area, to be used for such things as growing on young plants and housing container plants that are past their best or are yet to reach their prime. Such an area behind the scenes will help ensure that the garden – the stage itself – will look wonderful most of the time.

Tackling an overgrown garden

Unless your new garden belongs to a brand-new house, it is highly unlikely that it will be completely bare. It is even less likely that an existing garden will contain a well designed selection of plants that are in need of very little attention! Inheriting someone else's established and overgrown garden can be a mixed blessing indeed – on the one hand the plants do give the garden an air of maturity, but on the other there is a good chance that you will be faced with a jungle of over-mature plants that are approaching or have passed their horticultural 'sell-by' date.

Adopting a wait-and-see policy is an excellent approach. Certain plants only reveal themselves in their full glory at one season – spring bulbs, for example, cannot be seen at all during summer and autumn – and a garden could contain many such treasures. In any case, most people are unlikely to start tackling a garden the minute they move in. Amid the welter of decorating and furniture-shuffling, take a few minutes every so often to pop outside and make notes on what is growing and flowering in the garden.

The difficulties of taking on an overgrown garden are compounded if you are new to gardening and one tangle of foliage looks much

---

CHECKLIST FOR A NEW GARDEN

- ■ Check out the garden's immediate surroundings, particularly any trees and buildings that cast shade.
- ■ Find out about the climate and any other relevant geographical details.
- ■ Establish the direction your garden faces (is it shady or sunny?).
- ■ Establish your soil type (clay, sand, chalk etc.) and its pH (is it acid or alkaline?).
- ■ Consider any practical features that need to be included.

like another. The temptation is to either hack the lot to the ground or not touch anything at all, but neither approach is ideal. How do you know which plant could be a choice but slow-growing shrub that is just reaching its peak of perfection, as opposed to a gangly, vigorous and easily grown variety that is best heaved out at 10 years old and replanted with a fresh specimen? Here a little expert knowledge will go a very long way indeed. Consider bringing in a garden consultant for a one-off, advisory visit – their fee can be more than adequately offset against the money you could spend on new plants, by selectively keeping and rejuvenating your existing ones. The consultant's advice should be well informed and impartial, too, which may not be the case with that given by well meaning gardening friends or relatives.

However, if plants really are past their best, now is the time to harden your heart and bring down the axe – far better to have all the upheaval at one go, rather than to start creating your garden and then face disruption later. Prime candidates for the chop are old deciduous shrubs such as cytisus, forsythia, deutzia and weigela, which are quick-growing anyway and would be much better planted afresh. Be chary, though, of taking out choice plants such as camellias and rhododendrons that take a long time to mature.

Renovating existing plants

Many overgrown shrubs have simply been neglected and can be rejuvenated by judicious pruning. As a general rule of thumb, remove one in three of the thickest, oldest stems, as near to the ground as possible. Light and air will flood through the centre of the plant and encourage new growth to develop from the base. In subsequent years, the one-in-three rule can be repeated until a balance of growth has been restored. Once pruning has been carried out, mulch around the plant with well rotted compost or manure and apply a dressing of fertilizer to kick-start new growth after such major surgery.

The time to prune varies according to the type of shrub. Evergreens are best tackled in the middle of spring, when the hardest frosts to which they can be susceptible should be well past. Shrubs like mock orange (*Philadelphus*) and weigela, which bloom in early summer, bear flowers on growth that has been produced during the previous season and should be pruned immediately after flowering. Late summer-flowering shrubs such as buddleia produce their flowers on the current year's growth and should be pruned in late winter. However, if you are wary of breaking out the saw and secateurs, just remember that even if you do prune at the wrong time, the worst result is usually the loss of a year's flowers and the plant should still perform much better in the future.

Herbaceous perennials that have formed large, overgrown clumps are much more straightforward to deal with. The way to rejuvenate them is to lift and divide the clump, discarding the congested, woody centre and

RENOVATION PRUNING OF AN OVERGROWN SHRUB

Remove about one-third of the oldest, thickest branches as close to the ground as possible. Repeat over several years until all old growth has gone

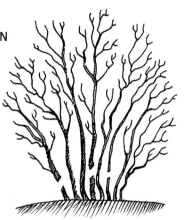

replanting pieces of the fresher outer growth. Perennials are best divided when dormant in autumn, winter and early spring.

When it comes to a tree, think long and hard before felling it, as trees are a valuable part of our heritage and obviously take many years to reach maturity. A large tree may be protected with a tree preservation order, and your local authority should be able to give further information as to whether this is the case. A tree growing near the house often raises concerns about its root system disturbing the foundations, but if this is the case felling it may not be the answer to the problem. The sudden removal of a mature tree that has been taking up many gallons of water can cause great disturbance due to the water, which is suddenly no longer taken up by the tree, and consequently the water table rises rapidly. The best solution in such a case is to allow the tree to remain, but with its crown of branches raised and thinned so that the tree draws up less water from the soil. Treated in this way, a tree that has seemed impossibly oppressive and overbearing can suddenly become an attractive and welcome feature in the garden. Employ a qualified tree surgeon for the job rather than a general landscape contractor, for surgery is indeed the key word and a tree can be maimed for life by unskilled hands. Your local garden centre may be able to recommend someone, or you can obtain a list of tree specialists from the relevant professional body.

Trees and tall hedges that belong to neighbours can become a source of great annoyance, as they are beyond your control but can affect your garden to a huge extent by blocking out light and taking up the lion's share of water and nutrients from your soil, thereby depriving your own precious plants. Check out the legal situation before carrying out any work on trees

CHECKLIST FOR A MATURE GARDEN
- Live with your garden for a year before carrying out any major work, to discover the full range of plants within it.
- Bear in mind that many large shrubs can be rejuvenated by careful pruning as an alternative to getting rid of them.
- Plants that are past their 'sell-by' date are best removed before starting on the new planting, in order to avoid future disruption.
- Remove trees only if absolutely necessary – pruning and thinning may give adequate results – and first check out the legal situation, as well as other implications such as possible subsidence.
- Consider bringing in a consultant to advise on how to tackle existing plants, particularly if you are new to gardening.

or boundary planting, as expensive court cases between neighbours have resulted from wrongful pruning where the ownership of the plants has been debatable. In the case of plants that actually overhang your plot from a neighbouring garden, you are usually entitled to trim back the growth that is 'trespassing', cutting it back to the boundary line but no further unless your neighbour consents. The same goes for roots, which can be cut back to the boundary too. However, there is a way of mitigating the plants' influence in the future: dig a narrow trench as close to the boundary as possible and as deep as you can make it, chopping off roots with the spade in the process. Then, line it with material such as old paving slabs or corrugated iron that will limit the spread of new root growth.

Planning your Planting

ADVANCE PLANNING of planting is the key to success with all gardens, but it is most crucial of all with a small plot, where a lot of juggling and contriving is necessary in order to cram everything in. Depending on your enthusiasm for such matters, planning can be carried out to different degrees – from drawing up a detailed planting plan to merely deciding on an overall style and working things out as you go along – but in my experience, the more the better. Time devoted to planning will undoubtedly help you to create a successful garden, as well as saving money on plants that would otherwise fail or disappoint due simply to their being in the wrong place. Although there will always be mistakes and

losses when planting a garden, some degree of planning will go a long way towards limiting them. Yet another advantage of having a plan to follow is that the garden can be created piecemeal as finances permit; even a small space can eat up money, particularly if a lot of construction is involved.

Garden style

Choosing a distinct style of planting will establish the character of your garden and give it an air of harmony – important in a small space, where conflicting styles and features can result in an impression of clutter rather than a feeling of space. It goes without saying that your chosen style must suit your personal taste – regardless of

Left: Planning means that the space can be crammed with plants that will provide a succession of colour throughout the year.

Right: A varied selection of plants is brought together successfully by having a firm structure or 'skeleton' to the garden.

Consider the garden's surroundings and plan your design to suit. A rural site is perfect for an informal, cottage-style garden.

the dictates of fashion, it is you who will be living with the garden, not the design gurus. An aspect that it is all too easy to overlook, however, is that the garden must also suit your lifestyle, and the planting design of your dreams could turn out in reality to be a nightmare to live with and look after. A selection of planting styles is outlined on the following pages; while contemplating which theme you prefer, give some serious consideration to the points discussed below. This will begin a process of elimination that will help to point you in the right direction – towards creating a garden that you can love and live with happily.

An important aspect to consider is planting your garden to fit its context. A town site is most suited to a formal layout that has a strong degree of symmetry, or an oriental style where the emphasis is on form and foliage, with few

flowers. A sun-filled courtyard is perfect for a Mediterranean garden, while a country setting is the obvious place for the rumpled exuberance of a cottage garden, or at the very least an informal style of planting. Where the garden's space and layout make it possible to divide it into sections that are completely separate and distinct from one another – as in the case of a long, thin garden, for example – more than one style can be adopted. In such a situation you may find it best to start with a formal style of planting adjacent to the house, becoming more informal further away, and perhaps even finishing with a 'wild' garden at the furthest point.

A garden that is completely enclosed can offer the greatest possibilities of all, for here the house is the only feature that needs to be taken into account and you can adopt whatever style you desire, within any practical limitations that the site may impose. If your taste inclines towards the theatrical, for example, a small garden could even be turned into an outdoor stage set, with murals, statuary and unusual or decorative features, all framed by careful planting.

Consider who is to use the garden and in what way. Are there children who need space to play? Do you just want somewhere to sit and relax, or would you like to spend more time actively gardening? How much time will you actually have available? Is the garden intended to be an extension of the house – an outside room – or a separate area with a different identity?

Think of your own preferences as a guide to garden style. Do you like a neat, uncluttered house with few ornaments and minimal furniture (formal), or a lived-in, ordered jumble of many things (informal) with lots of colour (cottage)?

And, of course, always consider your budget!

Last, but certainly not least, don't try to cram too much into your small space. In many cases, less really can appear to be more, and there are few more disheartening sights than a full-to-bursting small garden that is obviously a large one trying to get out. Recognize the limitations and work within them, and you will have much more chance of ending up with a garden that is a joy to look at and a pleasure to maintain.

Formal

A formal style can be eminently suitable for a small space. It is characterized by straight lines and a strong degree of symmetry, with hard landscaping materials usually playing a prominent role. Choose straight lines, squares, rectangles or circles for shaping borders and

A formal, symmetrical layout of paths and box hedges is perfect for a town garden. Climber-clad walls enhance the impression of an outdoor room.

other areas. Many people can be put off by the apparently spartan appearance of such a design on paper, but do bear in mind that plants will create their own informality within the disciplined structure.

Depending on your preference, the planting within a formal layout can either be very restrained – using low, clipped hedges of plants such as box (*Buxus sempervirens*), cotton lavender (*Santolina*) or lavender, and a very limited number of other plants to infill the planting space – or it could be a more exuberant mixture of shrubs, perennials and other plants within the formal framework to create a slightly more relaxed appearance. To emphasize a formal layout, the planting on one side of the garden should ideally match that of the other side. Key plants should either be those that are naturally formal in appearance, such as conical or pyramid-shaped conifers or trees with a fastigiate shape such as *Sorbus aucuparia* 'Fastigiata', or shrubs which lend themselves to trimming and shaping like pyracantha, golden privet (*Ligustrum ovalifolium* 'Aureum') and decorative cultivars of holly (*Ilex*). Foliage plants, and particularly evergreens, make up a large part of the planting in a formal garden.

Clipped hedges and topiary shapes such as spirals, balls or pyramids can form a major part of the structure, and not only in borders either as they also look marvellous in containers. Box is the traditional plant to use, although the advent of wire frames in a multitude of shapes makes it possible to take a short-cut by training small-leaved ivies (*Hedera helix* cultivars) over moss-filled frameworks.

Oriental

As with a formal garden, an oriental style of planting is very suitable for a small space. A traditional Japanese garden is very sparing in its use of plants and includes a high proportion of hard materials such as rocks, pebbles and gravel, the forms and layouts of which have great significance. Such a style is too minimalist for most people – a good compromise is to use the oriental style as inspiration but incorporate a wider range of plants. Again, foliage and form rather than drifts of flowers is the way to go.

Many of our garden plants come from the East and these are obviously ideal for this style; a good garden reference book will list plant origins. Plants for an oriental garden could include Japanese maples (*Acer palmatum*), which come in a huge number of varieties with leaves of many different, delicate shapes and colours. They range in size from compact shrubs that form a low mound to upright varieties that eventually become large shrubs or small trees. These maples are deciduous; the spotted laurel (*Aucuba*) is a handsome shrub for evergreen foliage. Tall ornamental grasses and bamboos such as *Miscanthus sinensis* and *Arundinaria murieliae* are excellent for rapid height. There are many more compact forms too, such as *A. viridistriata* and *Hakonechloa macra* 'Aureola' with golden leaves, *Carex comans* bronze form with bronze-red foliage and *Festuca glauca* with blue-green leaves. Still on the foliage theme, hostas are superb for shady spots and containers.

There are plenty of oriental-style plants to give some bursts of flower colour, too. Dwarf rhododendrons provide a stupendous display of spring blooms – they need an acid soil, although these dwarf varieties could be grown in pots. *Osmanthus* × *burkwoodii* is an excellent shrub with evergreen foliage and scented white spring

Right: By adopting the total contrast of an oriental style, a garden can be turned into a magical world of its own.

flowers, which responds well to trimming and shaping, too. Wisteria is a handsome climber for a sunny wall or pergola, and certain clematis would also work well in this setting, particularly those with pale blooms such as the *C. viticella* hybrid *C.* 'Alba Luxurians' and large-flowered hybrids like *C.* 'Marie Boisselot'.

Pebbles, rocks and stepping stones make an ideal surround for plants and cut down on weeding as well. Features in keeping with an oriental style include stone lanterns, water features such as a pebble fountain, timber decking and screens made of thin bamboo.

Informal

An informal style is more relaxed and natural in appearance. It is characterized by sweeping curves and plants that are placed singly or in odd-numbered groups, either in curved drifts or rough ovals, or, in the case of bulbs, scattered to give a seemingly natural appearance. The planting is exuberant and plentiful, perhaps mingling together with climbers growing through shrubs and trees, and perennial flowers peeping through the foliage of neighbouring shrubs. Hard surfaces such as paths and a patio can be softened at the edges by plants such as lavender and parahebe tumbling over from their borders, and gaps in paving can be planted with low-growing, aromatic herbs like chamomile (*Chamaemelum nobile*) and pennyroyal mint (*Mentha pulegium*).

Many plants are suitable for an informal garden, although a strong element of form is still vital to achieve structure and long-lasting interest within the planting. Include a good proportion of evergreens for winter interest, such as mahonia, *Viburnum davidii* and *V. tinus*, and Mexican orange blossom (*Choisya*). Deciduous shrubs with attractive foliage will give interest

for half the year; good choices include *Cornus alba* varieties with golden or variegated leaves, *Berberis thunbergii* varieties and the strong-smelling curry plant (*Helichrysum italicum* subsp. *serotinum*). Flowering shrubs like hebes, lavender, tree mallow (*Lavatera*), potentilla and Cape figwort (*Phygelius*) will give lots of summer colour while still adding an element of form. Vertical features such as arches, and obelisks within borders, can support the luxuriant growth of climbers such as jasmine, clematis, passion flower (*Passiflora caerulea*), perennial pea (*Lathyrus latifolius*), climbing and rambler roses, and honeysuckle.

Cottage garden

A cottage garden takes the informal style to its limits. The traditional cottage garden was first and foremost a practical one, with priority given to productive plants – fruit, vegetables and herbs – while flowers were jumbled in between as space and time permitted. Now the priorities have switched and it is old-fashioned flowers that are the essence of today's cottage gardens, with vegetables and fruit grown in small patches among the ornamental plants or maybe not at all. However, do bear in mind that although this style looks like an effortlessly created mass of colour, a fair degree of planning and horticultural expertise goes into the creation of a successful cottage garden, and it requires quite a lot of maintenance, too.

The flowers need not be genuinely old varieties in order to create the desired effect. Many traditional cottage-garden flowers, such as roses and pinks (*Dianthus*), have now been bred

A blend of informal and formal styles can be very successful, with plants tumbling exuberantly within a strong layout.

to produce varieties that combine the most favourable characteristics of the old – fragrance and an old-fashioned appearance – with a compact, sturdy habit and resistance to disease. The same goes for annuals like pot marigold (*Calendula*) and Californian poppy (*Eschscholtzia*). Where herbs are concerned, select plants for their ornamental appearance, such as the coloured forms of sage, marjoram and lemon balm, and avoid rampant or scruffy growers like angelica, lovage and tarragon. A similar approach can be adopted with vegetables, some of which are very attractive in appearance. Plants like runner beans, ruby chard and lettuce with red or frilled

Lupins, roses, sweet williams and many other traditional plants jostle together in this gloriously colourful and fragrant cottage garden.

leaves look superb, and of course have the added bonus of being edible too.

Many popular cottage-garden shrubs such as mock orange (*Philadelphus*) and lilac (*Syringa*) do, in the main, grow far too large to be suitable for a small space. However, with a bit of selectiveness and searching, a few compact forms of these lovely old favourites can be found. They include *Philadelphus* 'Manteau d'Hermine', which grows to around 0.9m (3ft) high, as does the delightful dwarf lilac *Syringa meyeri* 'Palibin'. Both these plants are fragrant, and scent is an important consideration when planning a cottage garden – as, indeed, it is in many other garden styles too (see panel).

Spring and summer are the glory times for a cottage garden, although in a small space winter colour and interest must be borne in mind too. To this end, evergreens need to be incorporated, although they must be chosen carefully to fit the garden's style. Ivies, both green and variegated types, can be grown on walls and up supports from containers; *Viburnum tinus* 'Eve Price' is excellent value with evergreen foliage and winter flowers, and Christmas box (*Sarcococca*) has pointed evergreen leaves and deliciously fragrant winter flowers. For extra colour at each end of the year, squeeze in plenty of bulbs beneath and between existing plants and in containers, plus a few biennials like wallflowers, sweet rocket (*Hesperis matronalis*), and forget-me-nots (*Myosotis*).

Mediterranean

A sunny, sheltered site is essential for the creation of a Mediterranean garden, preferably accompanied by soil that is sharply drained or which can be made so to accommodate those sun-loving plants that detest having wet roots in winter. Walls are a definite asset, particularly for their storage-heater effect, which can be a life-saver for plants in cold areas over winter. To heighten the Mediterranean effect, walls are best painted white or in pale, pastel colours, and perhaps adorned with painted tiles. You can put up a pergola or a couple of beams on which to train a vine – either a grape vine or the vigorous ornamental species *Vitis coignetiae* – to create a soft, dappled shade in which to sit.

Vibrant flower colours – blues, reds, oranges, yellows and deep pinks – are necessary to hold their own in strong sunlight, particularly if it is reflected by pale walls. Typical Mediterranean

---

PLANTS WITH FRAGRANT FLOWERS

Trees	Climbers
Malus	*Akebia quinata*
	Clematis armandii
Shrubs	*Jasminum officinale*
Choisya ternata	*Lonicera* (most)
'Sundance'	*Rosa* (many)
Daphne laureola	*Trachelospermum*
Daphne odora	*Wisteria*
'Aureomarginata'	
Lavandula	There are a number
Mahonia aquifolium	of annuals and
'Smaragd'	biennials with
Osmanthus x	fragrant flowers,
burkwoodii	such as tobacco
Philadelphus	plants *(Nicotiana)*,
'Manteau	wallflowers and
d'Hermine'	sweet rocket, sweet
Rosa (many)	peas, and bulbs
Sarcococca	such as lilies.
Skimmia japonica	
'Rubella'	
Syringa meyeri	
'Palibin'	
Viburnum x *juddii*	

plants are those of the *maquis* and *garrigue* – particularly those with aromatic foliage such as lavender and rosemary. Spiky foliage such as that of yuccas, phormiums and cordylines provides strong visual contrast to the rounded shapes of the flowering plants and gives evergreen interest. Containers can be filled with colourful frost-tender perennials – geraniums (*Pelargonium*) for that authentic touch, although many others can be used including African daises (*Osteospermum*), Zulu daisies (*Arctotis*) and diascias. Terracotta is an excellent choice for a Mediterranean garden, and there is a huge range of sizes and styles of container to suit every budget. If the bank balance allows, a couple of *pithoi* (large storage jars) would add a gloriously authentic touch.

For a more comprehensive list of plants for a Mediterranean garden, see pages 55–6.

Plant enthusiasts

The yearning to possess a vast range of desirable plants can lead to conflict in a small plot. Trying to cram one of everything into a limited space can result in an horrendous jungle of plants all struggling for light and air, and the overall effect this creates in a small garden can end up as one of complete confusion.

A strong design helps to make a good backbone for a garden that is likely to contain a wide variety of plants. Pay particular attention to the layout of hard landscaping features such as paths and the patio, and to choosing the largest plants for the garden. Some discipline is absolutely vital when choosing these key plants –

The keen gardener can cram in an enormous number of plants by keeping lawns and paths to a minimum.

few sights are sadder than shrubs and trees crammed together and pruned so hard that the grace and attraction of their overall shape is lost. More leeway is offered by smaller plants; developing a taste for alpines, for example, which offer the opportunity to create a landscape on a miniature scale, would be very helpful! Containers can be a real boon, with potential to mix and match an enormous range of plants.

Finding a corner for a nursery area is an excellent idea for the enthusiast. This could include a small greenhouse, or failing that a cold frame, for propagating new plants and overwintering tender ones, a little nursery bed for growing on seasonal plants, and a standing area for containers that are past their prime or waiting to reach their peak of perfection.

Make the most of every available space by gardening on the vertical, planting up walls and fences and introducing features such as arches and obelisks. Climbers can be grown through established shrubs and trees, small shade-tolerant shrubs and perennials can be planted under larger specimens, and bulbs can be squeezed into a multitude of places. Of course, these techniques are applicable when planting any small space, but are particularly essential to the plant-lover who wants to grow as many plants as possible.

Family

A family garden is the most difficult of all to plan and plant, as a small space has to fulfil a host of different needs. Children need space in which to play, which must be surrounded by plants of cast-iron toughness. Bark chippings make a good, safe base for a play area, and in later years this could be adapted and planted with a woodland theme, with one or two trees underplanted with shade-loving shrubs,

perennials and bulbs. For younger children, a concrete-lined sandpit can be earmarked for later conversion to a pond or bog garden for moisture-loving plants. An area of gravel will keep a toddler happy for hours, and it can be made equally pleasing for adults by planting the edges with subjects like sisyrinchium and lady's mantle (*Alchemilla mollis*), which will self-seed readily to create an informal effect.

Safety must be paramount, so avoid poisonous plants (see page 36). The labelling of potentially dangerous plants has improved greatly in recent years, although it would still be worth a final check with a knowledgeable member of staff at the nursery or garden centre when buying. In addition, avoid plants with the potential to cause physical harm; those with prickly leaves or stems, some that have sharp-edged leaves such as pampas grass (*Cortaderia*), and those with spiky-tipped leaves like cordylines, which could be dangerous to eyes.

On the positive side, there are many plants that are excellent in a family garden, for a variety of reasons. Attracting wildlife to the garden is fascinating for children of all ages – not to mention the adults, too. Choose fruiting trees and shrubs to provide winter food for birds, such as crab-apples (*Malus*), sorbus and cotoneaster. Certain flowers are very attractive to butterflies, including Michaelmas daisies (*Aster*) and *Sedum spectabile*.

Children love to have natural hiding places under trees. Although a massive weeping willow is an obvious no-no, a smaller weeping tree – such as the weeping silver-leaved pear (*Pyrus salicifolia* 'Pendula') and weeping purple willow (*Salix purpurea* 'Pendula') – can still offer some seclusion under their umbrella of branches.

Plants to please the senses can be appreciated by children from a surprisingly early age – my daughter started homing in on scented flowers at 16 months. Tactile plants tend to be firm favourites too; these include those with woolly leaves such as lamb's ears (*Stachys byzantina*) and rustling ornamental grasses.

POISONOUS PLANTS

A few garden plants are toxic and may cause poisoning if eaten. Those with colourful berries can be a particular danger to very young children, who could be tempted to eat the fruits. The following is a select list of commonly grown plants that are poisonous: it is not intended as a comprehensive list of all those which may be dangerous.

Aconitum	*Laburnum*
Arum italicum subsp.	*Lantana camara*
marmoratum	*Nerium oleander*
Brugmansia	*Gaultheria*
Colchicum	*mucronata*
Convallaria	*Prunus laurocerasus*
Daphne mezereum	*Ricinus communis*
Digitalis	*Taxus baccata*

Wild

A 'wild' garden is rarely an option for the whole of a small garden, unless you happen to be a very keen conservationist. However, where the size and shape of the garden permit it can be an excellent choice for part of it – at the end of a long, narrow plot which borders straight on to countryside, for example.

However, 'wild gardening' needs to be approached with circumspection, and I am wary of the common misunderstanding that a wildflower garden can be made with little work and even less maintenance. Scattering handfuls of flower seed and leaving it to its fate is a great way of throwing money away and burying your enthusiasm for gardening at the same time. The only exceptions are 'cornfield' annuals – plants like field poppies, corn marigold, corncockle and cornflower – which can be sown in a dry, sunny spot and the ground simply raked lightly to cover the seed. Otherwise, to achieve good results requires the same care over ground preparation as for all garden plants. Seed has to be sown with due attention to detail or, better still, grown in pots for planting out, and selective weeding and thinning must be carried out to ensure that a balance is maintained.

For a small plot, the best approach to wild gardening is usually a compromise. Choose perennials, shrubs, ornamental grasses, hardy ferns and bulbs that are cultivated forms of native plants or because their appearance would blend in well with this style of planting. These plants can sit happily alongside selected varieties of native plants – those that look attractive enough to be gardenworthy yet aren't invasive.

A shady site, or one which is overhung by trees, is a wonderful spot for woodland flowers. A pageant of spring colour can be created with primroses, sweet violets and bugle, along with bulbs such as bluebells, winter aconites and snowdrops. For summer there are tall spires of foxgloves and clumps of red campion. If the ground is reasonably moist, include a few hardy ferns; this wonderful and under-used group of plants offers a tremendous range of foliage shapes and styles.

Many nurseries offer a good range of native plants so there is absolutely no excuse for taking plants or seeds from the wild – a practice that in most cases is illegal in any case. Be wary of the illegally harvested wild bulbs that are often offered for sale – particularly snowdrops,

bluebells and hardy cyclamen. Check the source and only buy from a responsible retailer.

Planting native flowers can literally be a life-saver for some creatures. Not least of these is the humble bumblebee, which fills the summer garden with its relaxing hum, as many modern flowers that have been bred for features such as new colours or double blooms either don't produce nectar or are shaped so that it is not readily available to bumblebees. It is salutary to think that planting wildflowers, an exercise in horticultural nostalgia for us, can mean the difference between life and death for those creatures that we take for granted.

Making plans

Before you can begin to draw up a detailed planting plan for your garden, you will need to have an understanding of planting distances and plant groupings.

Wild flowers, carefully chosen for their garden-worthiness, look every bit as good as cultivated ones. A cowslip-studded lawn makes an enchanting feature.

Planting distances

How far apart to plant? This is the perpetual question that vexes gardeners and to which, unfortunately, there is no hard-and-fast answer. Much depends on how quickly you wish to achieve a mature look to your garden. If you are likely to be moving on in a few years' time, closer planting will be more desirable than if your new house will be your home for the foreseeable future.

Bear in mind that overplanting, rather than the opposite, is by far the most common trap for the unwary, particularly if planting takes place in autumn or winter, when leafless shrubs and trees are a shadow of their summer selves. Come the growing season, plants burgeon and fling out long stems, and will be nestling cheek by jowl before you know it. Overplanting tends to be treated by disfiguring pruning rather than the better option of outright removal of plants and, as already mentioned (see page 35), few sights are more depressing.

So, when planning your borders make it a priority to check out the height and spread of your chosen plants. Focus on the larger plants that will form the backbone of the garden – trees, large shrubs, climbers, roses and conifers – choosing and placing these before the smaller infill plants like compact shrubs, herbaceous perennials and so on. The Plant Directory (see page 126) gives the size after 10 years, although this is necessarily approximate, as growth will vary according to factors such as soil fertility and the availability of water. As a rough guide, allow 4–6m (12–20ft) between trees and 1.5–2.5m (5–8ft) between large shrubs.

For the first year, and maybe two, your borders will undeniably look rather bare and gappy if you have given plants sufficient room for future development. However, this can be rectified by filling the spaces with short-lived plants: hardy annuals such as pot marigold (*Calendula*), love-in-a-mist (*Nigella damascena*) and poppies (*Papaver*) conveniently last for only one season and also self-seed with alacrity, as do biennials like foxglove (*Digitalis*) and sweet rocket (*Hesperis matronalis*) that grow from seed one year to flower the next. Herbaceous perennials are tremendously useful gap-fillers too, as the vast majority are more than happy to be transplanted once the main planting begins to thicken. In fact, virtually all perennials benefit from being lifted, divided and replanted every few years in order to rejuvenate large, established clumps (see page 125), so are ideal for infilling in this way, as well as getting more plants for your money.

Grouping plants

Where large to medium-sized plants are concerned, planting singly in a border is the usual choice and these key plants should always be given priority. When it comes to small shrubs, low-growing to medium-sized perennials and ground-cover plants, however, grouping is by far and away the most effective way of placing them within a border.

Planting in groups gives a more harmonious overall effect to the garden and ensures that the planting will have plenty of impact, whether it is viewed close up or from a distance. This avoids the biggest pitfall of planting a small space – putting in one of everything and ending up with a confusing clutter of different plants that give a 'liquorice allsorts' effect.

As a guide to quantities, always use odd numbers for a more natural appearance: threes, fives and sevens tend to be ideal, unless your design uses a very limited range of plants laid out in large drifts. Otherwise, the smaller the plant, the greater the number that can be used. Within each group, place the plants in an informal shape such as a rough oval rather than in straight rows. In all cases, check the ultimate size of your plants and space them accordingly. Bulbs, particularly dwarf varieties such as snowdrops (*Galanthus*), scillas and glory-of-the-snow (*Chionodoxa*), look most effective when planted in large drifts rather than small patches. Planting such bulbs in drifts of 50 or 100, rather than measly tens or twenties, will give a glorious spring display. For the most natural appearance, take a handful of bulbs, scatter them on the ground and plant where they fall.

The chief exception to the above guidelines is planting a formal design. Here plants are often laid out in straight lines, with one side of the garden reflecting the other in order to create a

GROUPING PLANTS

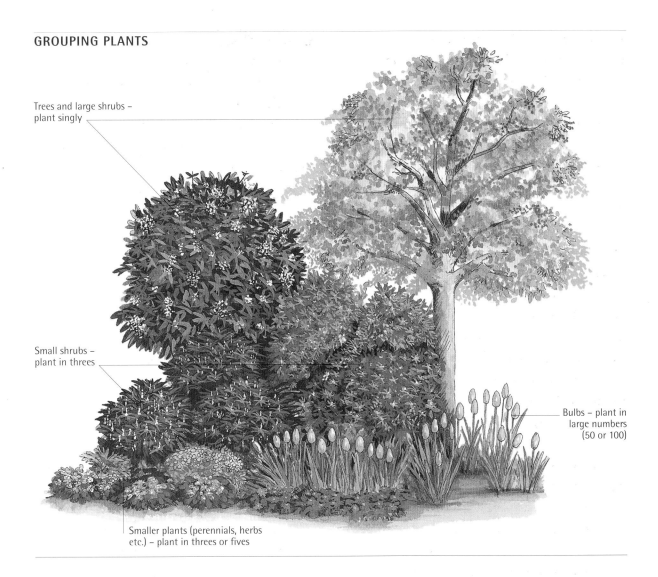

Trees and large shrubs – plant singly

Small shrubs – plant in threes

Bulbs – plant in large numbers (50 or 100)

Smaller plants (perennials, herbs etc.) – plant in threes or fives

symmetrical appearance and an air of harmony.

At the same time as planning your plant groupings, give some thought to colour and to grouping together plants of contrasting shape and texture. That way, your borders will look good for long periods of time, regardless of what may be in flower (see pages 65 and 68).

Drawing up a plan

Making a plan is by far the best way to tackle the future planting of your garden. In order to be really effective, a plan must be drawn up to scale, so first of all the garden has to be surveyed – that is, measured in detail. Start by taking a board

and large piece of paper outside (preferably on a mild, dry and windless day to avoid the risk of rushing the job) and make a rough sketch plan of the garden. Then, starting with the boundaries, the house and any other buildings, take measurements and write them on the plan as you go. Existing features of fixed size, such as fence panels and paving slabs, can be used as a useful guide to speed up the job.

Don't forget to take into account every existing feature, such as house doors and windows, paths, patio, trees, shrubs or other plants that you plan to keep in the same place, as well as plants that overhang from next door. Note any change in level, particularly if you wish to alter it. Note also the location of any services such as water and electricity. Mark down which areas are sunny or shady, any special characteristics of the soil and the influence of outside factors (see pages 10–16).

SURVEYING THE GARDEN

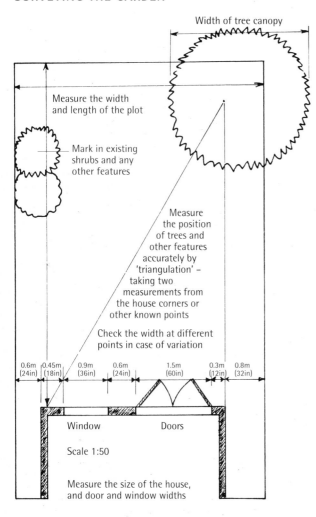

Width of tree canopy

Measure the width and length of the plot

Mark in existing shrubs and any other features

Measure the position of trees and other features accurately by 'triangulation' – taking two measurements from the house corners or other known points

Check the width at different points in case of variation

0.6m (24in) | 0.45m (18in) | 0.9m (36in) | 0.6m (24in) | 1.5m (60in) | 0.3m (12in) | 0.8m (32in)

Window   Doors

Scale 1:50

Measure the size of the house, and door and window widths

MEASURING LEVELS

Take a plank of wood of known length, eg 1.8m (6ft). Put one end on the ground and support the other with a wooden peg hammered into the ground. Adjust the peg until the spirit level is correct. Measurement A will show the fall over a distance of 1.8m (6ft)

Spirit level

A

Once you are satisfied that absolutely everything has been included, draw up the survey neatly and to scale, on graph paper. A useful working scale to use is 1:50 (2cm = 1m); you can buy a scale ruler to do the conversions for you. When the drawing is complete, take it back outside, spend a few minutes looking at it and the garden at the same time and check a few key measurements. If any mistakes have been made, now is the time to pick them up before you progress any further – remember that the survey is the basis of your plan and any errors will be compounded as work continues.

Now lay tracing paper over the top of the survey drawing, and you are ready to start drawing in your borders and new plants. All this may sound like a lot of work, and it is, but it's also very absorbing and good fun. Take plenty of time over the job – leave your plan for

---

SURVEY CHECKLIST

To survey a garden and draw up a plan, you will need:

■ Graph paper – A2 size is usually adequate
■ Board, to lean on
■ Sticky tape or drawing pins, to hold paper in place
■ Tape measure – very long if possible; if not, use several shorter ones
■ Tracing paper
■ Ruler, pencil and eraser
■ Scale ruler (optional)
■ Directional compass – not essential, but useful to determine the correct orientation of the garden

---

Right: A photograph from an upstairs window can provide a handy alternative to measuring up the whole garden.

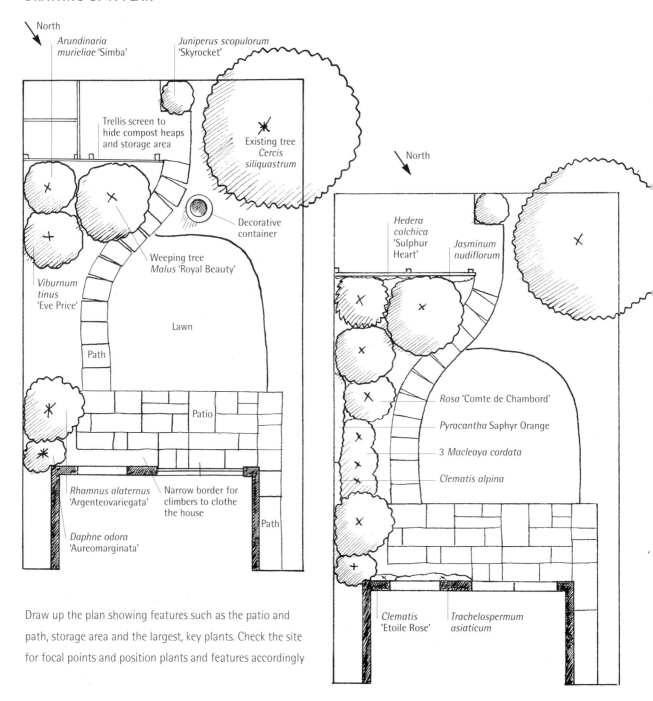

North

Arundinaria murieliae 'Simba'

Juniperus scopulorum 'Skyrocket'

Trellis screen to hide compost heaps and storage area

Existing tree *Cercis siliquastrum*

Decorative container

Weeping tree *Malus* 'Royal Beauty'

Viburnum tinus 'Eve Price'

Lawn

Path

Patio

Rhamnus alaternus 'Argenteovariegata'

Narrow border for climbers to clothe the house

Path

Daphne odora 'Aureomarginata'

North

Hedera colchica 'Sulphur Heart'

Jasminum nudiflorum

Rosa 'Comte de Chambord'

Pyracantha Saphyr Orange

3 *Macleaya cordata*

Clematis alpina

Clematis 'Etoile Rose'

Trachelospermum asiaticum

Draw up the plan showing features such as the patio and path, storage area and the largest, key plants. Check the site for focal points and position plants and features accordingly

Add the rest of the 'backbone' planting – climbers, larger shrubs and perennials. Include a good proportion of evergreens for year-round structure and interest

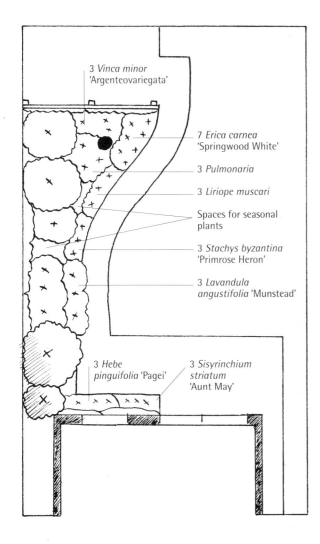

3 *Vinca minor*
'Argenteovariegata'

7 *Erica carnea*
'Springwood White'

3 *Pulmonaria*

3 *Liriope muscari*

Spaces for seasonal
plants

3 *Stachys byzantina*
'Primrose Heron'

3 *Lavandula
angustifolia* 'Munstead'

3 *Hebe
pinguifolia* 'Pagei'

3 *Sisyrinchium
striatum*
'Aunt May'

Put in the smaller 'decorative' plants such as smaller perennials, shrubs and ground-cover plants. Note the spaces left for seasonal plants, such as annuals and tender perennials, to provide long-lasting summer colour. Bulbs can also be interplanted throughout for extra flowers

a day or a week and mull over your progress, then return to it with fresh ideas. Winter is a great time to do this, when the long, dark evenings can be filled with dreams of the garden's future glory.

Not surprisingly, many people find it hard to visualize the garden's layout on the basis of a plan alone. An alternative approach is to take a photograph of your garden from the best vantage point – usually an upstairs window – and have it enlarged. Then lay tracing paper over the top and sketch in the shape of your new borders and their planting, as well as any new features.

When drawing up your planting plan, try to concentrate first and foremost on the larger shrubs and trees that will form the skeleton of the garden. Mark them on your plan, making a cross to show the exact planting position, and then sketch in their approximate eventual spread to be sure that you aren't placing plants too close together. Once you are satisfied with the backbone planting, infill with smaller plants such as herbaceous perennials, small shrubs and ground cover plants.

Having completed your plan on paper, check that it actually works in practice before buying the plants and digging the borders. Mark out the border outlines, using a hosepipe for curving borders and pegs and string for straight edges. Put in markers to indicate the sites for the largest, key plants, using tall canes or even garden chairs. Any fine-tuning of your plan that may be required is much easier this way than after the plants have been put in!

The Secrets of Successful Planting

PLANTS ARE LIKE PEOPLE, with differing likes and dislikes – in their case, as to where they grow in a garden. And, like people, plants vary in their sensitivity. A few are happy-go-lucky creatures that thrive almost anywhere, but the majority are choosy to a lesser or greater degree. However, the wonderful thing about plants is that regardless of how extreme the conditions in your garden may be, there will be at least a few – and usually a lot more – that will like what you can offer. The route to success is through careful match-making to ensure that the likes of the plants match the conditions of their site, so that they can perform at their best. The amount of sun or shade a site receives, whether the soil is dry and free-draining or heavy and moisture-retentive, and its acidity or alkalinity, are the chief aspects to consider when selecting plants for your garden, along with climatic influences. These factors are covered in detail on pages 15–16.

Right plant, right place

Choosing the right plants to match the conditions in your garden is important for several reasons. Most significant is that you will achieve far more rewarding results, and with less work,

by working *with* the conditions you have rather than *against* them. Plants chosen to suit their environment will flourish with the minimum of attention – contrast this with, for example, the amount of watering that would be required if you attempted to grow moisture-loving plants in a sunny, well-drained site. It goes without saying that this approach also saves money on replacing plants that sicken or die when grown in unsuitable places.

What is less immediately obvious are the benefits to the appearance of the garden as a whole. Plants that like the same conditions automatically tend to look good together, so a little time spent on selecting the right plants for your garden's environment will pay off handsomely in terms of creating the best-looking plant combinations for your borders. Shade or sun, dry or damp: each site has its own special appeal and can be planted to generate its own distinct character.

Planting in shade

Shade: the very word reeks of gloom and despondency, which is perhaps part of the reason why many people view a shady plot as a difficult place in which to garden. Fortunately, the reality is very different and shade is a definite asset that I would hate to do without. Plenty of plants thrive out of the sun, and most are particularly good for the small garden because much of their appeal comes from attractive shapes and decorative foliage, which give excellent long-lasting interest. There are plenty of flowers for shade, too, in colours that tend to be the more subtle ones of white, cream, pink and blue rather than the vivid tones generally produced by sun-loving varieties. An added bonus of shade is that flowers will last for a much longer period as a result of being kept out of direct sunlight.

There are, however, degrees of shade, and greater scope in planting can be achieved if this is recognized at the start. The deepest, darkest shade, such as a tunnel-like alley at the back of a terraced house or a site facing away from the sun that is also overhung by a densely canopied tree, can only be planted with a relatively small selection of plants that will tolerate such severe

Shade-loving plants create a textured and softly coloured tapestry of foliage.

gloom. By contrast, a border underneath a lightly foliaged tree such as a birch or sorbus will receive a greater amount of light and is therefore suitable for a wider range of plants.

DRY SHADE

By far the most common of conditions encountered in a small garden, dry shade occurs where dense cover is provided by overhanging trees and large shrubs, which prevent much of the rain from reaching the ground and also take up the lion's share of whatever moisture there is. Buildings and nearby walls – especially common in a town garden – also shield the soil from the rain. Conditions are further exacerbated if the soil is light and free-draining.

Thorough soil preparation can make a world of difference to the health of your plants and will certainly get them off to a good start in life. Enriching the ground with organic matter will improve the water-holding capacity of the soil, as

Right: A plant-framed seat brightens a dark corner.

well as lessening the speed at which nutrients are washed out of a light soil. Dig in the organic matter if possible, but if existing plants or tree roots make this impossible, just lay it on the surface of the bare soil as a mulch and the worms and other soil organisms will take the material down into the ground to enrich it thoroughly (see page 117).

Deep, dry shade

The darkest corners rely chiefly on variegated or coloured foliage to lighten the gloom. Ivies – magnificent, ultra-tolerant yet undervalued plants – are without parallel for lightening the deepest shade right through the year. A large expanse of wall is a suitable spot for the vigorous Persian ivy *Hedera colchica* 'Dentata Variegata', with its bold, glossy white-and-green leaves, while the many forms of English ivy (*H. helix*)

PLANTING FOR DEEP, DRY SHADE

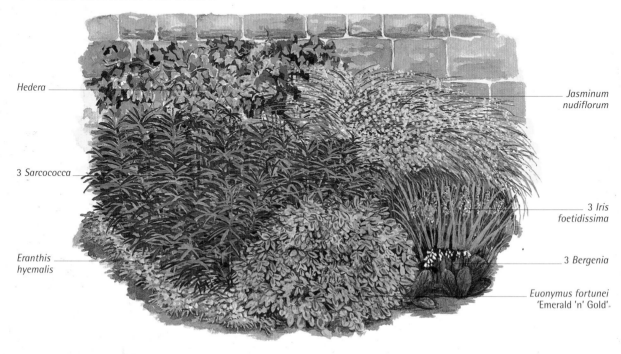

Hedera

Jasminum nudiflorum

3 *Sarcococca*

3 *Iris foetidissima*

Eranthis hyemalis

3 *Bergenia*

Euonymus fortunei 'Emerald 'n' Gold'.

are less vigorous and excellent in a smaller space. Near a house or in a formal setting, the smaller ivies can be trained into topiary shapes by using wire frames, which are available in many different designs; grow them in pairs to flank a doorway, path or flight of steps. Although ivies are mostly used as climbers, they make excellent ground cover as well. Also good for a shady wall, although deciduous, is the climbing hydrangea (*Hydrangea anomala* subsp. *petiolaris*), slow to get going but lovely when established, with frothy white heads of summer flowers and green leaves that turn yellow before falling.

Evergreens should have priority for high-profile sites near the house. *Daphne laureola*, handsome yet understated, has glossy dark green leaves and clusters of scented, subtle greeny-yellow flowers in early spring. Also fragrant is Christmas box (*Sarcococca*) with dark, glossy foliage and tassels of vanilla-scented flowers in mid- to late winter, while *Viburnum tinus* 'Eve Price' flowers at around the same time. *Euonymus fortunei* varieties, many of which have brightly variegated foliage, are invaluable both as ground cover and to scramble up a wall if trained in the right direction.

Certain perennials retain their leaves all year. The best include bergenias, aptly named 'elephant's ears' for the shape of their rounded,

Purple honesty and the arching stems of Solomon's seal lighten this shady border.

shiny leaves, with pink, purple or white flower clusters on short stems in early spring. Contrast these rounded leaves with the sword-like foliage of the Gladwyn, or Gladdon, iris (*Iris foetidissima*) – 'Gladdon' meaning 'sword' in Old English – which, unlike most irises, is noted less for its blooms than for its autumn pods of bright orange seeds and evergreen leaves that smell faintly of roast beef when crushed. Hellebores are superb and flower for a long period, from late winter until well into spring; most beautiful is the Lenten rose (*Helleborus orientalis*) that produces its open, four-petalled blooms in many shades of pink and purple. Lastly, for a really difficult site that is bone dry and packed with tree roots, grow the near-indestructible *Euphorbia robbiae*, a real thug of a plant whose vigour is restrained to acceptable levels where conditions are poor. Its glossy, evergreen rosettes of dark green leaves are enlivened with tall bracts of lime-yellow flowers in spring.

Deciduous plants can add extra colour in a variety of ways. Perennials like pulmonarias and *Geranium macrorrhizum* provide spring and summer blooms respectively. Bulbs are marvellous in dry conditions, as they carry their own stocks of nourishment and are less reliant on outside supplies. In deep shade, choose snowdrops, bluebells and winter aconites for spring, and for autumn the delightful little hardy cyclamen *C. hederifolium*, with its dainty pink blooms which are followed by attractively marbled leaves.

Light, dry shade

Away from the intense gloom of the shadiest spots and out into areas that are still sunless but receive more light, the range of plants that can be grown broadens considerably. All the plants described previously for deep shade will certainly flourish with thanks for a lighter site, but there is no need now to be so ruthlessly selective.

The choice of plants to clothe walls, fences and other supports is excellent. Most clematis species will do well, apart from the real sun-lovers like *C. armandii* and *C. texensis*. A surprising number of large-flowered hybrids prefer light shade too, particularly those with pale or bicoloured blooms, which have a tendency to become bleached in full sun. Partner a clematis with pyracantha, a wall shrub that can be trimmed closely against its support and gives all-year interest with spring flowers, autumn berries and evergreen foliage, or with one of the climbing roses that tolerate shade (see panel on page 50). An expanse of wall, or a garden building such as a shed or garage, can be covered with the vigorous ornamental vine (*Vitis coignetiae*) whose exceptionally large, lobed leaves make a dramatic display, particularly with their rich autumn colours, as do the silver-veined leaves of *Parthenocissus henryana*.

Many shrubs perform well in light shade, including hollies (*Ilex*), with spiky leaves in beautiful variegations and unusual shapes, *Lonicera nitida* 'Baggesen's Gold', with tiny golden, evergreen leaves, and *Viburnum davidii*, with bold, ridged, dark evergreen leaves. Certain shrubs need to be out of midday sun in order to give of their best, notably those with golden foliage that tends to scorch in direct sun but fails to colour well in deep shade. These include the golden-variegated *Aucuba japonica* 'Crotonifolia', golden Mexican orange blossom (*Choisya ternata* 'Sundance'), and *Berberis thunbergii* 'Aurea'.

Perennials to grow under large shrubs, or just to be planted on their own, are many and varied. Virtually all the winter- and spring-flowering perennials listed in the Plant Directory (see pages 149–50) are happy in light shade, including the

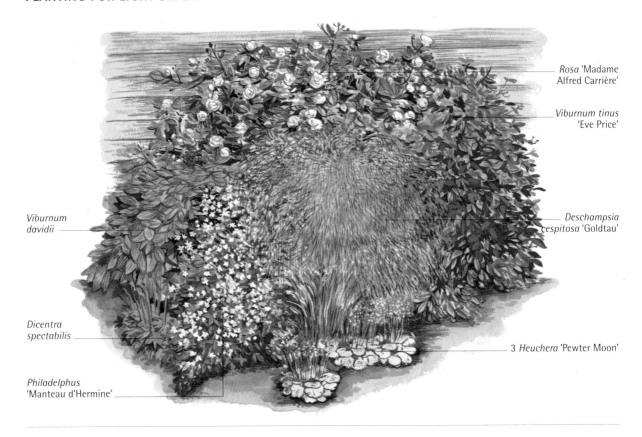

Rosa 'Madame Alfred Carrière'

Viburnum tinus 'Eve Price'

Deschampsia cespitosa 'Goldtau'

Viburnum davidii

Dicentra spectabilis

Philadelphus 'Manteau d'Hermine'

3 Heuchera 'Pewter Moon'

horned violet (*Viola cornuta*), with dainty white or pale blue flowers, which forms a carpet on its own or will clamber enchantingly through a low-growing shrub such as euonymus. Plants with attractive foliage such as lady's mantle (*Alchemilla mollis*), epimediums and heucheras look good from spring to autumn, while the lilyturf (*Liriope muscari*) gives late-season colour with its deep purple blooms. Most bulbs are happiest in light shade, so they can be used to infill any bare patches or just to pop up among groups and through carpets of other plants, which then conveniently conceal the unsightly dying bulb foliage.

CLIMBING ROSES FOR A SHADY SITE

'Aloha'

'Danse de Feu'

'Gloire de Dijon'

'Golden Showers'

'Madame Alfred Carrière'

'New Dawn'

'Parkdirektor Riggers'

DAMP SHADE

A moisture-retentive soil in a shady site offers the chance to grow a wonderful range of plants, many of which have lush, attractive foliage or colourful flowers. However, damp shade is less common than dry shade in a small garden, due to the rain-shielding effects of trees, large shrubs and nearby structures already explained. Most of the plants discussed previously will also be happy in damp, although not wet, soil.

Deep shade

In deep shade, the bold, sculpted leaves of hostas create spectacular foliage interest with a wealth of different colours and variegations. Of the ornamental grasses, sedges (*Carex*) prefer a retentive soil, forming little arching clumps of elegant leaves that are gold, bronze or green-and-white in colour, while the purple moor grass (*Molinia caerulea* 'Variegata') produces a wonderful display of elegant yellow stems topped with purple spikelets of flowers. Skimmias provide year-round interest with glossy evergreen leaves and long-lasting flower buds, while the female and hermaphrodite varieties bear red berries in autumn, too.

Although most annuals are sun-lovers, there is a handful of varieties that prefer shade and these few can be incredibly useful for lightening gloomy spots in summer. Annuals are wonderfully flexible plants, suitable for all manner of containers – pots, hanging baskets and window boxes – plus, of course, beds and borders. Busy lizzies (*Impatiens*) are available in a wealth of colours, as are fuchsias, which come in a number of shapes too – bushes, trailers, standards and cordons – while trailing lobelia in blue, white or pink is an excellent gap-filler.

Light shade and moist soil

Light or dappled shade and moist, acid soil is a site to treasure, for in come some of the plant genera that comprise a huge selection of species and cultivars. There are Japanese maples (*Acer palmatum*) with delicate, finely cut leaves and shapes that vary from a neat 'mushroom' mound to an upright, branching shrub that slowly attains the size of a small tree. Dwarf rhododendrons produce a spectacular display of

PLANTING FOR SHADE AND RETENTIVE SOIL

Clematis 'Nelly Moser'

Cornus alba 'Sibirica'

Lonicera nitida 'Baggesen's Gold'

3 *Hosta sieboldiana* var. *elegans*

3 *Anemone* x *hybrida*

3 *Epimedium* x *rubrum*

brightly coloured spring blooms: *R. yakushim-anum* hybrids are the best for small gardens, being compact in habit, with good-looking foliage as well as flowers in a magnificent range of colours. Heaths (*Calluna*) are excellent low-growing shrubs for summer flowers, and the 'bud-blooming' varieties give colour over a particularly long period. Other shrubs that need acid soil include evergreen or Japanese azaleas, pieris and camellias.

Planting in sun

A sunny site has the potential to grow a wonderful selection of plants. Many are at their best in summer when there is a profusion of flowering plants available, so be aware of the dangers of falling for a plethora of summer beauties and neglecting plants for other times of the year. There are a great many vivid flowers from which to choose, so it is wise to plan a colour scheme if clashes of the most dreadful kind are not to occur. Although bright colours predominate – which is no bad thing, as intense sunlight drains colour – do not overlook white, which comes into its own in the evening, as well as attractive foliage to offset and enhance all the different flowers.

As a great many plants thrive in sun, it is often easier in the first instance to look at what *not* to grow – so start by consulting the previous section on plants for shade. The vast majority of shade-lovers will make their dislike of sun quite plain by developing brown, scorched patches on their leaves, or bearing flowers that appear almost to sizzle and shrivel up, so quickly do they fade and die in bright sun.

PLANTING FOR SUN

Ipomoea tricolor 'Heavenly Blue'

Miscanthus sinensis

Choisya ternata 'Sundance'

Artemisia 'Powis Castle' with *Clematis* x *durandii*

3 *Salvia officinalis* Purpurascens Group

As is always the best procedure where the choice is wide, begin with the largest plants. In an open site, one or two trees or large shrubs will, when established, cast some very welcome shade. A tree with attractive foliage looks in keeping with a sunny site: good examples are the ferny golden leaves of the honey locust (*Gleditsia triacanthos* 'Sunburst') or the small lobed, tricoloured ones of *Acer negundo* 'Flamingo'. They cast a shade that is gently dappled, enabling a wide range of plants to be grown underneath. The Judas tree (*Cercis siliquastrum*) throws a deeper shade: it comes from the Mediterranean and delights in sun, producing a plentiful show of magenta-pink spring flowers if the previous summer has been warm. Certain quick-growing shrubs can soon do duty as shade providers, such as the Italian buckthorn (*Rhamnus alaternus* 'Argenteovariegata'), which has the bonus of colourful evergreen foliage.

All the summer-flowering shrubs in the Plant Directory (see page 131) thrive in sun and some, such as caryopteris, lavender and rosemary, are immensely popular with bees, their soothing hum being the very essence of the garden in summer. Most annuals and tender perennials revel in full sun and can be packed into any gaps to ensure that there is no shortage of summer colour. For shrubs that provide foliage interest, look to hebes with leaves in green, silver, purple and yellow ochre, *Lonicera nitida* 'Baggesen's Gold' with tiny yellow leaves, New Zealand flax (*Phormium*) with bold sword-like foliage in many colours including cream and red, and *Physocarpus opulifolius* 'Diablo' with dark purple foliage.

Ornamental grasses blend beautifully with other plants and the contrast of their arching, slender leaves and airy flowerheads with the heavier foliage of shrubs, perennials and conifers makes an enchanting combination. At the back of the border, plant *Miscanthus sinensis* varieties, which will form tall clumps of bamboo-like foliage – tall varieties of the true bamboos are excellent here, too – and in the border centre place the tufted hair grass, *Deschampsia cespitosa* 'Goldtau'. At the very front, small grasses like *Carex* and *Festuca* make a neat edging that finishes off the border to perfection.

Roses, too, are part and parcel of the summer garden, bearing a glorious profusion of blooms. Climbers and ramblers can be trained against walls and fences, and over pergolas, arches and arbours. In the border, where roses have to rub shoulders with lots of other plants, choose shrub roses which are happy in company, as opposed to hybrid tea and floribunda varieties which perform best when grown in a bed on their own. Many of the true old-fashioned varieties grow very large, or flower only once during the season, although some of the old groups of Portland, China and Polyantha roses are both compact in habit and repeat-flower well. There are also

English roses, which are new, old-fashioned lookalikes that combine the chief virtues of both old and modern varieties. For border edges and sunny banks, there is a goodly selection of ground-cover roses which are long-flowering and compact in habit. Many newer varieties such as 'Flower Carpet' and the County Series are extremely garden-worthy plants. Do beware, though, of exceptionally vigorous ground-cover roses such as the Gamebird Series, which are used for large-scale landscaping and have a spread of several metres.

Drought-tolerant plants

Soil that is very light and free-draining, such as sandy, stony or chalky ground, needs to be matched with plants that can thrive happily for long periods without water. These drought-tolerant plants are best grown on free-draining soil in any case, as most dislike having wet roots in winter, particularly in cold areas. Plants that originate in hot, dry countries have cleverly developed ways to cope with such conditions and

PLANTING FOR DRY, DROUGHT-PRONE SOIL IN SUN

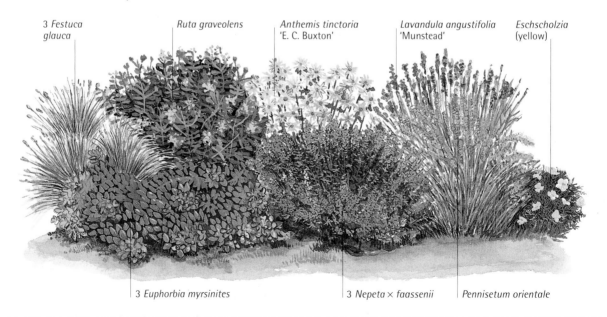

3 *Festuca glauca*

Ruta graveolens

Anthemis tinctoria 'E. C. Buxton'

Lavandula angustifolia 'Munstead'

Eschscholzia (yellow)

3 *Euphorbia myrsinites*

3 *Nepeta × faassenii*

Pennisetum orientale

Drought-tolerant plants often have glaucous foliage, such as the rue in the centre with its yellow flowers.

reduce water loss, by producing leaves that are grey, hairy, waxy or narrow.

Evergreen plants for year-round structure can easily be overlooked in favour of summer flowers. Spiky-leaved shrubs like cordylines and yuccas, both the plain green and variegated forms, are wonderful for winter interest as well as for providing a strong background to flowering plants. In cold areas, however, it is safest to grow these shrubs in pots so that they can be moved under cover if very low temperatures are forecast. Junipers, in a host of different shapes and foliage colours, are real sun-lovers, as is the variegated Italian buckthorn (*Rhamnus alaternus* 'Argenteo-variegata'). Any gaps can be filled with tender perennials. Particularly fond of sun-baked sites

DROUGHT-TOLERANT PLANTS

Artemisia 'Powis Castle'

Caryopteris x *clandonensis*

Convolvulus cneorum

Eschscholzia

Euphorbia myrsinites

Festuca glauca

Helichrysum italicum subsp. *serotinum*

Juniperus

Lavandula

Lotus hirsutus

Nepeta x *faassenii*

Pennisetum orientale

Ruta graveolens

Salvia officinalis

Sedum spectabile

Stachys byzantina

are the daisy-flowered varieties such as Zulu daisy (*Arctotis*) and African daisy (*Osteospermum*) which have large, showy blooms, *Felicia amelloides* with small, deep blue flowers, and *Bidens ferulifolia*, a superb trailing plant that bears masses of small, bright yellow flowers.

Choosing key plants

In a small garden, any plant of a reasonable size absolutely has to earn its keep and look good for the greater part of the year. Trees and medium-sized to large shrubs occupy a goodly proportion of the available ground and must all be chosen with this point foremost in your mind: there can be no slackers where space is at a premium. If your garden is to look good for a long period of time, sentiment and impulse need to be firmly sat upon for the moment – they can be given a freer rein later with the smaller plants to grow in, around and through these key specimens.

Planting to scale

Achieving the right balance of scale and proportion is a matter of choosing plants that will attain an eventual height and spread which are in keeping with the overall size of your garden, the house and any other structures. Putting in plants that will become too large is

the biggest danger, although it is also quite likely that you will inherit planting mistakes made by previous owners which will need complete removal or rejuvenating with severe pruning. A stroll around any town or suburb will usually turn up some classic examples of out-of-scale planting, such as an outsize tree, the height of which is several times the width of the garden, or a very tall, straggling hedge of Leyland cypress which dominates and dwarfs a small plot. Once seen and realized, such potential mistakes can be avoided much more easily.

On the other hand, erring too far on the side of caution can bring its own problems, albeit far less severe and more easily rectified than the scenarios described above. A narrow border edging a large lawn allows for only a few small plants to be grown and looks mean and niggardly. A border that is larger, but which contains all small plants and no large ones to provide a bit of 'oomph', will similarly look out of keeping. However, these situations can readily be remedied by enlarging the border or planting several bold specimens, such as those described on page 60. Even a miniature landscape of alpines needs a few plants to provide impact, although still in keeping with the scale, such as dwarf conifers or shrubs that reach 30cm (12in)

PLANTING TO SCALE

Good: the hedge is approximately ¼ – ½ the height of the house and the two look in balance

Bad: the hedge is far too tall and completely dominates the plot, throwing the whole scene out of proportion

or so in height. Similarly, a border of summer bedding plants benefits from a few tall 'dot' plants such as marguerites (*Argyranthemum*). Successful planting depends on balance in order to achieve an harmonious appearance in the garden as a whole.

Plants as focal points

Focal points are a valuable way of providing structure and interest within a garden. Any view, whether from inside the house, from the patio, or out in the garden, benefits by having a key plant or feature as its centrepiece. A plant that looks particularly striking can be placed so that it is seen from the viewpoint and deliberately draws the eye towards it. One is all that is needed – two or more focal points in the same view cause confusion and dilute the overall effect. Just as importantly, a focal point can also be used to draw

Above: Plants with spiky foliage, such as the cordyline in the foreground, make superb focal points to draw the eye around the garden.

the eye *away* from an unsightly view or object.

In all but the tiniest of gardens, focal points can be sited at strategic spots to draw the visitor away from the house, through the garden and back again – a visual way of taking someone by the hand and leading them around. For example, at the end of the lawn a weeping tree, or one with a seat placed temptingly underneath, can be seen from the patio or from inside the house. Once the visitor reaches the tree, an attractive plant in a container comes into view, perhaps at right angles behind a border. Then, when standing by the container, a clipped topiary specimen close to the house leads the visitor back by means of a path behind the border.

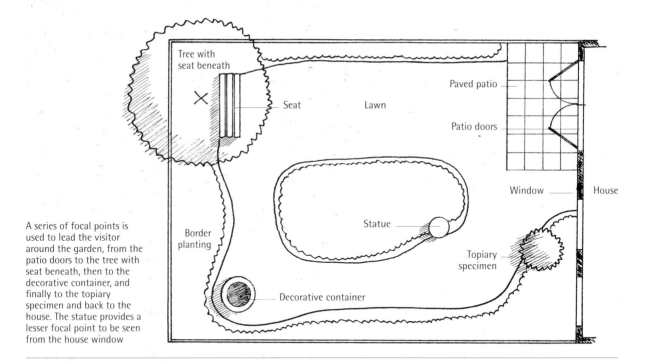

A series of focal points is used to lead the visitor around the garden, from the patio doors to the tree with seat beneath, then to the decorative container, and finally to the topiary specimen and back to the house. The statue provides a lesser focal point to be seen from the house window

Plants for focal points can range in size from a small shrub to a tree, but regardless of size, it is imperative that they look good for the whole year. A tree could have a distinctive shape, such as a weeping or columnar habit (see panels below and on page 59), or decorative bark, such as the shining mahogany trunk of the Tibetan cherry (*Prunus serrula*) and the dazzling white stems of the Himalayan birch (*Betula utilis* var. *jacquemontii*). Trees with variegated foliage, like *Acer negundo* 'Flamingo', are better used as focal points than in general planting, as they stand out from the surrounding plants and really catch the eye. Evergreen shrubs can be clipped to form distinctive shapes of all sizes, from small pyramids of box (*Buxus sempervirens*) to tall cones of variegated holly (*Ilex*) or domes of golden privet (*Ligustrum ovalifolium* 'Aureum').

For it to be most effective as a focal point, the backdrop to the chosen plant should be a neutral one such as a hedge, a group of plants with plain green foliage, a fence or a wall. A smaller specimen can be emphasized by framing it with an arch, or placed so that it is seen through a 'doorway' clipped in a hedge.

Trees for small gardens

The grace, beauty and size of trees ensure that they play a starring role in any garden. Most small gardens, however, can house only one or two, and so these prima donnas need to be exceptionally hardworking in terms of

UPRIGHT OR COLUMNAR TREES

Juniperus scopulorum 'Skyrocket'
Malus 'John Downie'
M. 'Van Eseltine'
Prunus 'Amanogawa'
Sorbus 'Joseph Rock'
S. aucuparia 'Fastigiata'

Most small gardens can only house one or two trees, so choose and site them with great care.

ornamental value. It is simply not enough for a tree to flower in spring and then do nothing for the remaining 11 months of the year: to be worthy of selection, there must be at least two seasons of interest, such as spring flowers followed by autumn fruit, ornamental foliage that looks good from spring to autumn, or

WEEPING TREES
Fagus sylvatica 'Purpurea Pendula'
Malus 'Royal Beauty'
Prunus 'Kiku-shidare-zakura'
P. x yedoensis 'Shidare-yoshino'
Pyrus salicifolia 'Pendula'
Salix caprea 'Kilmarnock'
S. purpurea 'Pendula'

TREE SHAPES

Upright/conical

Weeping

Rounded

Fastigiate

Wide-spreading

attractive leaves plus decorative bark that really comes into its own in winter. Only where there is space for several trees to be grown is it a good idea to include a less versatile variety, such as a flowering cherry (*Prunus*).

Any trees that grow too large are out of the running to begin with, although there are plenty of small ones that reach around 5–6m (15–20ft), as you will see in the Plant Directory on pages 127–30. Grafted varieties are more compact still, notably weeping trees like the Kilmarnock willow (*Salix caprea* 'Kilmarnock'), purple willow (*S. purpurea* 'Pendula') and Cheal's weeping cherry (*Prunus* 'Kiku-shidare-zakura'), which attain a height of around 1.8–2.5m (6–8ft).

The overall shape of a tree can also have a strong influence on its suitability for a particular site. Although many trees have a rounded head of upright or arching branches, there are some with a narrowly upright or vase shape and others so narrow as to be columnar in habit, while the branches of some varieties weep down to the ground (see pages 58 and 59). Most rounded, upright or columnar trees can be grown in a border and underplanted with shrubs, perennials and other plants, while weeping trees need adequate space around them so that their shape can be fully appreciated, and can only be underplanted with exceptionally shade-tolerant ground-cover plants as their canopy of branches darkens the ground underneath considerably. Fruiting trees are best avoided where they would overhang a patio or path, as the fallen fruits will be squashed underfoot, making the paving dangerously slippery as well as unsightly.

When choosing the planting site, allow enough distance from the house so that the roots cannot interfere with foundations or drains. The smallest weeping trees which have been grafted and will not grow beyond around 1.8m (6ft) can be planted within a few metres of the house, while as a general rule of thumb larger ones should certainly be no closer than their eventual height.

Specimen plants

Plants that are particularly eyecatching, such as those with an attractive shape or long-lasting ornamental features, can become key features around the garden. In a mixed border, they provide a focus to the planting and make a good

---

ARCHITECTURAL PLANTS
The plants listed below either have a bold shape or particularly striking foliage.

Acer palmatum cultivars
Aucuba japonica 'Crotonifolia'
Bamboos: *Arundinaria murieliae*, *A. nitida*,
    Phyllostachys and other tall varieties
Berberis thunbergii 'Helmond Pillar'
Conifers: *Juniperus scopulorum* 'Skyrocket',
    Taxus baccata 'Standishii' and many other
    columnar varieties
Cordyline
Euphorbia characias subsp. *wulfenii*
Ilex
Miscanthus sinensis cultivars
Phormium
Macleaya cordata
Rhododendron yakushimanum hybrids
Sambucus racemosa 'Plumosa Aurea'
Skimmia japonica 'Rubella'
Viburnum davidii
Yucca

Right: Architectural plants, such as this clipped box and a spiky-leaved cordyline, are very dramatic in appearance.

ARCHITECTURAL PLANTS

Formal, trimmed shape –
box topiary

Bold, spiky leaves –
phormium

Attractive shape and
decorative foliage –
Japanese maple

Distinctive columnar
shape – *Prunus*
'Amanogawa'

Upright, clump-forming
bamboo

contrast to the soft lines of the surrounding plants. Placed on either side of a door, path or gateway, such plants enhance and emphasize whatever they are flanking. When used singly in a lawn, a small border or on a patio, with sufficient space to be appreciated individually, they become key features in their own right.

A number of evergreen shrubs respond well to clipping and trimming to create dense, neat shapes such as domes, pyramids or cones (see panel below). Such a clipped, formal shape will provide a visual 'full stop' within the border or garden, drawing the eye and breaking up a planting. If left untrimmed, however, these plants will merge into the general overall appearance of the border. An illusion of space can be created by planting specimens of plants suitable for clipping at regular intervals down the garden: trim them all to the same shape, but gradually reduce the size of each plant so that they appear to recede into the distance.

'Architectural' plants – those which have large, bold leaves or strong form – are invaluable in any garden, although in a small space they should be used with a little restraint. Too many strongly shaped plants close together can be overpowering, but a few thoughtfully placed specimens bring year-round dramatic impact to a garden. Architectural plants are eyecatching and naturally draw attention to themselves, and as such should be placed close to the house. Here they will be an immediate attraction, and the rest of the garden will then be noticed more gradually. Conversely, if such strong shapes were to be used in the middle to far distance, they would instantly catch the eye and make the garden appear to be shorter than it actually is. Their structural shape also makes a good

SHRUBS SUITABLE FOR TRIMMING

A number of shrubs respond well to clipping into formal shapes such as balls, pyramids, spirals or domes. On average, two cuts in the growing season should be sufficient, although slower-growing varieties such as yew (*Taxus baccata*) often need only one cut while the vigorous ones like golden privet (*Ligustrum ovalifolium* 'Aureum') may need three. Do not clip after early autumn or the soft young growth that is subsequently produced may be susceptible to frost damage.

Buxus sempervirens
Ilex
Laurus nobilis
Ligustrum ovalifolium 'Aureum'
Lonicera nitida 'Baggesen's Gold'
Taxus baccata

A box 'ball' makes an excellent contrast to the lax growth of *Hemerocallis, Knautia* and phlox.

BORDER PLANTED FOR YEAR–ROUND INTEREST

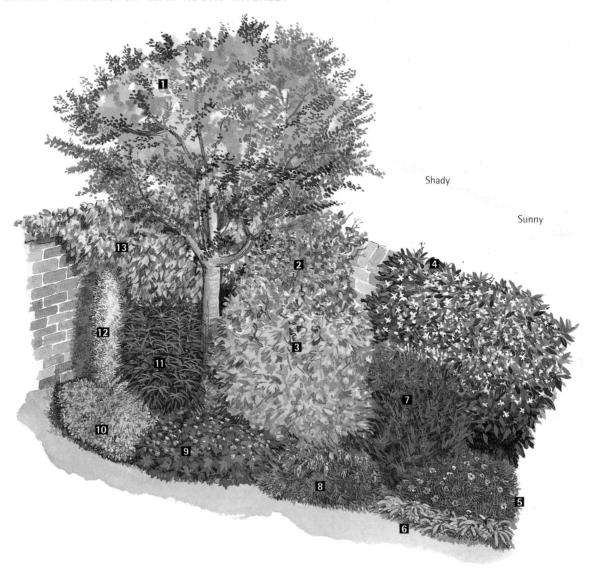

Shady

Sunny

1 *Sorbus cashmiriana* Compact tree with spring flowers, attractive leaves and clusters of white berries in autumn

2 *Lathyrus latifolius* Herbaceous climber with bright pink flowers in summer

3 *Physocarpus opulifolius* 'Dart's Gold' Rounded deciduous shrub with attractive yellow-green leaves

4 *Trachelospermum asiaticum* Self-clinging evergreen climber bearing jasmine-like, deliciously scented flowers in summer

5 *Nigella damascena* Hardy annual with feathery foliage, white or blue flowers and decorative seed pods. Good gap-filler

6 *Stachys byzantina* 'Primrose Heron' Ground-cover plant with woolly leaves in an unusual shade of yellow-green

7 *Caryopteris* x *clandonensis* 'Heavenly Blue' Late-summer shrub bearing deep blue flowers in small, spiky clusters, loved by bees

8 *Dicentra* 'Stuart Boothman' Useful perennial for underplanting with fern-like, divided, blue-grey leaves. Deep pink, locket-like flowers appear from early summer onwards

9 *Geranium wallichianum* 'Buxton's Variety' Low-growing perennial with divided green leaves and in summer bearing sky-blue flowers with large white centres

10 *Hebe* 'Red Edge' Mound-forming evergreen shrub with glaucous red-tinged foliage. Red tints deepen in winter

11 *Sarcococca hookeriana* var. *digyna* Compact, evergreen shrub with glossy, dark green foliage and deliciously scented, creamy-white flowers in mid- to late winter

12 *Taxus baccata* 'Standishii' Columnar conifer with colourful foliage in a beautiful shade of old gold

13 *Hedera colchica* 'Sulphur Heart' Ivy with large, dark green leaves splashed with lime-green

transition from the hard, formal lines of the house to the softer planting further out in the garden. Many of the plants listed in the panel on page 60 are shrubs that will take several years at least to attain a reasonable size. There are other plants, however, that reach decent proportions reasonably quickly. One such is the plume poppy (*Macleaya cordata*), a superb plant that deserves much wider use: it quickly throws up tall, stout stems, which rarely need staking, clad with lobed grey-green leaves and topped with beautiful plumes of flowers.

If the budget permits, it may be worth buying one or more of the key shrubs and conifers for the garden as mature, ready-grown specimens. In a very small plot where the total number of plants will be limited anyway, spending a relatively large sum of money on one stunningly gorgeous specimen can be perfectly justified. In this case, the plant would be such an eyecatcher that money could be saved on the surrounding infill plants by buying smaller sizes and waiting for them to grow.

Year-round interest and seasonal impact

Ask most small-garden owners what they want to achieve from their plot, and the likely answer will be 'colour and interest all year round'. And if not, it ought to be! For, as most if not all of a small garden will be in full view from the house for the whole year, there needs to be something good to look at through every month.

The best way to achieve year-round interest is by planting mixed borders – that is, a blend of different plants such as trees, shrubs, conifers, roses, herbaceous perennials, bulbs and ornamental grasses, with an extra garnish of seasonal flowers from annuals and tender perennials if desired. The single-plant border,

---

HARDY EVERGREENS FOR COLD AREAS

Buxus sempervirens

Cotoneaster frigidus 'Cornubia'

Euonymus fortunei cultivars

Hebe: H. ochracea 'James Stirling',

H. pinguifolia 'Pagei' and other small-leaved varieties only

Hedera colchica cultivars

Hedera helix cultivars

Ilex

Ligustrum ovalifolium 'Aureum'

Mahonia aquifolium 'Smaragd'

Pyracantha

Rhododendron yakushimanum hybrids

Sarcococca

Viburnum davidii

Vinca minor

---

such as a rose bed, or herbaceous border, is a luxury that looks good for a limited period and one that can be afforded only by those with larger gardens.

Within these various plant groups, choose plants that flower at different times of the year to provide successional interest. However, although flowers tend to grab one's attention first, it is of even greater importance also to include plants with other, longer-lasting attributes. Decorative effects can be provided by evergreen foliage, attractively shaped, coloured or variegated leaves, autumn berries and leaf colour, and ornamental bark. In their various ways, these plants will then all contribute to the year-round pageant of colour that is the mixed border.

Some advance planning is definitely recommended in order to achieve a successful mix of plants. Otherwise, a single visit to the garden centre – geared as it is to tempting the customer to buy on impulse – is likely to result in a carload of plants that only look good at that particular time. Start by choosing plants for winter interest, the time when good-looking plants are most scarce, then autumn, spring and summer, in that order.

Structural planting with evergreens

Evergreens make up the skeleton of the garden and are vital for creating structure as well as all-year interest. In summer they provide a foil and backdrop to flowering plants, but when perennials have died back and deciduous plants have lost their leaves, the true value of evergreens can really be appreciated. Let it not be forgotten that this leafless period in the garden can last for fully half the year in colder areas.

In a small space, evergreens should make up about one-third of all the medium-sized to large plants. This will give plenty of winter interest without making the garden look static and boring, which can happen if a greater percentage of evergreens is used. Include plants which have a bold, architectural shape to introduce some strong form and impact to a border; this element can be strengthened further by clipping or training certain varieties (see page 62). Take care not to overdo the number of evergreens with brightly coloured foliage: a few such plants give the garden a real lift in winter, particularly in shady areas, but too many will look gaudy and ill at ease with each other. Green is nature's true colour and one which is restful rather than unsettling.

Evergreens vary in their level of hardiness and can be particularly susceptible to frost damage. This is because, unlike deciduous plants which become dormant in winter, evergreens keep their leaves and remain in active growth, needing to take up water continually. Most of the time this isn't a problem as water loss is minimal in cold weather, but if the ground is frozen and the plant is exposed to cold, drying winds yet is unable to take up water, the leaves will become scorched and shrivelled, and the plant may die back partly or even completely. So, in cold areas site evergreens in sheltered spots. Make the most of the shelter provided by walls and fences, and in open sites surround newly planted evergreens with a circular windbreak of plastic netting for their first winter. Mulching the roots also helps to protect the plants from the worst weather.

Foliage plants for long-lasting interest

Attractive foliage plants are the stalwarts of the border, producing an unflagging display of colour from the moment their leaves unfurl in spring right up to autumn leaf-fall, or in the case of evergreens, right through the year. A good proportion make first-class background plants, providing a contrast for flowers, or for plants that have a bold, architectural shape. Others, however, are flamboyant eyecatchers in their own right and deserve a site at the centre of the stage.

Foliage plants can be divided broadly into two groups: those with coloured or variegated leaves, and those that have green leaves which are attractively shaped. Variegated plants are currently all the rage, with a steady stream of new varieties coming on to the market every year. Not all these plants are particularly gardenworthy, however, so choose carefully. Some variegations are caused by virus, resulting in a mottled, speckled or blotched leaf which can often make a plant look sick, and my instinct is to avoid such varieties for this reason. Watch out, too, for a potential clash of flowers and foliage, although this is more dependent on personal preference: pink flowers with golden foliage is one such combination which, to my mind, is somewhat nauseating. In many cases, though, flowers and foliage complement each other, as in *Caryopteris* × *clandonensis* 'Worcester Gold', which has the gorgeous combination of golden leaves and blue flowers. One final general point about variegated plants is that they are slower-growing than their green-leaved cousins because they have less chlorophyll (the green pigment which a plant uses to manufacture energy). So, if speed of growth is of the essence stick to plants with green leaves.

For the purposes of grouping and placing coloured-leaved and variegated plants, it is useful to divide varieties according to their appearance. There are four main groups: white-and-green variegations; yellow or gold leaves, or yellow/gold-and-green variegations; silver; and multicolours. Different plants in the same group are far more likely to look at ease with each other

Contrasting foliage shapes and colours are subtle yet immensely appealing. Plants here include purple sage at the top with skimmia on the right.

PLANTS WITH COLOURED FOLIAGE

(E) = evergreen

Yellow, gold or yellow-/gold-variegated

Arundinaria viridistriata (E)

Aucuba japonica 'Crotonifolia' (E)

Berberis thunbergii 'Aurea'

Carex hachijoensis 'Evergold' (E)

Caryopteris x *clandonensis* 'Worcester Gold'

Ceanothus 'Diamond Heights' (E)

Choisya ternata 'Sundance' (E)

Conifers: many, eg *Thuja occidentalis* 'Rheingold' (E)

Cornus alba 'Aurea', *C. a.* 'Spaethii'

Erica carnea 'Foxhollow' (E)

Euonymus fortunei 'Emerald 'n' Gold' (E)

Gleditsia triacanthos 'Sunburst'

Hakonechloa macra 'Aureola'

Hedera helix cultivars, eg H. h. 'Buttercup',
    H. h. 'Goldheart' (E)

Humulus lupulus 'Aureus'

Ilex cultivars, eg *I.* x *altaclerensis* 'Golden King',
    I. a. 'Lawsoniana' (E)

Jasminum officinale 'Fiona Sunrise'

Ligustrum ovalifolium 'Aureum' (E)

Liriope muscari 'Gold-banded',
    L. m. 'John Burch' (E)

Lonicera nitida 'Baggesen's Gold' (E)

Physocarpus opulifolius 'Dart's Gold'

Sambucus racemosa 'Plumosa Aurea'

Vinca minor 'Aureovariegata' (E)

Yucca filamentosa 'Bright Edge' (E)

Yucca flaccida 'Golden Sword' (E)

Red or purple

Acer palmatum cultivars (many)

Berberis thunbergii 'Dart's Red Lady',
    B. t. 'Helmond Pillar', *B. t.* 'Rose Glow'

Fagus sylvatica 'Purpurea Pendula'

Heuchera cultivars, eg *H. micrantha* var.
    diversifolia 'Palace Purple', H. 'Pewter Moon'

Houttuynia cordata 'Chameleon'

Phormium cultivars, eg P. 'Bronze Baby,
    P. 'Dazzler' (E)

Physocarpus opulifolius 'Diablo'

Salvia officinalis Purpurascens Group (E)

Silver or glaucous

Artemisia 'Powis Castle' (E)

Convolvulus cneorum (E)

Dicentra 'Pearl Drops', *D.* 'Stuart Boothman'

Echinops bannaticus

Euphorbia myrsinites (E)

Festuca glauca (E)

Hebe pimeleoides 'Quicksilver' (E)

Hebe pinguifolia 'Pagei '(E)

Helichrysum italicum subsp. *serotinum* (E)

Hosta cultivars (many)

Lavandula (E)

Lotus hirsutus (E)

Macleaya cordata

Nepeta x *faassenii*

Pulmonaria saccharata Argentea Group

Pyrus salicifolia 'Pendula'

Ruta graveolens 'Jackman's Blue' (E)

Santolina chamaecyparissus (E)

Santolina pinnata subsp. *neapolitana* (E)

Sedum spectabile

Stachys byzantina 'Silver Carpet'

Teucrium fruticans (E)

than if a selection from across the board is jumbled together. Another effective way of grouping plants is to place a variegated variety alongside its green-leaved counterpart – *Euonymus fortunei* 'Emerald Gaiety' with *E. f.* 'Dart's Blanket', for example.

However, having said that, do bear in mind that coloured and variegated foliage may be especially attractive when seen in isolation but, as with choosing evergreens (see page 65), you should keep such plants in the minority in a mixed border or the overall effect can be a little stomach-churning. Golden or gold-variegated foliage in particular can be extremely eyecatching and therefore could dominate a border if not used with care. The exception is with a colour-themed planting, such as a yellow border with lots of golden foliage, or a 'hot' border which can include plenty of red- and purple-leaved plants. Silver and white-and-green variegated foliage are more restful and can be used more liberally.

Plants with attractively shaped green leaves can be used in greater numbers than those with coloured foliage, as they create interest without being overpowering. A few good examples include bamboos and grasses, shrubs like rosemary, Japanese maples (*Acer palmatum*) and *Rhododendron yakushimanum*, and many foliage perennials such as hostas, lady's mantle (*Alchemilla mollis*) and euphorbias, which all have green leaves that look extremely ornamental.

The importance of shape and texture

Still leaving flowers aside for the time being, the shapes and textures of different leaves and, indeed, the shape of the plants themselves, can add enormously to the visual appeal of a border.

COMBINING CONTRASTING SHAPES AND TEXTURES

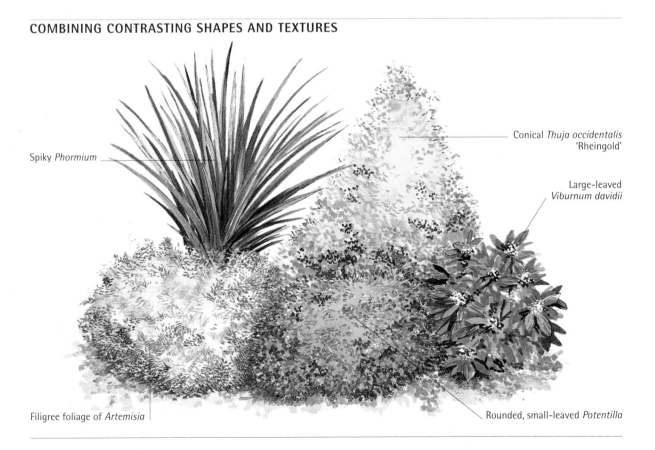

Spiky *Phormium*

Conical *Thuja occidentalis* 'Rheingold'

Large-leaved *Viburnum davidii*

Filigree foliage of *Artemisia*

Rounded, small-leaved *Potentilla*

Looking at overall plant shapes first, those with a rounded habit of growth are well in the majority, although there is also a good selection of varieties that are spiky-leaved, narrow and upright, spreading or prostrate and mat-forming. Now picture a border made up entirely of rounded plants. It relies entirely on flower and foliage colour for interest, and even at its seasonal peak the overall appearance is rather dull, as there is no contrast whatsoever. However, by grouping plants so that their shapes contrast – spiky shapes against rounded ones, fronted by carpet-forming plants, for example – the border will look attractive and interesting even when there is nothing in flower.

The many different shapes and textures of the leaves of individual plants can also be partnered to good effect. Leaf size varies from the finely cut, feathery foliage of love-in-a-mist (*Nigella damascena*) to the bold, sword-shaped leaves of New Zealand flax (*Phormium*), and two such plants placed together make a very attractive combination. Combining a contrast of both colour and texture can be extremely decorative. For example, the silver filigree foliage of *Artemisia* 'Powis Castle' looks magnificent with the bronze-edged, apricot-and-pink striped leaves of *Phormium* 'Maori Sunrise'.

Achieving maximum impact

There are several specific planting techniques you can use in order to produce the absolute maximum impact from a small plot.

Planting in tiers

Much can be gained from a limited area of ground if plants of different sizes are put together in tiers, or layers. For example, starting with the largest plants and at the back of the border, a tree can be underplanted with medium-

If space allows, the lime-yellow flowers of lady's mantle can tumble outwards to soften a path edge.

sized shrubs and tall perennials that are tolerant of some shade. The middle to front of the border can then be filled with small to medium-sized plants, with compact, spreading ones at the front to make a neat edge. So far, this is all pretty obvious, but then under any plant that spreads upwards to leave a bit of bare soil beneath you can squeeze in ground-covering plants to create maximum interest. The shade-tolerant perennials described on pages 48–50 are suitable for this purpose, as are spreading, evergreen shrubs such as *Euonymus fortunei* varieties, with glossy leaves of green-and-white or gold-and-green. Where there is a little sun, the dwarf *Hebe pinguifolia* 'Pagei' makes an attractive carpet of blue-grey leaves. A bonus of carpeting the soil with plants is that, once established, there is much less

1 Pure white *Rosa* 'Iceberg' grows up a post to give rapid height (2.5m/8ft)

2 *Vinca minor* 'Gertrude Jekyll' provides shade-tolerant, evergreen ground cover plus white flowers (15cm/6in)

3 The dense growing habit of *Artemisia* 'Powis Castle' forms a bushy mound of neat silver foliage (60cm/24in)

4 *Viburnum* x *juddii* (1.2m/4ft) produces fragrant, pink-tinged white flowers in spring. *Clematis* 'Madame Julia Correvon' grows through it for wine-red summer flowers

5 Shade-tolerant *Cyclamen hederifolium* beneath the viburnum produce pink and white flowers in autumn (7.5cm/3in)

6 Striking, almost black-leaved *Ophiopogon planiscapus* 'Nigrescens' makes a neat evergreen edging (15cm/6in)

7 Annual *Cosmos bipinnatus* provide long-lasting summer blooms (0.9–1.2m/3–4ft)

8 A standard juniper gives rapid height and can also be underplanted (1.5m/5ft)

9 Evergreen pyracantha, with creamy-white flowers followed by colourful berries, can be trained closely against the fence (1.8m/6ft)

10 *Gleditsia triacanthos* 'Sunburst' is a light-canopied tree so other plants will grow happily underneath it (3–4m/10–12ft)

11 *Lavatera* 'Rosea' gives rapid height and bears long-lasting, pink-white flowers in summer. Cut back in spring to reveal the *Vinca minor* 'Gertrude Jekyll' in flower underneath (1.8m/6ft)

12 *Humulus lupulus* 'Aureus' (5.2m/16ft) and *Clematis* 'Hagley Hybrid' (1.8m/6ft) climb together for added interest from one space

opportunity for any weeds to grow there.

Areas of ground that are left bare at certain times of the year can be filled with colour for that season only. Prime sites for such treatment are the spaces around shrubs like tree mallow (*Lavatera*) and hardy fuchsias, which form substantial bushes for much of the year but are hard pruned in early spring, leaving the surrounding area empty for a couple of months until they regrow. Here, plant early-flowering perennials like azure-blue lungworts (*Pulmonaria*), elephant's ears (*Bergenia*) and the bleeding heart (*Dicentra spectabilis*). Spring bulbs are obvious candidates too (see page 74).

Choosing the right plants for the very front of a border or to edge a path is important. Such plants need to look good for a long period of time as well as being reasonably neat in habit, without tumbling and spreading in a large mass over a lawn – where eventually they would kill the grass – or obstructing a path. Photographs of plants spreading exuberantly over pathways may look appealing, but in most cases the path is a good metre or more wide and belongs to a large garden – not the smaller spaces that we are dealing with here. Neat, well mannered plants include lilyturf (*Liriope muscari*), with evergreen leaves and wands of violet flowers in autumn – it makes a lovely combination with hostas – and its close relative, the Japanese black grass (*Ophiopogon planiscapus* 'Nigrescens'), which is also evergreen. The scalloped, coloured leaves of heuchera hybrids are attractive from spring to autumn, while the fresh green of lady's mantle (*Alchemilla mollis*) is refreshing and provides a natural contrast. The latter plant is much maligned for its rampant self-seeding, but such seedlings do create a charming natural effect – otherwise, you can simply cut off the flowerheads before they mature to avoid the problem. For the darkest months of the year, put in drifts of winter-flowering heathers (*Erica carnea* varieties). They blend well into a mixed border and, if trimmed after flowering, the foliage will make a neat if insignificant edging for the summer months. Plants such as these, which are comparatively dull in summer, can be enlivened for that season by growing a *Clematis viticella* variety alongside. The clematis will scramble over the heathers and in autumn can be cut back in time for the heather to bloom in its turn.

Although the obvious way to plan a border is with tall plants at the back, medium-sized ones in the middle and low-growing varieties at the front, a border that is planted in such a fashion can sometimes appear just a little too organized.

Having the odd plant breaking ranks and pushing forwards can look a good deal more natural and attractive, particularly in an informal garden. A few plants which, at certain seasons of the year, are tall yet airy, are ideal for placing towards the front. Good examples are ornamental grasses like tufted hair grass (*Deschampsia cespitosa* 'Goldtau'), which bears tall stems of flowerheads followed by seeds in summer and autumn; Japanese anemones (*Anemone × hybrida*), with their elegant saucer-shaped, late-summer blooms; and the Cape figwort (*Phygelius*), which throws up tall stems clad with exotic tubular flowers.

Adding height to borders breaks up what might otherwise become a rather monotonous view of plants that are all on a similar level. On a large scale, climbing plants can be trained up a single, netting-wrapped rustic post or a tripod of

---

PLANTS SUITABLE AS STANDARDS

All the plants listed are evergreen, unless otherwise stated. A number are not included in the Plant Directory (see page 126), as if not trained as standards they will grow too large for the small garden.

Arbutus unedo
Cotoneaster x *suecicus* 'Coral Beauty'
Cupressus arizonica var. *glabra* 'Conica'
Cupressus macrocarpa 'Goldcrest'
Elaeagnus pungens 'Maculata'
Euonymus japonicus 'Ovatus Aureus'
Hibiscus syriacus (deciduous)
Ilex x *altaclerensis* cultivars
Ilex aquifolium cultivars
Laurus nobilis
Photinia x *fraseri* 'Red Robin'
Rosa (deciduous)

posts, and will quickly become a major feature of the border. On a slightly lower level, standard shrubs, roses and conifers are a wonderful way of introducing more visual interest – these plants are trained to form a 'lollipop' shape on top of a clear stem about 90–150cm (3–5ft) high. A number of different shrubs are available as ready-grown standards and they can be used in a variety of ways. The most familiar use is in containers, with a pair of standards flanking a path or door, and these are particularly well suited to a formal garden style. However, standards also look extremely good when used within a grouping of plants, either in containers or in a border, where they create instant height. Their stems, which can look rather bare and obvious, can be surrounded and disguised by smaller plants.

Plants in pots can be dropped into any bare patches to create instant height. Lastly, when the larger, permanent plants have had several years to become established, they can be swagged and garlanded with climbers to provide an even greater quantity of colour.

Doubling-up with climbers

The value and versatility of climbing plants in a small space is inestimable. Yet, although climbers are widely used on walls, fences, screens and vertical structures all around the garden, there is comparatively little use of a huge selection of perfect sites – other plants. Once a shrub, tree or conifer is several years old and has attained a reasonable size, it becomes the perfect support for a climber, which can garland its host with flowers and provide many weeks of extra

A climber grown through another plant provides extra colour as with this *Clematis* 'Ville de Lyon' with purple cotinus.

Clematis 'Prince Charles' makes a perfect partner for *Hebe* 'Watson's Pink'.

GROWING CLIMBERS THROUGH OTHER PLANTS

One problem with growing climbers through established plants like trees and shrubs is that the surrounding soil tends to be thoroughly colonized with roots, which means that any new plant is going to have a tough time competing for water and nutrients.

To make life easier for a new climber, plant it at the edge of the host plant's canopy of branches rather than near its trunk, where the roots are usually at their most dense. From here, train the climber upwards using canes, string or wires. Plant it on the shady side of the host if possible, where the soil will be cooler and damper. Dig out an area at least 60cm (24in) square and fill the hole with fresh topsoil mixed with lots of organic matter. To be really sure of success, frame the planting pit with a bottomless wooden box sunk into the ground. By the time the wood rots, the climber's root system should be well established and it will be able to hold its own in competition with the surrounding plants. Remember to give the climber a good mulch and feed every spring too.

Planting a climber to grow into an established tree

The climber is planted near the outer edge of the tree's canopy and trained up into the branches using canes and string

A bottomless wooden box frames the planting pit, which is filled with good soil enriched with plenty of organic matter – by the time the box rots, the climber will be well established

colour. A well established climber or wall shrub can also play host to another climber. Roses are prime candidates for such a partnership: the plants can flower at the same time to create a spectacular display of contrasting colour, such as the sky-blue flowers of *Clematis* 'Perle d'Azur' with the pale pink, apple-scented blooms of *Rosa* 'New Dawn', or the flowering times can be staggered to produce a longer display of colour, for example by partnering *Rosa* 'Maigold', which gives a spectacular display of apricot-yellow flowers in early summer, with the cup-and-saucer plant (*Cobaea scandens*), which bears large, bell-shaped, deep purple flowers later in the season.

Compatibility of vigour is the key to success when choosing climbers to grow through other plants. Take care to avoid planting a vigorous climber with a small to medium-sized shrub, as the shrub could easily become entwined in a fatal grip. It all depends on the size and age of the host. A well established tree, for example, could support a large climber such as a rambling rose or a vigorous clematis like *C. montana*, while a shrub such as a dogwood (*Cornus*) or berberis would be best partnered with something much less rampant. The plants described on pages 73–4 are less vigorous climbers that will be suitable for most situations.

Clematis are far and away the top choice of climber to grow through other plants. Large-flowered hybrids have the perfect disposition – preferring their heads in the sun and their roots in shade – and they clamber up by winding their leaf stalks gently around another plant. Stealthily they scramble upwards, until one day comes the delightful surprise of beautiful plate-sized flowers nestling among the growth of another plant. A huge range of varieties is available, offering an almost endless number of combinations with other plants. Certain clematis species are excellent, too. *C. viticella* hybrids bear a profusion of small flowers in late summer, and as they benefit from hard annual pruning almost to the ground the growth can easily be kept tidy. In a sheltered spot, *C. texensis* hybrids produce a glorious display of bell-shaped pink or ruby-red flowers. *C. × durandii* is semi-herbaceous in habit and can be grown over a small shrub.

Herbaceous climbers – those that die back to the ground in winter but regrow in spring – are perfect to partner with other plants. They include the golden hop (*Humulus lupulus* 'Aureus') which has large, lobed yellow leaves, and perennial pea (*Lathyrus latifolius*) with stems of pink or white flowers, similar to sweet peas in appearance but without scent. Annual climbers are also excellent (see page 92), although do bear in mind that most prefer a sunny spot.

To achieve the best effects, select flower colours that contrast with the foliage of the host plant. For example, grow a white-flowered climber such as the *Clematis vitcella* hybrid *C.* 'Alba Luxurians' through evergreen shrubs such as *Viburnum tinus* 'Eve Price' or a pyracantha, as the darker background will show up the pale flowers to perfection. Similarly, the dark foliage of a conifer or holly tree is excellent with the large, lobed yellow leaves of the golden

hop or the fresh green leaves and yellow flowers of the annual canary creeper (*Tropaeolum peregrinum*). The silver filigree leaves of *Artemisia* 'Powis Castle' look marvellous with the indigo-blue flowers of *Clematis × durandii*, while a glaucous-blue conifer is the ideal host for the rich shades of *C. texensis*. Variegated foliage, such as the white-and-green leaves of *Cornus alba* 'Elegantissima', makes an outstanding contrast with large-flowered clematis that have rich purple or blue flowers, as do the golden leaves of *Choisya ternata* 'Sundance'.

Infill planting

A garden filled with well established plants tends to have little left in the way of bare earth to house any permanent additions, but that doesn't mean you have to stop there. There are plenty of crafty ways of squeezing in a whole lot more seasonal colour by using bulbs, annuals, biennials and tender perennials.

BULBS AND BIENNIALS

Bulbs are a great friend to the small-space gardener, mainly because they carry their own store of energy, which allows them to be popped in just about everywhere. Early spring-flowering bulbs can be planted in carpets beneath deciduous shrubs and trees, to flower before their leaves unfurl and hide the ground from view. Similarly, underplant summer-flowering shrubs like hardy fuchsias and tree mallow (see page 70). For extra summer colour, put in lilies with their exotic, often richly scented blooms. Lilies are particularly good in a mixed border, as they are happy with their heads in the sun and their feet in the shade of other plants. They grow exceptionally well in containers, too, as do the vast majority of bulbs.

Different-sized bulbs can even be planted in

layers, one on top of the other, to make the absolute maximum use of the space available, both in containers (see page 109) and in the open ground. For example, narcissi are planted about 12.5–15cm (5–6in) deep, with grape hyacinths (*Muscari*) next at 7.5cm (3in) down and glory-of-the-snow (*Chionodoxa*) at 2.5–5cm (1–2in) deep. Don't worry about putting bulbs on top of each other, as the shoots of the lower ones will quite happily find their way around any obstacles. Even where the ground is completely covered with carpeting shrubs and perennials, bulbs will find a way through the foliage to bloom, and then their yellowing leaves can be tucked discreetly out of sight.

This is the only drawback with bulbs: to stock up with energy for the following year, the foliage has to be allowed to die back naturally without trimming or tying up. A dressing of slow-release fertilizer in spring will help to keep your bulbs performing well next year too, along with an occasional good soaking of water if the season is dry. If there are no plants to hide the dying leaves and the sight becomes too much to bear, dig up the bulbs and heel them into a trench out of view, laying netting underneath first so they can be lifted easily and replanted in autumn.

The choice of bulbs is huge, and it is far too easy to become carried away by all the glorious picture labels and try a handful of lots of different varieties. Even – or perhaps especially – in a small space it is far more effective to have lots of bulbs of a very few varieties, planted in drifts or carpets around the garden. Bulbs are one of the very few plants with which it is possible to think big in a small space, so plant lavishly (see page 38). Satisfy any craving for variety by choosing bulbs that flower at different times to create a succession of colour. The season starts in late winter, with snowdrops (*Galanthus*) and

winter aconites (*Eranthis hyemalis*), moving on to crocuses, the first narcissi, and dainty dwarves like glory-of-the-snow (*Chionodoxa*) with blue-and-white blooms. Plant a succession of narcissi to flower through the spring, then there are grape hyacinths (*Muscari*) in mid-spring, and tulips which bloom from spring right into early summer. Into summer, there are beauties like lilies, and finally crocus and hardy cyclamen for late summer and autumn.

Autumn is the peak period for bulb planting, but at this time of year the garden is still full of growth and it is perplexing to remember the whereabouts of all the bare earth that looked so obvious in the spring. There are two solutions: in spring, make a note of all the bare areas that could usefully be crammed with bulbs and fight your way through vegetation to plant them in autumn. Alternatively, plant your bulbs in large pots – the plastic ones that shrubs and trees come in are adequate, rather than using costly ornamental containers – and the following spring simply drop potfuls of bulbs in any spot that needs a bit of colour. If you miss the autumn planting completely, don't despair, as many garden centres now sell potted bulbs in flower. These are more expensive, it's true, but worthwhile so as not to miss out on the first breath of spring.

To partner this spring bonanza of bulbs, there are biennials. This group includes popular cottage-garden flowers like forget-me-nots (*Myosotis*) and wallflowers (*Erysimum*), which bloom in early to mid-spring, while for late spring and early summer there are foxgloves (*Digitalis*) and sweet rocket or dame's violet (*Hesperis matronalis*). All these plants are raised from seed sown in summer, grown on and transplanted – or bought and planted – into their flowering positions in autumn.

ANNUALS AND TENDER PERENNIALS

Once into summer, annuals and frost-tender perennials take over. Although not quite as flexible as bulbs for cramming into almost non-existent spaces, these seasonal plants are nevertheless invaluable for extra flower colour. Annuals, many of which are referred to as bedding plants, have long been popular, and although in recent times the emphasis has shifted to using them in all types of containers rather than for large bedding schemes in borders, they are still incredibly useful for filling small areas between permanent plants. In late summer, when the majority of shrubs and perennials have already flowered, annuals really do come into their own. Annual climbers (see page 92) are also magnificent small-garden plants. If you like to

enjoy a real extravaganza of summer colour from your garden, it's worth deliberately leaving some spaces between your permanent planting specifically for the purpose of filling with seasonal summer plants.

For growing purposes, it is important to recognize the difference between hardy and half-hardy annuals. Hardy varieties can be sown outside in spring or autumn, directly where they are to flower, whereas half-hardy types would be killed by frost and need to be grown under cover, then planted out in late spring when all danger of frost is past (see page 125).

The best annuals for a small space are those that have other attributes in addition to flowers. Cosmos, with its large daisy flowers, has delicate, feathery foliage, as does love-in-a-mist (*Nigella*) which produces inflated, decorative seed pods too. Another variety with attractive seed heads is the Californian poppy (*Eschscholzia*), which has pods that are long and pointed. Others have exceptionally fragrant flowers, such as tobacco plant (*Nicotiana*) – those with white flowers have the best scent. A few annuals are grown just for their foliage and these are very useful to provide a backdrop to offset the many flowers. When mixing in annuals with other plants, often the best ones to choose are plant species which have single flowers and a more natural appearance, rather than some of the over-bred monstrosities that have huge, bloated double flowers that look out of proportion on a squat, very dwarf plant.

Colour theming of annuals has developed enormously in popularity, and whereas plants and seed used to be sold mostly in mixtures, today it is easy to buy separate colours to create specific colour schemes. This is a great advantage, as with so many different colours on offer it would be easy to create some horrendous clashes. There have been considerable

Annuals give masses of summer flowers. Here fiery orange *Eschscholzia* combines dramatically with purple cabbage.

developments, too, in the range of annuals available. Plant breeders have developed many new forms of old favourites, as well as new strains that give improved garden performance.

Tender perennials can be used for interplanting in the same way as annuals, although as the vast majority are sun-lovers they generally dislike being overshadowed by larger plants. Tender perennials are ideal for containers and raised beds, so the patio tends to be their main home. However, they can still be used to brighten borders simply by strategically dropping the odd pot-grown plant into any area that needs cheering up. Tall plants like marguerites (*Argyranthemum*) can inject some instant height into a planting scheme.

Tender perennials can be kept from year to year if overwintered in a frost-free place such as a greenhouse, porch or conservatory, or they can be propagated readily from cuttings taken in late summer and kept indoors on a windowsill (see page 125) – but if this sounds like too much trouble, don't feel bad about throwing out your plants at the end of the year and buying new ones the following spring. Divide the purchase price into pence per every week that the plant has flowered and given you pleasure, and it will seem pretty insignificant compared to the cost of, say, the weekly groceries!

The importance of colour

The use of colour is perhaps the most challenging aspect of planting a garden. It is also the one which is most subject to the vagaries of fashion, which leads me to the most important point of all: colour preference is immensely personal and, regardless of what schemes are prominent at the current year's flower shows, remember that above all it is *your* garden and it is vitally important to choose what *you* like.

Blue (here *Hyacinth* 'Delft Blue') and yellow (here in the form of *Narcissus* 'Tête-à-tête') make a magnificent combination.

However, there are a few general guidelines which can be very useful, and these are outlined on the following pages.

Using colour to 'create' space

Crafty placing of colours can make all the difference to whether your garden appears spacious or cramped, however large or small it may be in reality. Bright colours immediately draw the eye, and so if placed at the end of the garden can destroy the perspective by appearing to leap into the foreground. Put the vivid shades of red, pink, orange and yellow close to the house, with paler ones such as blue, silver, cream, pink and soft yellow further away, and the end of the garden will appear to recede.

White may appear innocuous, but can actually have a similar effect to bright colours. By day the contrast of white flowers and green foliage may be just a little too stark, and after the sun has set and darkness has begun to fall, white flowers appear to reflect every last little bit of light and remain visible long after all other colours have faded. This makes white wonderful around the patio and close to the house, particularly in places where people will be sitting out in the evening, but not so good at the end of the garden where it, too, can destroy the perspective.

Colour schemes

Plants offer such an enormous range of colours, from foliage, fruits and bark as well as flowers, that planning a colour scheme can at first seem a bewildering prospect. However, by working through several choices in relation to your garden's conditions and your own preferences, the procedure becomes much simpler.

The geographical location, as well as the

THE COLOUR WHEEL

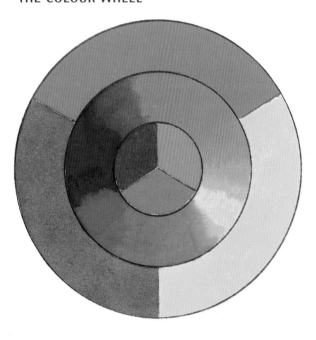

amount of sun or shade a particular garden receives, plays an important role when choosing colours. In cooler climates where the light tends to be soft, the pastel shades such as pale blues and pinks, mauve and silver look extremely effective – the same goes for shady spots. Where the climate is warm and sunny, and in a site that is in full sun, plants with brightly coloured flowers and foliage will create much more impact (see pages 52–5).

Next, assess your own preferences for colours. These may already be so obvious as to need no further consideration, or it may take a period of contemplation to decide on exactly which ones you prefer. The colour charts available from paint manufacturers can make a very useful study for this purpose, as will a few visits to gardens open to the public.

When it comes to matching one colour with another, the classic solution is to consult the colour wheel, where the colour spectrum can be divided into two. Colours from each half generally go well together, but mixing colours within one half is usually less successful. For example, blue and yellow look good together, but red, pink and orange simply argue among themselves.

After this, if bewilderment still has the upper hand, a good route to take is to imitate nature's colours with the passing of the seasons. Start in spring with yellows and blues – a lovely colour contrast – along with white and the fresh green of new foliage. Summer shades are paler blues along with pinks, mauve and red, offset by silver foliage. In autumn, there is a final blazing display of brilliant red, orange, bronze, scarlet and purple almost as though the garden is putting on a show of defiance against the coming winter. Then, in winter, it is a case of being grateful for whatever colour there is in the garden!

USING COLOUR TO CREATE AN ILLUSION OF SPACE

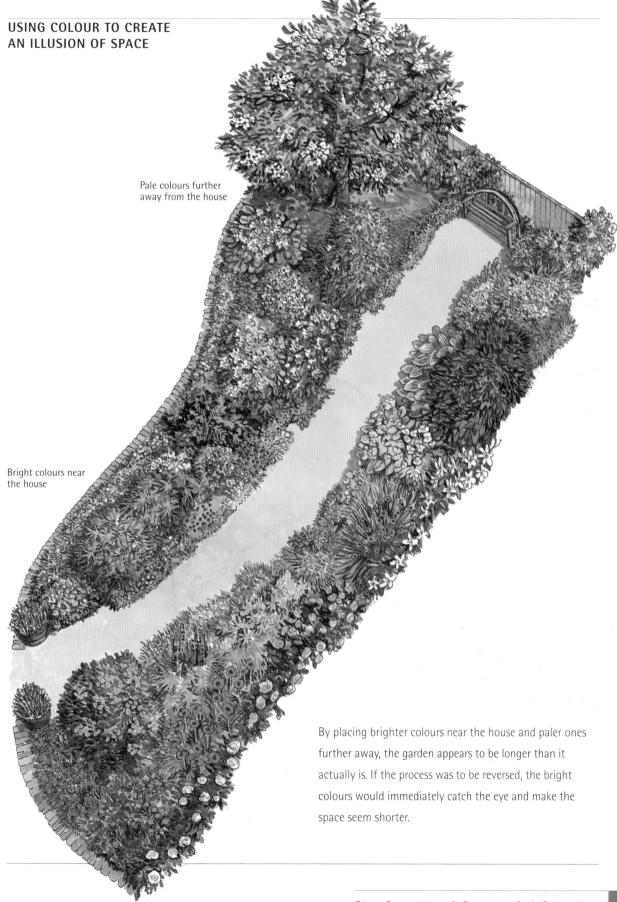

Pale colours further away from the house

Bright colours near the house

By placing brighter colours near the house and paler ones further away, the garden appears to be longer than it actually is. If the process was to be reversed, the bright colours would immediately catch the eye and make the space seem shorter.

Cool colours such as silver, grey, cream, pale pink, soft blue and mauve are most useful in a small garden in order to make it appear more spacious than it actually is (see page 78). Beware of going to the limits of refinement, however: sometimes a border composed entirely of 'cool' colours can look a little too subtle and simply cries out for a few brighter plants to give it a bit of bite. In this case, the excellent contrast created by blue and yellow can be the answer, being stimulating without overpowering the senses.

A 'hot' border, composed of colours such as reds, oranges, purples and bright pinks, can look dramatic and immensely exciting. It can also serve to divert the attention from an undesirable view or feature elsewhere in the garden. However, so much does a border of this type leap into the foreground that it is generally less than ideal for a small space, unless the planting and design are intended to look exotic or theatrical.

Single-colour themes should be weighed up with great caution before actually implementing such a scheme in a small space. An all-white garden is a popular single-colour scheme, considered by many to be the epitome of sophistication since Vita Sackville-West created her famous example at Sissinghurst Castle in Kent. In a large garden, however, there is more than adequate space to devote an area to a particular theme, whereas if there is only one colour to look at in your entire garden the appeal may soon begin to pall. If you still decide to go ahead with a white garden, take care to select only those flowers which are pure white, as cream and ivory can look grubby by contrast.

To round off all this talk of vibrant colours and pastel shades, there is one that tends to be widely overlooked by virtue of its familiarity – green. It is the most soothing and restful of nature's colours, and shows off all other shades to perfection. A border that is lacking in green – unless it is one that has been planned to a very specific theme such as a dazzling 'hot' border – will result in an overdose of colour that can be just too indigestible, in exactly the same way as a meal of rich food without any plain bread or potatoes. Once the initial colours have been seen and appreciated, the eye can then move on to enjoying the many different shades of green, as well as the textures and shapes of all the plants.

COLOUR CONTRASTS

Blue and yellow

1 *Cornus alba* 'Spaethii'

2 *Ceratostigma willmottianum* 'Forest Blue'

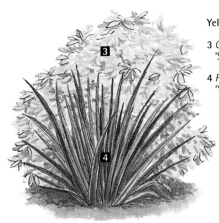

Yellow and green

3 *Choisya tenata* 'Sundance'

4 *Phormium* 'Yellow Wave'

COLOUR THEMES

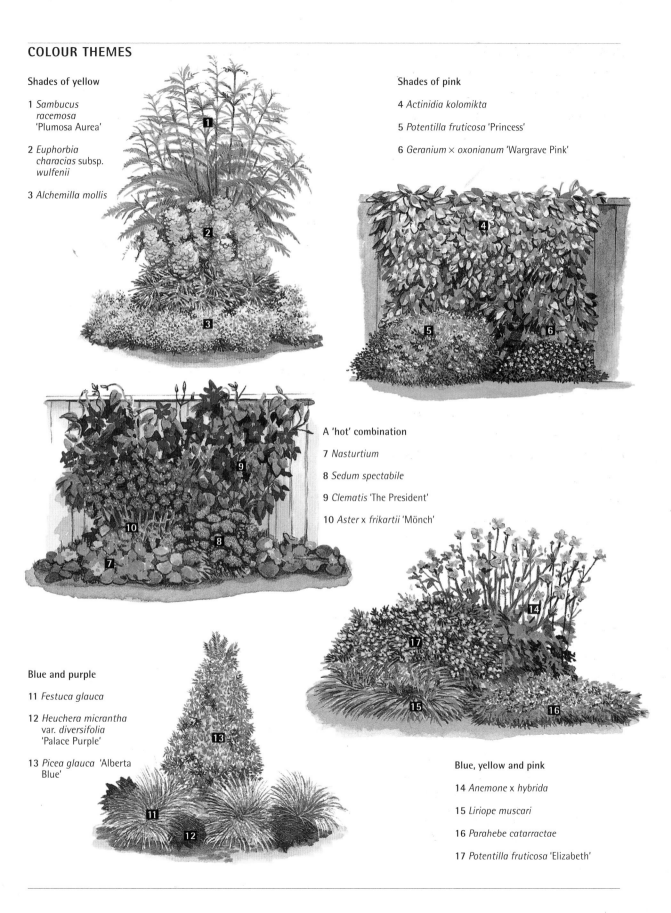

Shades of yellow

1 *Sambucus racemosa* 'Plumosa Aurea'

2 *Euphorbia characias* subsp. *wulfenii*

3 *Alchemilla mollis*

Shades of pink

4 *Actinidia kolomikta*

5 *Potentilla fruticosa* 'Princess'

6 *Geranium × oxonianum* 'Wargrave Pink'

A 'hot' combination

7 *Nasturtium*

8 *Sedum spectabile*

9 *Clematis* 'The President'

10 *Aster* x *frikartii* 'Mönch'

Blue and purple

11 *Festuca glauca*

12 *Heuchera micrantha* var. *diversifolia* 'Palace Purple'

13 *Picea glauca* 'Alberta Blue'

Blue, yellow and pink

14 *Anemone* x *hybrida*

15 *Liriope muscari*

16 *Parahebe catarractae*

17 *Potentilla fruticosa* 'Elizabeth'

Creative Planting

CLIMBERS AND WALL SHRUBS provide a wonderful way of getting more mileage out of a small plot. Where the ground area is very limited, often the only way left to go is up – by gardening on the vertical. Not only does this give more planting area for the keen gardener, but there is the added bonus of creating a greater impression of space into the bargain. This is done in two ways: first, the eye is encouraged to travel upwards rather than just looking along the ground, and second, climbers can be draped over boundary walls and fences so that the garden's limits are not immediately visible.

Vertical gardening

Of all the different plant groups, climbers are by far and away the most versatile, as they are both beautiful and immensely practical. On the practical side, climbing plants can be used to conceal ugly walls, fences, buildings and other objects. They can also be employed on trellis screens and other supports to create some privacy quickly (see page 98). From an aesthetic point of view, climbers can be used not only on walls and fences, but also on ornamental vertical structures such as arches, obelisks and pergolas, to create colourful and handsome features that fully exploit the vertical dimension of the garden. Natural supports can also be utilized to the full by threading climbers through established trees, shrubs and conifers to give an extra burst of flowers or contrasting foliage (see pages 72–4).

An excellent range of climbing plants is available which gives a good choice for different styles of garden. For example, an informal, cottage-style garden looks superb with colourful, luxuriant growers such as clematis, roses and honeysuckle (*Lonicera*), which together offer an enormous range of flower colours and scents. A formal garden is more suited to the restrained colours and bold leaf shapes of foliage plants like *Vitis coignetiae* and *Parthenocissus henryana*, which both develop attractive autumn tints, and ivies (*Hedera*), which come in a huge range of different leaf shapes and colours.

The main point to bear in mind when choosing climbers is the marked preference that many have for either shade or sun. Do check in advance of buying that your plant will enjoy its intended site, particularly if it is to go on a house wall where the amount of sun or shade it receives will be accentuated by the height and orientation of the building.

Regular pruning and training is a good habit to get into with climbers. Most occupy prime positions with ultra-visibility, so a neglected tangle of stems will look extremely unsightly. Frequent tying-in of stems and trimming of

Climbers are immensely versatile and can be practical – by screening an ugly building, as here – as well as beautiful.

unruly growth, plus annual feeding and mulching, will ensure that your plants remain a joy rather than a nuisance.

Walls and fences

The best place to begin planting climbers is on ready-made sites such as house walls and boundary fences, which tend to look unpleasantly bleak and naked without any plants. Sunny walls also have the advantage of a warm, sheltered microclimate that offers a wonderful opportunity to grow a selection of plants which could be subject to frost damage in the open garden, but will thrive if given the storage-heater benefit of a warm wall. In cold areas, such plants include

Choose flower colours that are enhanced by their background. *Rosa* 'Danse du Feu' glows against a stone wall.

the two evergreen clematis species *C. armandii* and *C. cirrhosa*, the summer-flowering species *C. texensis*, passion flower (*Passiflora caerulea*) and *Trachelospermum asiaticum*.

For optimum visual effect, ensure that the colour of the background enhances that of the plants it supports. For example, red-brick walls and dark fences look superb with golden or variegated foliage, such as that of the golden hop (*Humulus lupulus* 'Aureus'), or an ivy with brightly variegated leaves like *Hedera colchica* 'Dentata Variegata', with its striking green-and-cream foliage. Similarly, choose pale flower colours that will be shown up by the dark backdrop. These include clematis with white or pale pink blooms, like *C*. 'Duchess of Edinburgh' which has beautiful double white flowers with golden stamens, *C. montana* with masses of small, snow-white blooms, or *C*. 'Silver Moon' which is an unusual shade of pearly grey. Summer jasmine (*Jasminum officinale*) bears clusters of pure white flowers against dark green foliage, and *Solanum jasminoides* 'Album' makes a handsome display of white flowers that have prettily contrasting sheaves of bright yellow stamens.

Pale stone or whitewashed walls, on the other hand, make an excellent backdrop for rich, vibrant flower colours and dark foliage. Many clematis have richly coloured blooms, such as the petunia-red flowers of *C*. 'Ernest Markham' or the deep, velvety purple of the *C.viticella* hybrid *C*. 'Etiole Violette'. Rather more exotic in appearance is the Chilean glory flower (*Eccremocarpus scaber*), which scrambles rapidly upwards to create a mass of attractive, deeply cut leaves that make an attractive backdrop for its clusters of bright orange flowers. In addition to flowering plants, those for foliage interest include *Actinidia kolomikta* with its spectacular pink, cream and green leaves, and *Ampelopsis*

TOP 10 CLIMBERS AND WALL PLANTS FOR SHADE

Chaenomeles

Clematis 'Nelly Moser'

Clematis alpina

Euonymus fortunei 'Silver Queen'

Hedera colchica and
   Hedera helix cultivars

Hydrangea anomala subsp. *petiolaris*

Jasminum nudiflorum

Lonicera x *tellmanniana*

Parthenocissus henryana

Pyracantha

TOP 10 CLIMBERS AND WALL PLANTS FOR FULL SUN

Eccremocarpus scaber

Ipomoea tricolor 'Heavenly Blue'

Lathyrus latifolius

Passiflora caerulea

Piptanthus nepalensis

Rosa (all)

Jasminum officinale

Teucrium fruticans

Trachelospermum asiaticum

Wisteria floribunda

glandulosa var. *brevipedunculata* 'Elegans', which has lobed leaves heavily mottled with pink, cream and green.

For the future health of your walls and fences, a couple of points are worthy of note. Self-clinging climbers like ivy, Virginia creeper (*Parthenocissus*) and climbing hydrangea (*H. anomala* subsp. *petiolaris*) are fine on walls where the bricks and mortar are sound, but should be avoided on sites where the material is unsound as the plants' aerial roots will creep into the cracks and speed up deterioration. Keep the growth of these self-clingers trimmed well away from paintwork, downpipes and guttering to avoid any damage. They are best avoided on fences, but if they are already growing on such sites you should make regular checks to see whether any shoots have crept through the joints of an overlap or close-board fence. If left to develop, the shoots will grow and thicken, eventually forcing the wooden slats apart and distorting the fence.

Although a few climbers are self-clinging by means of aerial roots, the vast majority need some form of support up which to grow (see pages 118–9).

Vertical features

The beauty of climbers is that their use need not be limited solely to walls and fences. There is a whole range of vertical features that can be built in different sites around the garden, ranging from very simple to quite complex structures, and just a single feature can effect an amazing transformation in the garden's overall appearance. These features can be adapted to virtually any size to fit the available space, even in a very tiny garden.

When choosing the style and material for your structure, first consider your DIY enthusiasms and abilities. If they are close to zero, go for a ready-made feature. At the more affordable end of the range are structures made from imitation wrought iron, and at the other there are craftsman-made arbours of hardwood and Victorian-style wirework. However, if your aim is to cover the feature with plants, there is little point in investing in something that is intended to be highly ornamental. Far better to opt for wood: sawn timber for an informal setting or planed and colour-treated for a smarter and more stylish, formal effect. Several manufacturers produce wooden structures in kit form ready to put up, which is obviously a lot less work than starting from scratch.

Unless the structure is actually an intricate, craftsman-made one that looks good with the barest dressing of foliage, it is the choice of plants that will turn your feature into something really special. In order to create a display of year-round colour, choose a selection of plants that flower at different times, not forgetting foliage plants to provide long-lasting interest. You can even achieve double the amount of colour by planting two flowering climbers to grow together (see pages 72–3).

Right: A pergola provides shade and seclusion, plus extra sites for these geranium-filled hanging baskets.

PERGOLAS

A pergola can be built in one of a number of designs to suit its site. A timber pergola can form a large square or rectangle over a sunny patio, with the house supporting one side of the cross-beams and pillars of timber or brick on the other. Here it helps to integrate house and garden, as well as making a focal point for relaxing and entertaining. A path along one side of the house can be covered with a pergola to create a stylish walkway, again with the house supporting one side of the beams, or the pergola can stand on its own over a long pathway to

SITES FOR CLIMBERS IN THE GARDEN

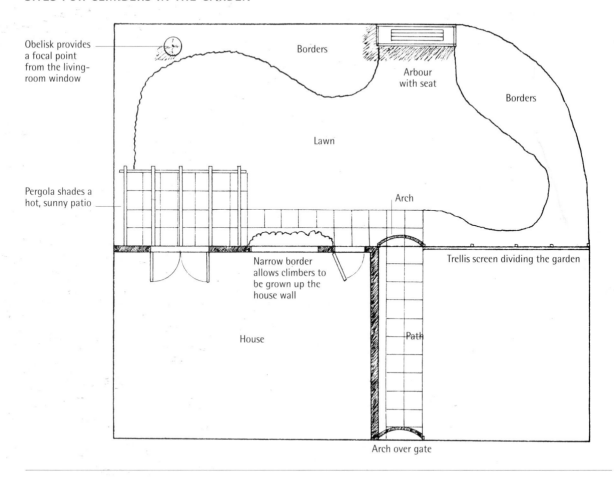

Obelisk provides a focal point from the living-room window

Borders

Arbour with seat

Borders

Lawn

Pergola shades a hot, sunny patio

Arch

Narrow border allows climbers to be grown up the house wall

Trellis screen dividing the garden

House

Path

Arch over gate

accentuate the transition from one part of the garden to another.

Pergolas tend to be reasonably large structures and provide an excellent opportunity to grow vigorous climbers such as wisteria, provided there is adequate headroom for the long racemes of scented flowers to dangle down, or the ornamental vine *Vitis coignetiae*, which can create a dappled shade reminiscent of Continental cafés. If the pergola runs above a window, be sure to choose a climber which will shed its leaves in winter to make way for scarce winter sunlight. If even the sight of leafless winter stems does not appeal, choose climbers with an herbaceous habit, such as the fast-growing golden hop (*Humulus lupulus* 'Aureus') with large, decorative, lobed leaves, golden in spring and greeny-gold in summer, or perennial pea (*Lathyrus latifolius*), which bears stems of bright pink flowers in summer. *Clematis viticella* varieties can be hard pruned in autumn, passion flower (*Passiflora caerulea*) can be treated likewise in spring if frost hasn't done the job already, while annual climbers are all ideal too (see page 92).

ARBOURS

A little arbour, clothed in plants and with a bench underneath, makes a wonderful secluded retreat. Until you actually have somewhere to sit away from the house, it is difficult to appreciate how thoroughly enjoyable it can be. Tucked out of sight from the family, casual callers and the intrusive demands of the telephone, you will be able to indulge in some complete relaxation – and admire your garden from a different perspective, too. Adding sides to your arbour helps to keep out draughts, as well as heightening the atmosphere of privacy and seclusion. Trellis can quickly be clothed with plants and suits most settings. Hurdles of woven

hazel look wonderful in a cottage garden, while bamboo screens are suited to a formal or oriental-style garden.

Plants grown over the framework create a pleasant dappled shade. Give top priority to fragrant climbers for a bit of home-grown aromatherapy that helps to intensify relaxation. Plants to choose include honeysuckles (*Lonicera*) which have an intoxifying perfume, although you should avoid *L.* × *tellmanniana* and *L. tragophylla* which are all show and no scent. Summer jasmine (*Jasminum officinale*) bears pure white, coconut-scented flowers, while the richly scented, dark red blooms of *Akebia quinata* are a must for chocaholics. For a sunny, sheltered site, *Trachelospermum asiaticum* bears jasmine-like blooms.

Roses are part and parcel of the garden's summer glory. First choose between ramblers or climbers, according to your gardening style. The informal gardener tends to prefer ramblers, with long, unruly stems scrambling and tumbling over their support and producing a one-off, exuberant mass of small blooms that lasts for several weeks. The formal gardener, on the other hand, may prefer climbing roses, which do best when tied in neatly to a framework. They have

---

A SELECTION OF SCENTED CLIMBING ROSES

'Compassion' (medium)

'Gloire de Dijon' (large)

'Madame Alfred Carrière' (large)

'Maigold' (large)

'New Dawn' (medium)

'Nice Day' (small)

'Pink Perpétué' (medium)

'Warm Welcome' (small)

'Zéphirine Drouhin' (large)

Clad with honeysuckle, this little arbour makes a fragrant and delightful retreat.

large blooms that are produced in less quantity but over a longer period. Many roses are scented, some with a rich and heavy perfume and others with a light, apple-blossom scent, so if fragrance is an important consideration it is well worth visiting a nursery or rose garden in summer in order to make a note of your preferred varieties, then ordering them for autumn supply.

To avoid ending up with a jumble of plants, limit numbers to two or three different varieties, or even just one if you have chosen a very vigorous plant such as a wisteria. Any gaps in the early years can always be filled with annuals such as *Cobaea scandens* and nasturtiums, or perennial climbers that can be treated as annuals like *Eccremocarpus scaber*.

ARCHES

An arch is quick and straightforward to put up and can be adapted in a variety of ways to suit the garden layout. In the case of an ordinary path or gateway, simply putting an arch over the top will transform it into a striking and attractive throughway – particularly important with a front entrance, where an attractive planting will welcome you home every day. Within a long, narrow garden or an L-shaped plot, an arch can be combined with a trellis screen to make a very effective divider, and the separation of certain areas means that they can then be planted to different themes if desired. A similar arch/trellis arrangement can also be used to conceal functional objects such as a shed, dustbins and compost heap. An arch can be used to frame and emphasize a focal point such as an urn or statue, or an attractive view. Several arches can even be combined over a long pathway, spaced at 3m (10ft) intervals, to give a lighter effect than one long pergola. To allow a comfortable space to

A walk-through trellis screen frames a tempting view of the garden with *Clematis* 'Comtesse de Bouchard' on the left combined with honeysuckle.

pass through, bearing in mind that plant growth will take up some room, an arch should be at least 1.2m (4ft) wide and 2.2m (7ft) high.

Climbers for an archway can reflect the area of the garden in which it is sited. A front gateway, for example, needs to look good all year round, so an evergreen such as ivy can be planted for winter interest, or use winter jasmine (*Jasminum nudiflorum*) with its starry yellow flowers, which does well when trained up a post. Either of these could be partnered with another climber such as a clematis for summer colour. A rose looks wonderful on an arch, although it is best to choose a compact climber such as one from either the modern or miniature group, rather than a rambler that will fling out thorny branches to snag unwary passers-by. If an arch borders a vegetable garden, plant edible climbers such as a thornless blackberry and runner beans, adding extra colour with climbing nasturtiums, all parts of which are edible.

An arch is also an ideal site for a climber with fragrant flowers (see panel on page 33), which give off intoxicating wafts of perfume as you pass by and are at just the right height to be appreciated, too. One last point: avoid using a vigorous climber on an arch, as the structure will soon become smothered with foliage and appear unbalanced and top-heavy, as well as being dangerously unstable in high winds.

OBELISKS

Obelisks are ideal for creating instant height and impact in a small space, yet are quick and easy to put up. In a mixed border, an obelisk clothed with a climber will become a column or pyramid of spectacular flowers and foliage in a short space of time, rather than having to wait years for trees and shrubs to reach a decent height. An obelisk can also be used as a stand-alone feature in a lawn, or as a focal point to be seen through an archway. As already mentioned (see page 85), there's no need to be a DIY expert either, as many different designs are available ready-made or in kit form.

Making your own plant support from scratch is, however, pretty straightforward, and cheap too. Just about the most basic structure is three rustic fence-posts put together to form a tripod, preferably with the bases buried a little way into the ground for stability. Another easy option is one such fence post knocked into the ground, with some wire mesh or netting wrapped loosely around it – ideal for scramblers such as clematis. A smarter alternative is four pieces of trellis, each measuring 0.3 × 1.5m (1 × 5ft), wired together and slipped over a post for stability.

Unless your obelisk is a particularly large and sturdy one, clothe it with one or, at most, two plants, which are compact in habit. Clematis are ideal for summer flowers; choose one of the

Instant height within a border is created by an obelisk and *Lathyrus latifolius* soon provides masses of flowers.

versatile *C. viticella* hybrids, or a compact large-flowered type such as *C.* 'Arctic Queen' or *C.* 'Royalty'. *C. texensis* hybrids are excellent in a sheltered site, and bear richly coloured blooms that bring an exotic flavour to the border, as do the beautiful blue flowers of the annual morning glory (*Ipomoea tricolor* 'Heavenly Blue'). A small-leaved ivy (*Hedera helix* cultivars) will give year-round interest with its decorative evergreen foliage in many shapes and colours.

ANNUAL CLIMBERS

Annual climbers are magnificent plants for a small garden: they are quick to grow, provide lots of summer and autumn colour, and are excellent for infilling any gaps or growing through existing plants. Most varieties can be raised easily from seed sown under cover in late winter or early spring. Sweet peas (*Lathyrus odoratus*) are old favourites which are everlastingly popular, with their long-stemmed blooms that are ideal for cutting and often wonderfully scented into the bargain. Also easy to grow is canary creeper (*Tropaeolum peregrinum*) which has lobed, fresh green leaves on quick-growing stems that are covered with bright yellow, prettily fringed flowers from late spring to the end of summer.

In a sunny site, even on poor soil, climbing nasturtiums are absolutely unbeatable, bearing masses of brightly coloured blooms. They thrive with virtually no attention at all, whereas morning glory (*Ipomoea tricolor* 'Heavenly Blue') needs a bit of coddling in a sunny site and rich soil to bear a good quantity of its large saucers of stunningly blue flowers, but they are so beautiful that they are well worth the effort. There are other less usual varieties of *Ipomoea* which are well worth trying too.

Lastly, the perennial Chilean glory flower (*Eccremocarpus scaber*), with its showy clusters of orange-red flowers, can be treated as an annual plant if desired, as it flowers well in its first year from an early spring sowing.

RAISING ANNUAL CLIMBERS FROM SEED

Growing frost-tender annual climbers from seed requires no special equipment – just a sunny windowsill and a bit of tender loving care. The time to sow is early to mid-spring. All you need is some deep pots, potting compost, clear polythene bags, rubber bands, labels and, of course, the seeds.

Large seeds which have a hard coat, such as sweet peas or morning glory, are best soaked overnight in tepid water to soften the outer coating. Fill the pots with moist compost and put in the seeds at the depth directed on the packet. A few plants, such as *Eccremocarpus scaber*, need light in order to germinate, so sow the seed on the surface of the compost and cover with perlite or horticultural vermiculite, which allows light through while preventing the seed from drying out. Cover the pots with polythene held in place with rubber bands, to keep the compost moist.

Put the pots in a warm place such as an airing cupboard (unless light is required) and check daily for signs of growth. As soon as the first shoots appear, move to a well lit spot. Thin to the strongest seedling, water as necessary and support the plants with stakes as growth increases.

Wait until all danger of frost has passed before planting out. Acclimatize the plants to the outside world for a couple of weeks first by standing them out during the day for increasing periods of time.

Planting for privacy

Lack of privacy tends to be the greatest bugbear of having a small garden. However well people get on with their neighbours, most prefer some degree of privacy in order to relax completely and enjoy their garden. Unfortunately, the knee-jerk reaction to having an overlooked garden tends to be to erect a tall fence or plant a fast-growing conifer hedge, but do be wary of creating the impression of a grim fortress or growing a hedge that would be ideal for the Sleeping Beauty's palace. A compromise can usually be reached by selective and thoughtful planting at strategic points.

The first priority is to assess how much privacy is needed and where. It might not be necessary to screen the whole garden; concentrate instead on making just one area private, such as the patio and back of the house, or any area that will be used for seating. Tall fence panels could be used on the boundary of just this part of the garden, clothed with climbers to soften their stark lines. Alternatively, use shorter fence panels topped with a strip of trellis through which climbers can be woven, letting in more light while still affording plenty of screening and privacy. If complete privacy is not essential, trellis with climbing plants is an excellent choice to give a reasonable amount of screening without any danger of creating a claustrophobic effect, while the overhead beams of a pergola, or alternatively a large parasol, offer a marvellous hiding place from any intrusive upstairs windows.

CREATING PRIVACY

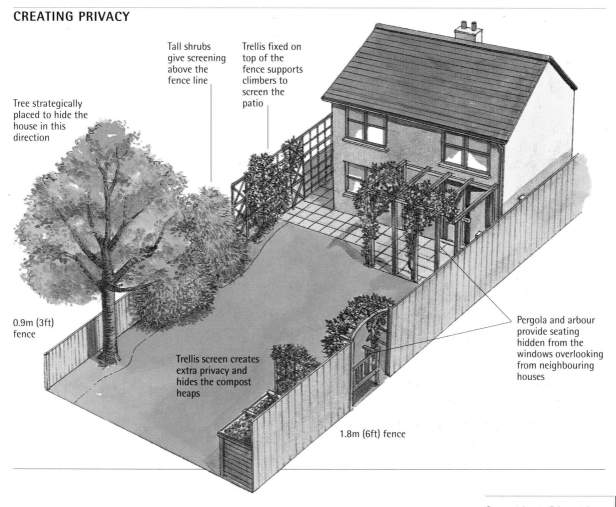

Tall shrubs give screening above the fence line

Trellis fixed on top of the fence supports climbers to screen the patio

Tree strategically placed to hide the house in this direction

0.9m (3ft) fence

Trellis screen creates extra privacy and hides the compost heaps

Pergola and arbour provide seating hidden from the windows overlooking from neighbouring houses

1.8m (6ft) fence

Trees for screening

First-floor windows that overlook your garden and tall eyesores like telegraph poles can be particularly aggravating, but here a bit of strategic planting can work wonders. Just one or two trees in exactly the right spots can soon block out these irritants, yet without dominating your own garden.

Placing the trees is a two-person job: one to stand or sit where screening is needed, and the other to move around with a marker cane to place in the exact spot. Bear in mind that although there is an automatic tendency to plant trees on the very edge of the plot, the nearer the tree is to the area that needs to be screened, the quicker it will provide privacy.

A strategically placed tree makes a secret little patio area within the garden.

If the tree's main purpose is to provide some screening from a narrow vantage point such as a window, or to hide an eyesore like a telegraph pole, the ideal variety is one with a columnar or fastigiate habit (with vertical branches close together) or a pyramidal shape (see page 59). Good small-garden trees with these shapes include *Sorbus aucuparia* 'Sheerwater Seedling', which has white spring flowers, attractive foliage and clusters of decorative berries in autumn; the crab-apple *Malus* 'Van Eseltine', which makes a magnificent spring display with large, semi-double flowers that are red in bud and open to pink flushed with white, followed by yellow autumn fruits; and the Lombardy cherry (*Prunus* 'Amanogawa'), which bears profuse quantities of large pink flowers in spring and has a very narrow habit.

Conifers are excellent if year-round screening

is required, but careful choice of varieties is essential as many upright types do eventually reach a considerable size. Most slender of all the conifers is *Juniperus scopulorum* 'Skyrocket', bluish-green in colour with a very narrow, columnar habit.

Hedges

A tall boundary hedge can become extremely dominant in a small garden and should only be planted after careful consideration. Bear in mind that it will eventually attain a width of at least 0.9m (3ft), even with regular trimming, and thereby cuts down your overall space by a fair percentage. However, having looked at the negatives first, there are plenty of positive aspects to growing a hedge. The right variety, well planted and maintained, is second to none as an attractive backdrop to the entire garden. On a cold, exposed site or one which suffers from

Overlooking buildings are almost completely screened with a clipped conifer hedge, while the weeping pear conceals the seat.

PLANTING AND MAINTAINING A HEDGE

■ Prepare the ground thoroughly, as a hedge will be in place for a long time. Dig a trench which is a minimum of 45cm (18in) wide, removing the top layer of soil to one spade's depth and putting it to one side. Fork over the soil in the base of the trench so that the roots can penetrate deeply into the subsoil. Mix in lots of bulky organic matter such as compost or well rotted manure, and replace the top layer of soil.

■ For optimum effect, use only a single variety of plant to make up the hedge. Mixing different plants tends to look bitty and creates a confused impression.

■ Put plants in a single line, spaced evenly 45–60cm (18–24in) apart. Use string to ensure a straight line, and a cane or marker as you plant to check that all the plants are the same distance apart, as any mistakes will show up like a sore thumb later on.

■ Formal or clipped hedges should be trimmed once or twice a year to maintain a good shape. Cut so that the bottom is wider than the top, with the sides gradually tapering upwards. Trim in summer, with an additional trim earlier or later in the growing season if a very neat finish is required. When trimming, use a guideline to ensure that the top is level by stretching a string between two canes.

■ Annual mulching and feeding with a slow-release fertilizer in spring will keep your hedge in prime condition. All too often hedges are overlooked in the yearly round of feeding.

strong winds, a hedge offers the prospect of excellent shelter, creating a very protected environment over an area twice its height and giving some degree of shelter to a distance of around seven times its height.

The choice of hedging plant is all-important. Avoid exceptionally vigorous plants like green privet (*Ligustrum ovalifolium*), which has a spreading root system that robs any nearby plants of water and nutrients. And do not, I beg you, plant that ubiquitous suburban blight, Leyland cypress (x *Cupressocyparis leylandii*), which is so incredibly fast-growing that it has been the cause of ferocious and expensive court cases between neighbours. Such plants are indeed cheap – and bear in mind that the cost is low simply because they grow so fast and are easy to produce – and this can be very tempting when you have a fair number to buy. But innumerable people have planted such a hedge, thinking that regular pruning will keep it within bounds, and have bitterly regretted their decision.

Dire warnings aside, there are some excellent plants for hedging that won't take over a small plot, and those described here all respond well to trimming, so the hedge can be kept reasonably narrow. For this reason, I have concentrated on plants with attractive foliage, as informal hedges of flowering plants generally take up more space. Good evergreen shrubs include golden privet (*Ligustrum ovalifolium* 'Aureum'), which has brightly coloured green and gold leaves and is far more attractive and less vigorous than its green-leaved cousin. There are many varieties of holly which have green or variegated leaves – the green-leaved forms are faster-growing – and the prickly foliage will form an intruder-proof barrier. *Lonicera nitida* 'Baggesen's Gold' has tiny yellow leaves and is reasonably quick-growing. In a mild area, the variegated Italian buckthorn (*Rhamnus alaternus* 'Argenteovariegata') is an excellent choice with its small, attractive, variegated leaves, although it is a plant which is best avoided in cold areas. The best conifers for a hedge are those that respond well to trimming and are reasonably quick-growing yet not overwhelmingly so, such as western red cedar (*Thuja plicata* 'Atrovirens'). Yew (*Taxus baccata*) is slower-growing but still reasonably quick to make a wonderful formal hedge.

Screening with specimen plants

In many cases, the screening required is a halfway house between the two options outlined above: not as large as a tree or as long and substantial as a hedge, but still growing to about 1.8–2.5m (6–8ft) high. A small grouping of tall plants can be the perfect solution. Bamboos such as *Arundinaria murieliae* and *Phyllostachys nigra* are excellent for screening, as they form a narrow, upright clump of canes clad with evergreen leaves. Shrubs such as golden privet (*Ligustrum ovalifolium* 'Aureum') will quickly grow to form a billowing mass of evergreen foliage, yet can be trimmed whenever it becomes necessary to restrict growth. The same goes for *Cornus alba* varieties, which are usually cut hard back each year to encourage good stem colour but can be left untrimmed. Lastly, tall herbaceous perennials like the plume poppy (*Macleaya cordata*) rapidly produce elegant, upright stems that can reach 2.5m (8ft) high, ideal for breaking up the harsh horizontal lines of a fence and providing a little in the way of screening.

Pleached hedges

A pleached hedge is basically a hedge on legs, which has been trained to have around 1.8m (6ft) of clear stem with the branches woven or trained together to form a neat, narrow hedge. Although labour intensive and obviously taking a number of years to achieve appreciable results, such a hedge can be an excellent solution to creating privacy in a small space without darkening the plot and making it feel oppressive. The design fits in well with a formal garden, and the 'legs' of the hedge allow lots of room for ornamental underplanting too.

During the early years the trees need to be trained on to a framework, which should be put up before the trees are planted. Set up a row of stout stakes about 2.5–3m (8–10ft) high and 2.5m (8ft) apart. Then, fix strong bamboo canes or wooden battens horizontally, allowing about 60cm (24in) between them and with the lowest one about 1.8m (6ft) from the ground, or wherever the growth of the hedge is planned to start. (See drawing on page 98.)

Plant the young trees with one by each stake. As lateral shoots develop, tie them in to the horizontal canes and cut out any that are awkward to tie in. As growth thickens, the branches can be interwoven rather than tied in. In future years, sideshoots that appear on these laterals should be cut back to two or three buds to encourage bushy growth. On the main stem, cut back any shoots that appear below the lowest point of the hedge. Once the leading shoot of the tree has reached the top of the stake, bend it over and tie it in, or simply prune out the tip. The framework can be dismantled after several years, once the hedge is well established.

Trees that have traditionally been used for pleaching include beech (*Fagus sylvatica*), lime (*Tilia platyphyllos* and *T.* × *euchlora*) and also hornbeam (*Carpinus betulus*). The larger types of

The tall 'legs' of this pleached lime hedge give screening where it matters while still allowing plenty of plants to be grown below.

TRAINING A PLEACHED HEDGE

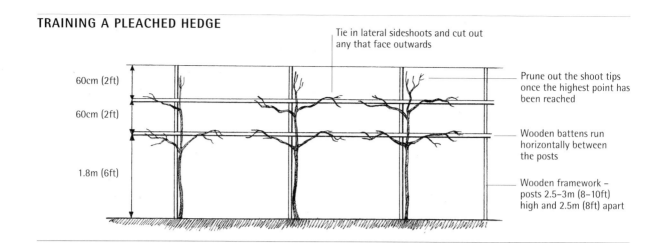

Tie in lateral sideshoots and cut out any that face outwards

60cm (2ft)

60cm (2ft)

1.8m (6ft)

Prune out the shoot tips once the highest point has been reached

Wooden battens run horizontally between the posts

Wooden framework – posts 2.5–3m (8–10ft) high and 2.5m (8ft) apart

ornamental maple such as *Acer platanoides* 'Drummondii' and *A. p.* 'Crimson King' can be used if variegated or coloured foliage is desired.

Climbing plants and wall shrubs

Climbers on a framework are second only to fences for speed and effectiveness where privacy is desired. As supports, use trellis where appearance is important, or a wire fence where it is less so. A low fence can be topped with trellis to give a combined height of around 1.8m (6ft). For extra height, place several arches next to each other along the fence, and the serpentine line of the arches above it will give a stylish look to your boundary. Where windows overlook from above, erect a pergola or large arbour and train a vigorous climber over the top, to create a snug and private area in which to eat and relax.

Plants that are reasonably fast-growing are best for screening. However, one to avoid at all costs is the rampant Russian vine (*Fallopia baldschuanica*), which is certainly not called 'mile-a-minute' for nothing! Deciduous climbers are faster-growing than evergreens, although a mix of the two is best if year-round privacy is required. Quick deciduous plants include *Clematis montana* varieties, which bear a profusion of white or pink spring flowers, and *C. orientalis*,

with 'lanterns' of golden-yellow flowers in late summer, while summer jasmine (*Jasminum officinale*) has dark green leaves and scented white flowers in summer. Passion flower (*Passiflora caerulea*) romps away in a very sunny spot. The Japanese honeysuckle (*Lonicera japonica* 'Halliana') is semi-evergreen, with small clusters of sweetly scented yellow-and-white summer flowers, and is excellent for covering wire fencing, as are *Parthenocissus* species with their attractive foliage and blazing autumn colour.

The choice of evergreens for screening is more limited. Ivy is the top choice, being an enormously versatile plant for sun or shade with glossy evergreen leaves that come in a wealth of different variegations. *Hedera helix* varieties tend to be the best choice for trellis, as varieties of *H. colchica* will eventually form a large mass of growth which, if left unpruned, will become too heavy for its support. Also happy in sun or shade is *Euonymus fortunei* 'Silver Queen', which is fairly slow-growing but makes very effective cover to about 1.2m (4ft), with glossy variegated leaves. *Trachelospermum asiaticum* does well in a sunny, sheltered spot and bears jasmine-like, exquisitely scented flowers in summer.

Initial pruning and training immediately after planting are important to form the basis of a good screen. Most plants will be supported by canes when purchased, and these need to be removed and any ties taken off. Untangle the stems and cut them back by about half. Spread them out in a wide fan shape with the lower ones as near to horizontal as possible, and tie in to the trellis or fence using soft string. Do not use wire, as it may cut into the stems as they grow.

A number of shrubs can be trained on to trellis or a post-and-wire framework to create a first-class screen. A framework can be made using fence posts at each end, with intermediate ones every 3m (10ft) or so. Run strong galvanized wire horizontally between the posts with 23–30cm (9–12in) between them, stretching the wire tightly to prevent it sagging when it is supporting lots of plant growth.

Many shrubs can be trained to grow flat against their support, with regular tying-in and removal of outward-facing shoots at the appropriate time. Good candidates for shade or sun include pyracantha, an evergreen which has clusters of white spring flowers followed by red, orange or yellow autumn berries. Flowering quince (*Chaenomeles*) bears many colourful, saucer-shaped flowers along its naked branches in spring, followed by autumn fruits. Winter jasmine (*Jasminum nudiflorum*) has yellow star-shaped flowers through the winter.

Gardening in containers

In a small garden, containers are an absolute boon. They offer unrivalled scope for growing a huge range of plants right through the year, and can be moved about to create an ever-changing display. Plants can be brought to centre stage as

Magnificently versatile, containers make it possible to create a constantly changing display in even the smallest gardens.

they reach their peak of perfection, then tucked discreetly behind the scenes once past their best, to grow on or die back in decent privacy. Impossibly tiny spaces and inconvenient corners can be enlivened with a few pots, and where there is no garden at all – such as at the front of a town house – hanging baskets and window boxes can be used to create a feast of colour.

Although summer-flowering bedding and tender plants remain top of the popularity charts, the greatest benefits for a small garden come with growing a selection of plants across the board to create permanent as well as seasonal colour. Permanent plants make a substantial backdrop to ephemeral flowers with the considerable advantage of requiring very little work, as opposed to bedding which needs to be replaced in totality twice a year. Evergreen and deciduous shrubs, dwarf conifers, ornamental grasses and certain herbaceous perennials offer a wonderful selection of foliage and flower colour. In frost-prone areas, a greenhouse, conservatory or porch will widen the scope even further, making it possible to grow what I call 'inside-outside' plants – tender shrubs that need winter protection but can move outside for the summer.

Types of container

There is a huge range of containers available to today's gardener. Choice is obviously a very personal matter, depending on individual taste and budget, although it is best to restrict the number of container materials and designs as too many different ones can produce a rather muddled effect. Most pots and containers are designed to sit directly on the ground, although wall pots are flat on one side so that they can be hung against a wall or fence.

At the lower end of the price range there is a wide variety of containers made from plastic, some of which are fair imitations of terracotta or stone. These are fine for short-lived plants, but you should avoid this type for permanent plants as the thin walls result in a wide fluctuation in temperature – too hot in summer and very cold in winter. Wooden containers come in a number of sizes and designs, including window boxes, elegant Versailles tubs and rustic half-barrels. Terracotta – both glazed and unglazed – is very popular and again there is a considerable selection of sizes and designs on the market. Prices vary according to the size and the amount of decoration on the pot, and also whether the pot is frost-proof or not – an important consideration in cold areas if the container is to stay outside all year. Brand-new terracotta is generally a bright orange colour that will soon weather and take on a more mellow appearance. Weathering takes at the very least a few months, although the process can be speeded up by giving the pot a wash of lime or spraying it regularly with liquid fertilizer.

Tall, free-standing containers or jardinières are very useful to lend height to a grouping of pots. Those made of wrought iron are most ornamental, although fairly expensive. However, cheaper ones made from plastic-covered metal are widely available, and remember that the container itself should soon be hidden by plant growth. Old chimney-pots are excellent, although their increasing popularity has ensured a corresponding rise in price.

The same goes for hanging containers such as baskets, flower pouches and swags. Although the containers themselves are not at all ornamental, if planted properly they should soon be hidden from view. They don't cost much either, which is

For overall harmony, choose containers made of just one material but vary the shapes to avoid monotony.

always a bonus! The main choice for hanging baskets falls between open-mesh types and those which have a solid base and sides – a hanging pot, in effect. When choosing, bear in mind that open-mesh baskets are much more versatile as the sides and base can be planted as well as the top, to create a glorious globe of colour. This type needs a liner to retain the compost and plants. Hanging baskets are usually suspended from brackets fixed to walls, posts or pergolas, although it is also possible to have a free-standing display by using a hanging basket 'tree' made from wrought iron. Designs are available to take anything from two to ten baskets.

Many items can be adapted for use as plant containers. Let your imagination run riot and use throwaway items such as old sinks and toilets, central heating tanks, buckets and even old boots, which can all be planted up. Pieces of wood can be nailed together to form a trough, window box or square pot. The only criterion to bear in mind is that any potential plant container must be provided with drainage holes, as plants with waterlogged roots will quickly die.

Choosing and positioning containers

With so many pot designs and materials available, it is easy to fall into the trap of buying a few of everything and end up creating an impression of jumble and clutter rather than harmony. Although different materials can certainly be used in sites around the garden to great effect, try not to get carried away when choosing containers for a patio or courtyard garden and stick to one or two materials. Within your chosen type of pot – terracotta is a popular

POSITIONING CONTAINERS AS A GROUP

For the best effect, group together containers of different sizes and shapes for contrast. The same principle applies to plants. Choose a selection of upright, bushy, spiky and trailing shapes.

example – the sizes and styles can be varied so that there is lots of visual interest, but without conflict. An informal or cottage garden is the chief exception, where old household items like zinc mop-buckets and wash-coppers can rub shoulders with wooden half-barrels and weathered terracotta pots. Such a mixed group of containers can still be linked by using similar plants, but in different cultivars or colours to give an air of harmony while still offering plenty of variety.

Although a group of pots that vary in size is ideal and easy to place, you can very often end up with lots of similar-sized containers – particularly if they are offered at a bargain price! Inject more interest by making 'steps' on which to raise several pots to the rear of a group, or even turn an empty pot upside-down to make a base for another. Height can also be added to a group of pots by using tall containers such as chimney-pots and jardinières, planting some climbers in containers (see page 107), and

SHORTCUTS TO SUMMER PLANTS

Once there were two main choices if you wanted plants for summer containers: grow your own bedding plants from seed or buy costly ready-grown ones. Now, however, there are two splendid shortcuts available in the form of ready-grown seedlings and rooted cuttings.

Seedlings strike the ideal balance between the rewards of raising your own bedding plants and the risks of starting from scratch with seed. They offer good savings in both time and money. Seed can be expensive, particularly the F1 hybrids of plants such as geraniums, begonias and busy lizzies. These need to be sown early in the year and grown on at a high temperature, which requires costly equipment such as a propagator and greenhouse for guaranteed results.

After purchase, keep the seedlings moist and prick out into trays as soon as possible, or they will quickly become overcrowded and leggy. Handle by the leaves as the stems bruise easily. Use fresh potting compost and, if the bag has been sitting outside, bring it indoors for a few hours first to avoid the shock of delicate roots going into cold compost. Similarly, water should be tepid rather than ice-cold straight from the tap. Grow the plants on in a warm and well lit place such as a heated greenhouse or on a sunny windowsill.

Frost-tender perennials can be bought as ready-rooted cuttings or young plantlets, often called 'starter plants', 'plugs' or 'tots'. Pot up soon after purchase into 9cm (3½in) pots. Solid pots should be removed before potting up, while net pots can be left on as the roots will grow through the holes. With hanging baskets, swags and flower pouches, you can get a real head start by planting the whole container in early spring. Plantlets are ideal for this purpose as their small rootballs can be slipped easily into place. However, you will need sufficient frost-free space in a greenhouse, porch or conservatory to grow the plants on in their containers for a few weeks.

All these tender plants need to be kept under cover until all danger of frost is past. Then, acclimatize them to the outside world and harden off for a week or two by placing them outside for increasing periods of time. By early summer, you will have well established plants that look absolutely superb and will give you a long season of vibrant colour.

including standard plants that are trained to have a length of clear stem (see page 71).

A single pot can look spectacular, too, and one large or stylish container can be used on its own to make a focal point. Look for the key viewpoints around the garden and place your pot accordingly. Emphasize it further by making a base of decorative tiles or paving setts, and plant a circle of one type of plant such as box (*Buxus sempervirens*) or catmint (*Nepeta × faassenii*) around the base. Containers in matching pairs also look very effective flanking a doorway or at the start of a path.

Security, alas, has to be borne in mind with containers that are to be positioned at the front of a house. Free-standing pots should be large, heavy and near-impossible to carry off, such as wooden half-barrels or large stone troughs. Hanging baskets can be secured to their brackets with a small padlock and chain, while window boxes can be held in place with wires passed through the drainage holes and around the back of the box to a couple of nails.

Once you have been bitten by the container bug, all sorts of potential sites for pots will become apparent. A series of small pots can be placed, Continental-style, up one or both sides of a flight of steps. Little grouplets of pots can be placed in odd corners, or next to a seat. And, for the truly organized, containers of plants such as annuals or tender perennials can be kept in reserve and dropped into borders to fill those nasty gaps that tend to appear in late summer, or to replace a plant's sudden demise.

Summer plants for pots

Summer is the time of fresh mornings, warm days and balmy evenings when we can enjoy our gardens to the full, so it is no wonder that summer-flowering plants remain the absolute favourites for containers. Traditional plants have undergone something of an upheaval in recent years, and now a huge range of bedding plants and frost-tender perennials offers a bewildering choice to the gardener. Many of the old favourites such as geraniums (*Pelargonium*), busy lizzies (*Impatiens*), petunias and begonias have been developed to produce new varieties, colours and shapes, along with improved performance. Many plants are now available in individual colours rather than the mixed shades that were previously on offer, making it easier to plant containers with a particular colour theme.

Frost-tender perennials have hit the gardening scene in a big way and are now immensely popular. These plants tolerate little or no frost, but produce a marvellous display of flowers within a short time of planting. In many cases their foliage is handsome, too. As the name suggests, these plants can be overwintered in a frost-free greenhouse or conservatory, to give another good display the following year. For the majority of people, who don't possess such a structure, take cuttings in mid- to late summer – most of these plants root with consummate ease – and keep them on a well lit windowsill until late spring.

With so many plants available, it is worth thinking about planting schemes before heading down to the garden centre. Colour theming works just as well in containers as in the borders and is perhaps even more vital, given that the vivid, brazen flower colours of summer plants can so easily end up screaming at each other.

Cool, pastel shades look elegant and are excellent against a dark background such as conifers, evergreens or red brick. White is particularly good on a patio that is used a lot in the evening, as the flowers stand out in the twilight long after others have faded from view.

There are white varieties of busy lizzies, *Sutera cordata*, which bears masses of tiny blooms, and white tobacco plants (*Nicotiana*), which have the considerable bonus of a rich and exotic perfume in the evening. For a cool combination, mix white flowers with silver foliage and blue or soft pink flowers. Blue and silver can be combined with yellow flowers for a colour contrast that is bright without being vivid.

Vibrant colours predominate and the range is immense, with many shades of red, pink and purple to choose from. For best effect, place these against a pale rather than a dark backing, to ensure that the blooms stand out and can be appreciated fully rather than blending into the background. These 'hot' colours can be combined to create a really eye-socking effect, and an overall air of harmony can be created by using one or two main plants, like geraniums or petunias, in a wide range of colours. Alternatively, bright flowers can be toned down by mixing in some foliage plants.

Most annuals and frost-tender perennials prefer a sunny site, particularly so in the case of plants like Zulu daisy (*Arctotis*), African daisy (*Osteospermum*) and nasturtiums (*Tropaeolum majus*). A few plants, notably fuchsias and busy lizzies, do prefer to be out of the sun and these are wonderful for brightening shady spots.

Permanent plants for containers

For the busy gardener, hardy plants that stay in the same containers for several years are a tremendous boon. With minimal maintenance, they provide colour and interest in their own right year after year, as well as making a substantial backdrop to seasonal flowering plants. Another bonus is that, unlike most seasonal summer plants, many permanent plants are happy in full or partial shade, a situation that tends to be more common than sun in small gardens, particularly close to the house.

Most permanent plants have vigorous root systems, and so are best grown in individual containers rather than planted with several other specimens in one large pot. For overall harmony use the same style and material of pot but in a range of different sizes to match the vigour of each plant. The minimum pot size should be 25cm (10in) wide and deep for a fairly small plant such as an herbaceous perennial, while a wooden half-barrel or similar is required for shrubs and climbers.

Herbaceous perennials that make a long-lasting display in pots are few and far between, but a select number are well worth growing.

Perennials in pots last for years with minimal care. Large-leaved *Heuchera* 'Pewter Moon' and hosta are excellent for shade.

LARGE-FLOWERED HYBRID CLEMATIS FOR CONTAINERS

'Arctic Queen' (pure white)

'Fireworks' (blue with a red stripe)

'Guernsey Cream' (creamy yellow)

'Haku-ôkan' (violet-blue)

'Lasurstern' (lavender-blue)

'Nelly Moser' (pale mauve-pink with a
   deeper bar)

'Niobe' (ruby-red)

'Royalty' (purple-mauve)

'The President' (purple-blue)

'Silver Moon' (pale mauve)

'Vyvyan Pennell' (violet-blue)

Clematis 'Comtesse de Bouchard' climbs and cascades to make a spectacular and unusual display.

Those with decorative foliage give interest over the longest period. Hostas, with their bold architectural leaves in a wealth of variegations and colours, are magnificent for a shady spot. Being raised off the ground in pots tends to make these delectable plants less prone to the depredations of slugs and snails, for whom the lush leaves are a gourmet treat. A final line of defence against determined pests is to put a layer of non-setting insect glue or petroleum jelly around the rim of the pot. For partial shade, there are heuchera varieties with lobed leaves in unusual colours and variegations, and the variegated lilyturf (*Liriope muscari* 'John Burch'), which forms a neat clump of gold-variegated leaves with the added bonus of deep violet-blue flowers borne on dense spikes in late summer. In full sun, plant *Euphorbia myrsinites* with its fleshy, glaucous leaves and lime-yellow flowers.

Ornamental grasses impart an elegance of shape and form to the patio. A single trio of varieties, planted in individual pots and grouped together, amply demonstrates the beauty of their different shapes and colour contrasts. There is

SHRUBS FOR CONTAINERS

Acer palmatum cultivars

Arundinaria

Ceanothus 'Diamond Heights'

Convolvulus cneorum

Cordyline

Hebe

Phormium

Phyllostachys

Rhododendron yakushimanum hybrids
   (ericaceous or lime-free compost)

Yucca

See also plants for winter interest on page 108.

CARE OF PERMANENT PLANTS

- Check that pots have drainage holes and put crocks in the bottom to ensure good drainage.

- Use a loam- or soil-based compost such as John Innes No 3, which has more 'body' than soil-less types and is a better buffer against drought.

- Keep plants in good condition by top-dressing every spring. Gently remove the top few centimetres of soil and replace with fresh potting compost.

- Once plants have become potbound and packed their containers with roots, they will perform poorly. So, either plant out in the border or pot up into a larger container.

- Rejuvenate perennials and grasses by dividing their rootstocks into several pieces in spring or autumn, discarding the old, woody centre and replanting the smaller divisions.

- Feed plants with controlled-release fertilizer mixed with the top-dressing of new compost, or apply a weekly liquid fertilizer.

- Do not feed after mid- to late summer, as this would encourage the growth of soft shoots that could be damaged by frost.

- Cut back foliage in autumn once it has yellowed completely and died back. Place plants in a sheltered spot, and lie pots on their sides if waterlogging from heavy rain is likely.

the Japanese golden grass (*Hakonechloa macra* 'Aureola'), which forms a cascading clump of slender, gold-and-green leaves; *Festuca glauca*, which makes a 'hedgehog' clump of intense blue, and *Carex comans* bronze form, in a rich rust-brown. Invasive plants should be avoided at all costs in the borders of a small garden, but are excellent when confined to containers out of harm's way. Such plants include *Houttuynia cordata* 'Chameleon', with unusually variegated leaves of red, cream and green.

Climbers with a compact habit can be grown in containers – particularly useful in the case of walls and fences that have no soil at the base – while on the patio they can make an unusual display to give extra height to a group of pots. Container-grown climbers can either be supported with a home-made tripod of bamboo canes, combined with wire mesh or netting for those plants that climb by means of tendrils, or there are some very attractive ready-made supports available such as wooden 'bells', trellis fans or wire obelisks. Small-leaved ivies (*Hedera helix* varieties) can be trained over wire topiary frames to create shapes like spirals and lollipops.

Large-flowered hybrid clematis are excellent in containers. The choice of varieties is tremendous, although for pots it is best to choose those which flower in early summer as their habit tends to be compact (see panel, page 106). Place varieties with deep-coloured flowers in sun so that they can be seen at their most lovely, while those with pale or striped flowers are best in partial or even full shade, as strong sun can bleach out the delicate colour in the blooms. In addition to these summer beauties, the less vigorous species clematis such as *C. alpina*, *C. macropetala* and *C. viticella* are also sufficiently compact for containers: the first two bloom in spring and the latter in late summer. Clematis dislike having their roots in the sun, so choose a cool site or place the pot in the middle of a group.

Plenty of other climbers can be grown in pots if given a large container, including passion flower (*Passiflora caerulea*), *Jasminum officinale* 'Fiona Sunrise' and *Trachelospermum asiaticum*. Until recently, climbing roses have definitely been off limits due to their deep root system, but in recent years a number of miniature climbing roses have arrived on the scene. They reach about 1.8m (6ft) in height and can be grown in a large container such as a half-barrel. Varieties include 'Laura Ford', 'Little Rambler', 'Warm Welcome' and 'Nice Day'.

A single fan-shaped piece of trellis, up to about 1.5m (5ft) high, is ideal for supporting a trained shrub to make a handsome and unusual free-standing feature. Good plants for such treatment include winter jasmine (*Jasminum nudiflorum*) which brings a welcome splash of winter colour to a drab patio, pyracantha, which has spring flowers followed by colourful autumn berries, and the shrubby germander (*Teucrium fruticans*), with attractive grey foliage and blue summer flowers. Tree mallows (*Lavatera*) could be treated as a relatively short-lived display and grown as fans for several years.

Container plants for autumn and winter colour

In addition to the huge range of tender plants for summer colour, there is a wide variety of hardy ones that can provide a magnificent display to brighten the darkest and most gloomy times of the year. Strategic positioning is the key to getting maximum enjoyment from containers that are planned to look good in autumn, winter and early spring. Place pots around the main entrance to the house so that you are welcomed home by a cheery display of colour. Look at the parts of the garden seen from your most frequently used windows and favourite armchair, and position your pots accordingly.

Plants with colourful foliage will provide the main structure of a winter display. Golden-leaved shrubs such as *Aucuba japonica* 'Crotonifolia', *Choisya ternata* 'Sundance', *Euonymus fortunei* Emerald 'n' Gold, and variegated hollies (*Ilex*) all create a real splash of sunshine. Contrast these with *Hebe* 'Red Edge', its glaucous foliage developing darker red tints in winter, and the unusual 'whipcord' foliage of *Hebe ochracea* 'James Stirling'. A few evergreen shrubs have the added bonus of winter flowers, including Christmas box (*Sarcococca*) which also has a delicious fragrance, and *Viburnum tinus* 'Eve Price'. Others, such as *Gaultheria procumbens* and *Skimmia japonica* subsp. *reevesiana*, bear bright red berries in autumn that last for months. Compact-growing conifers are perfect for pots, offering a wonderful range of foliage including gold, silver, green and blue.

After the summer's display, there is plenty of autumn colour in pots: *Erica gracilis*, *Calluna vulgaris* 'Dark Star', ivies and *Viola* 'Blueberry Cream'.

PLANTING AND CARING FOR WINTER CONTAINERS

In cold areas where winter frosts are likely to be severe, the right planting, placing and care of plants is vital to their success and survival. Here are some guidelines:

■ Check that pots are frost-proof before using them outside in winter, particularly terracotta and glazed types.

■ Avoid very exposed, windy spots.

■ Make sure surplus water can drain away easily by 'crocking' pots well and raising them a little way off the ground, or the rootball could freeze solid and kill the plants.

■ Do not overlook the need for occasional watering – water sparingly when the compost is starting to dry out.

■ During very cold spells, container-grown plants are particularly vulnerable to frost damage as their roots are completely above ground. Move hanging baskets into a porch or greenhouse; stand containers close together in a sheltered spot, such as against the house, and wrap the pots in bubble polythene.

■ Protect the foliage of evergreens from frost and wind scorch by wrapping plants in horticultural fleece during severe weather. Remove it as soon as the weather improves.

PLANTING BULBS IN CONTAINERS

The outstanding versatility of bulbs is amply demonstrated by planting bulbs of different sizes in a large container.

First, prepare the container by checking that it has drainage holes in the base and putting a layer of crocks or drainage materials in the bottom, as bulbs tend to rot quickly in waterlogged compost. Then, put a little potting compost in the container and place the largest bulbs, such as daffodils, as the bottom layer. Cover these bulbs with a layer of compost and then put in the medium-sized bulbs, such as tulips. In turn, put compost over these bulbs and then finish with a layer of the smallest bulbs, like crocus, covering these with a final layer of compost. As a rough guide to planting depths, a bulb should be covered with compost to three times its own height. There is no need to worry about the careful placing of one layer on top of another, as the stems will work their way around any obstructions and you will end up with a wonderful display of spring blooms all in one container.

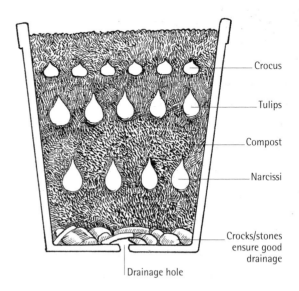

Layering bulbs in a container

Such shrubs and conifers can be planted in individual pots to be used as the fancy takes you on their own, grouped together or moved around to ring the changes, or they can be planted as centrepieces in large containers. In the latter situation, add extra colour with winter bedding plants such as pansies, or ornamental cabbage and kale with purple, cream or green foliage, and put in bulbs for spring blooms. For the summer, the centre plant stays put, and the surrounding plants are swapped for summer bedding. When changing plants over, always replace some of the old soil with fresh potting compost.

Hanging baskets and window boxes can also be planted for winter colour. Bedding plants and dwarf bulbs are ideal in these smaller containers, along with young plants of evergreen shrubs and conifers which can be used here for one season and then planted out in borders or larger containers. In addition there are winter-flowering heathers (*Erica carnea* varieties), which have a low, spreading habit, while ivies and lesser periwinkle (*Vinca minor* varieties) trail over the sides.

Raised beds

The inclusion of one or more raised beds in a small space can effect an amazing transformation, introducing a dramatic change of level as well as creating interest as features in their own right. Being reasonably formal in appearance, raised beds are ideal for a courtyard garden, a patio or near the house. The material should ideally match the surroundings; natural stone, wood or railway sleepers for a cottage or an older house, sawn logs for a natural setting, and brick or stone blocks to go with a new or formal town house. A bed could be finished with a coping wide enough to sit on, also providing useful extra seating.

Gardeners who find it uncomfortable to bend down to ground level will find that raised beds

are an absolute boon, and the fact that most of the work can be done from a sitting position also makes gardening accessible for the disabled. In this case, the height of the bed must be tailored carefully to that of the user, and it should be of a suitable width too.

From a horticultural point of view, such beds make it possible to control the growing conditions to a much greater extent than elsewhere in the garden. If the border soil is limy, the soil within the raised beds could be acid, making it possible to grow lime-haters such as rhododendrons, azaleas, camellias and pieris. In the case of a brick-built bed, line the inside with plastic or rubber sheeting – the type used for making ponds – to prevent lime from the mortar leaching into the soil. The drainage can be manipulated too, to suit plants such as alpines

CONSTRUCTING A RAISED BED

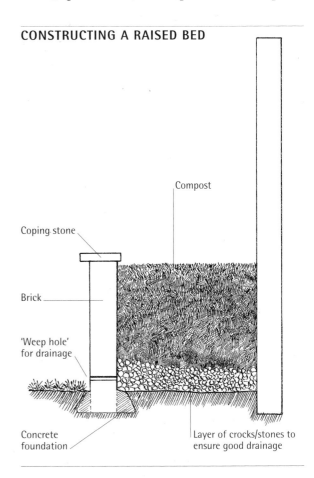

Compost

Coping stone

Brick

'Weep hole' for drainage

Concrete foundation

Layer of crocks/stones to ensure good drainage

that love a gritty, sharply drained soil, or for Mediterranean plants that detest having wet roots in winter. In all cases, make provision for adequate drainage by building in small drainage channels or 'weep holes' near the base of the walls, and putting a layer of drainage material such as broken bricks in the bottom of the bed.

The care and maintenance requirements for raised beds are similar to those for containers.

A raised bed is just container gardening on a large scale. Pansies, pinks and lilies create a pageant of colour.

Being raised off the ground results in faster drainage than in soil in garden borders, so watering will still need to be carried out regularly, although not as frequently as for containers. Feed plants with a controlled-release fertilizer in spring.

Practical Matters

ALL PLANTS BENEFIT FROM thorough soil preparation before planting in order to get off to a good start in life. Such advance groundwork is particularly important in a small garden as the plants are likely to be packed closely together, often with ground-cover shrubs under larger specimens and climbers growing through shrubs and trees. All these plants need to take up large quantities of water and nutrients in relation to the amount of space they occupy. The soil for climbers requires particular attention, as these plants have access to a very small area compared to their overall size; in addition, the influence of the supporting wall or fence has to be taken into account, particularly if it is a house wall with overhanging eaves, as this will prevent a good proportion of any rain from reaching the soil around the plants.

Preparing the soil

To prepare the soil for planting, dig it over, ideally down to two spades' depths ('spits') to ensure that the deeper subsoil is broken up sufficiently to allow roots to penetrate, and also so that plenty of organic matter can be thoroughly incorporated. Digging can be carried out at any time of year provided that the ground is not wet and sticky, as in these conditions your weight could compact the soil badly and damage its structure. Heavy clay soils are the hardest to cultivate, being waterlogged in winter and rock-solid when dry in summer. In this instance, let nature give a helping hand: if you dig the ground over in autumn and leave it in rough clods over winter, the frost will get into the soil and help to break it down into a workable, crumbly tilth.

When digging, work the ground in strips or

DOUBLE-DIGGING NEW GROUND

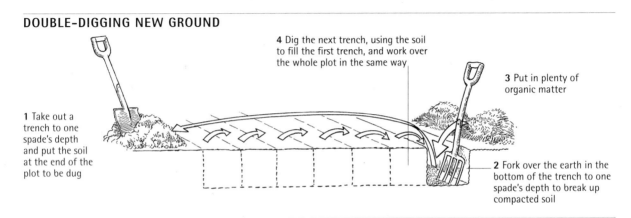

4 Dig the next trench, using the soil to fill the first trench, and work over the whole plot in the same way

3 Put in plenty of organic matter

1 Take out a trench to one spade's depth and put the soil at the end of the plot to be dug

2 Fork over the earth in the bottom of the trench to one spade's depth to break up compacted soil

Dense planting in a small garden means that thorough ground preparation is essential for success.

including well rotted manure, garden compost or a proprietary planting compost. Save money by investigating local sources of manure such as riding stables or farms; the classified advertisements in your local paper are often useful, too. Manure must be well rotted – at least six months old – to prevent it scorching the roots of plants. Alternatively, dig in fresh manure and leave it to rot down *in situ* for several months before doing any sowing or planting.

Weed control

A vital stage of preparing the ground for planting is to clear all weeds, some of which can be the absolute bane of a gardener's life. The oft-quoted adage of 'a weed is only a plant growing in the wrong place' is of little comfort when you are faced with the horrors of perennial weeds like nettles, brambles, thistles, ground elder and bindweed, all bursting with health and vigour. Annuals like chickweed and cleavers aren't nearly so bad as they can be hoed off easily, although it is best to do so at the seedling stage before they have a chance to mature and set seed themselves.

Perennial weeds need to be cleared meticulously, as they will regrow from the tiniest piece of root left behind. For this reason it is a huge mistake to rotovate a weedy site, as the blades will chop up the roots and you will end up with hundreds more plants than when you started! Perennial weeds can be tackled in three different ways: digging by hand, killing with weedkiller, or covering the ground completely to exclude all light for up to a year.

A combination of the first two methods is usually the best choice where results are required fairly quickly. To start with, dig up as much of the weed growth as possible, particularly the roots, and take it to the rubbish tip – *do not* compost the roots or they will simply regrow.

trenches so that no area is overlooked. Shovel the top layer to one side to keep the good quality, humus-rich topsoil separate from any poorer quality subsoil. Remove all weed growth (see below). Fork over the lower layer of soil, break up any compacted lumps and take out any bricks, stones or other large lumps of debris. Put plenty of organic matter in the trench, then finish by shovelling back the top spit of soil and levelling it roughly with a rake.

All soils benefit from the addition of bulky organic matter. Light, free-draining, sandy or stony soils need it in order to hold water and nutrients that would otherwise drain out quickly, and with heavy clay or silty ground it helps to open up and improve the soil structure. A number of different materials can be used

Then, when fresh shoots appear and the plant is growing strongly, apply a systemic weedkiller such as glyphosate to the leaves – spring and early summer are the best times for this – and the plant will draw the poison right down to the roots. Several applications may be required to finish off tough perennials once and for all. Obviously, you should take great care to follow the manufacturer's instructions when using and storing any chemical weedkillers.

The third option – the 'cover-up' method – is the easiest, but takes time, patience and the ability to ignore your garden looking a mess for months. This method works by excluding all light and so, eventually, even the toughest weeds will succumb. Materials that can be used include rolls of black polythene, old carpet or sheets of cardboard. Lay them on the ground with a good

INEXPENSIVE SOIL IMPROVERS

Unless your garden is absolutely tiny, buying bags of a proprietary soil conditioner to add vital organic matter to your soil can be very expensive. Here are the main choices of materials that won't cost a fortune.

Material	Advantages	Disadvantages
Manure	Mixed with straw or wood shavings and then left to rot down, makes an excellent soil improver. Usually contains a reasonable quantity of nutrients. Riding stables often supply free if you collect; farmers may deliver a bulk trailer load at a reasonable price.	Must be at least six months old or could scorch and kill plant roots. Manure containing wood shavings should be twelve months old before using. May contain weed seeds if the heap did not rot at a sufficiently high temperature.
Garden compost	Excellent way to recycle most garden and kitchen waste. Contains plenty of nutrients. Costs nothing after initial purchase of compost container.	Vital to be selective about what's included – avoid perennial weed roots, diseased plant material and cooked food. May contain weed seeds (see above).
Leafmould	Free natural resource and an excellent soil conditioner. Leaves can be rotted easily in large polythene bags. Collected leaves may be available in bulk from public parks or councils. Clean to handle.	Takes at least 12 months to rot down. Contains few nutrients.
Spent mushroom compost	Well composted manure and straw which is clean and easy to handle. Usually available in bags or loose in bulk direct from suppliers.	Unsuitable for acid-loving plants as includes lime. Contains few nutrients. May harbour chemical residues.

overlap where any joints occur, and either weigh down or bury the edges. After 6–12 months the weeds should all have died. A bonus of this method is that the weed growth will have rotted down to add useful organic matter to the soil and, having been covered for so long, the soil will be reasonably dry and in perfect condition for digging over.

Having worked hard on cleaning the soil of weeds, take a few minutes every week during the growing season to keep it that way. On a dry day, hoe the surface to kill off any newly germinated seedlings. If any of the detested perennial weeds appear, dig up the roots and bin them. When plants are in full, exuberant summer growth, watch out for weeds that have been thriving

KILLING WEEDS USING THE COVER-UP METHOD

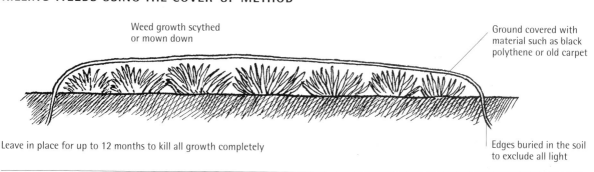

Weed growth scythed or mown down

Ground covered with material such as black polythene or old carpet

Leave in place for up to 12 months to kill all growth completely

Edges buried in the soil to exclude all light

MAKING GARDEN COMPOST

Most garden and kitchen waste can be turned into a wonderful soil conditioner and source of nutrients for your plants, simply by rotting it down to make garden compost.

Compost bins are a good investment as they contain the waste neatly and, because the material inside heats up quickly, the rotting process is faster than if the waste is just piled in a heap. Ready-made bins come in a range of sizes and designs; alternatively, make your own cheap and cheerful container by fixing wire mesh around four posts and lining it with carpet. Ideally, have two bins, so that one can be 'cooking' while the other fills up.

First, put a layer of woody prunings in the base of the bin, in contact with the soil, so that air can circulate more readily. Then, fill the bin with a mixture of dense, soggy material such as lawn clippings and kitchen waste like vegetable

peelings and teabags, along with drier material such as weeds and soft prunings. Woody branches should be shredded before being added to the heap. In a small garden, hiring a shredder for the occasional clear-up is generally a better option than buying one. As the bin fills up, a proprietary compost activator can be added from time to time to speed up rotting. Ideally the mixture should be moist, but not too wet or too dry, so cover the heap with a lid or a piece of carpet and add water if necessary. After about six months, the mixture should be brown and crumbly, and ready to use.

To make really top quality compost, turn out the heap after a couple of months, then fork it back, turning the compost sides to the middle. However, the material will rot down adequately – although a little more slowly – if left undisturbed.

unnoticed and suddenly pop out, full of seed waiting to be shed. Once the ground is clean, a mulch will help enormously in keeping it weed-free in future (see page 117).

Planting

Certain times of year are much better for planting than others. For hardy plants like trees, shrubs, roses and perennials, autumn is far and away the best time. Once the autumn rains have soaked the soil it will be warm and moist, so plants that go in then will make lots of root growth through autumn and during mild spells in winter, becoming well established in time for an explosion of growth the following spring. In colder areas, the chief exception to autumn planting is those plants that are obviously frost tender, and any which are on the borderline of hardiness such as ceanothus and cistus. Such potentially tender plants should be planted in spring to give a good period of establishment before the winter frosts.

Planting in autumn means that the need for subsequent watering is greatly reduced and should only really be necessary during any long, dry spells that occur the following year. By contrast, plants that are put in through spring and summer will need frequent watering, even daily during hot weather, as they struggle to establish their root systems and make top growth at the same time. Another bonus of autumn planting is that bare-rooted or field-grown plants are often available – principally trees, hedging, roses and fruit – and in most cases these are cheaper than container-grown plants. Bare-rooted plants are easily supplied by mail order, which is useful in out-of-the-way locations or if unusual varieties are required.

Whatever the time of year, before planting give the plant's rootball a good soaking by

The slowing of growth in autumn, coupled with warm, moist soil, make this the perfect time to put in new hardy plants.

standing it in a bucket of water for an hour or two. Dig a hole slightly larger than the rootball and mix some compost plus slow-release fertilizer (proprietary planting composts usually have fertilizer included) into the bottom of the hole and the excavated soil. If planting against a wall, dig the hole about 30cm (12in) away from it, as the bricks will take vital moisture away from the plant's roots. Gently knock the plant from its pot. If there is a mass of roots spiralling around the bottom of the rootball, tease them loose, then put the plant in the prepared hole so that the top of the rootball is level with the ground. Backfill the planting hole, firming the soil with your heel to avoid leaving any air pockets, and give the plant a thorough watering.

Regular watering of plants put in during spring and summer can be made more effective by using a large plastic bottle to ensure that the water goes directly to the roots. Simply remove the top, cut off the base and sink the bottle upside-down in the ground next to the rootball.

Fill the bottle with water every couple of days during dry spells. An entire border of new plants can be watered easily using seep hose, also known as porous pipe, which is made from recycled car tyres and designed so that water trickles out slowly along its entire length.

Mulching

The chief benefits of a mulch can be summed up as less watering and less weeds – which, of course, means a lot less work into the bargain. Mulching immediately after planting is a useful aid to plant establishment, as it slows the loss of water by evaporation as well as preventing competition from weed growth.

A mulch can be one material on its own, or a combination of two – a good-looking top layer to hide the ugly one underneath. Organic mulches such as well rotted manure, garden compost, leafmould, mushroom compost, bark chippings and cocoa shell all help to improve the soil to varying degrees and also make an attractive backdrop to plants. However, bear in mind that although manure and garden compost are the cheapest, they are quite likely to contain weed

Mulching the soil around new plants helps them become established by reducing water loss and weed growth.

PLANTING A SHRUB

To improve watering efficiency, cut the base off a large plastic bottle and sink it into the ground so that the water will go straight to the roots

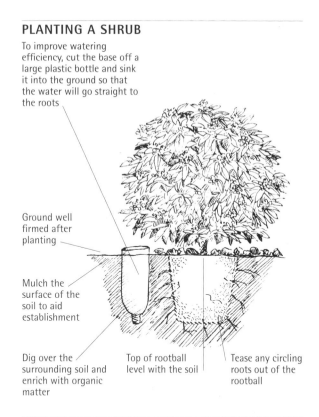

Ground well firmed after planting

Mulch the surface of the soil to aid establishment

Dig over the surrounding soil and enrich with organic matter

Top of rootball level with the soil

Tease any circling roots out of the rootball

seeds (see panel on page 114). All these materials should be applied in a layer at least 5cm (2in) thick on moist, weed-free soil between plants, leaving a gap around stems and leaves.

Woody prunings can be shredded to make a good home-made mulch. Stack the chippings for at least six months before use, otherwise they will take nitrogen from the soil as they begin to break down and will leave your plants short of this vital nutrient.

Man-made materials such as woven geotextile matting and tough black polythene are effective at suppressing weeds and retaining moisture. Home-made mulches made of cardboard or thick layers of newspaper also work well, with the added bonus of costing nothing at all. None of these materials is attractive to look at, however, so in prominent areas they are best covered with a thin layer of organic mulch such as cocoa shell or bark chippings.

Staking trees

Trees are top-heavy and need to be staked for a couple of years until their root system is well established. Otherwise, a new tree will sway in the wind, continually loosening and tearing its roots as they try to develop. In recent years the thinking on tree stakes has switched to using a short stake rather than one that is almost as high as the tree itself. A short stake prevents too much movement while at the same time encourageing a good root system to develop, while the longer stake acts as a permanent 'crutch' to the tree and may prevent it becoming self-supporting.

Choose a stout stake that is about one-third of the tree's height. Hammer it into the hole before planting – roots will be damaged if it is put in afterwards – and secure the tree using a tree tie. Do not use wire or string which could easily damage the bark, creating wounds through which disease can enter or, at worst, eventually killing the tree. If you do not have a proper tie, use lengths of nylon stocking as a temporary measure, as these will stretch as the stem expands and won't rub the bark. Ties must be checked regularly and loosened as the tree grows. They should fit snugly without being over-tight, but not so loosely that the bark could be rubbed off in a high wind.

Supporting climbers

Most climbers and all wall shrubs need some form of support when growing on walls and fences. The only exceptions are self-clinging plants such as ivy, climbing hydrangea and Virginia creeper. Climbing plants twine or scramble up their support, while wall plants need to be tied in regularly and their outward-growing shoots pruned back in order to keep them neat.

The main choice of support is between strong galvanized wire or wire mesh, and trellis. Galvanized wire is the most economical and easiest to put up over a large area of wall or a long fence. Run wires in single strands through vine eyes, either horizontally or in a fan shape, depending on the plant's habit. On a wall, run the wires along the mortar courses and they will be barely visible. Large-mesh wire fencing is also relatively cheap. It can be fixed to a wall or fence, and is ideal for scramblers like clematis, passion flower and eccremocarpus. Wire mesh is not attractive, so it is important that it will eventually be covered completely with climbers.

Trellis looks attractive and is therefore excellent for a high-profile position, although it is much more costly than wire. Styles range from basic squared trellis to stylish designs, and the price goes up accordingly. Do bear in mind that there is little point in choosing trellis if your main aim is to cover the wall or fence completely

PLANTING AND STAKING A TREE

Dig over the surrounding soil and enrich with organic matter

Secure with a plastic buckle-type tree tie

Stake, approximately one-third of the tree's height, put in before planting

Tease any circling roots out of the rootball

SUPPORTING CLIMBERS

Trellis
Screw the trellis to wooden battens approximately 5cm (2in) thick, to allow room for plants to twine around the trellis

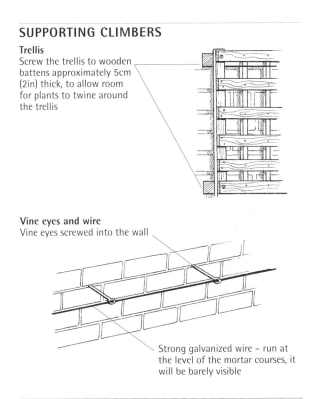

Vine eyes and wire
Vine eyes screwed into the wall

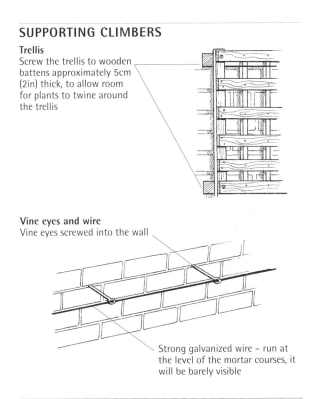

Strong galvanized wire – run at the level of the mortar courses, it will be barely visible

with plants. There is a wide range of sizes and designs to suit just about every taste and budget, and it's a good idea to obtain brochures from a number of manufacturers first, or inspect displays at several garden centres or at garden shows. When putting up trellis, fix wooden battens between the trellis and the wall or fence, to create a space of around 5cm (2in). This gives the plants sufficient room to twine around the trellis, which wouldn't be at all easy if it was fixed directly against the wall. Such spacing also allows good air movement around the plants, thus reducing the chance of fungal diseases appearing, as these flourish in humid conditions.

It is worth emphasizing once again that good ground preparation is crucial to the future health of climbing plants, as the soil by a wall or fence is generally poorer than elsewhere in the garden and receives less rain due to its sheltered position. Add plenty of organic matter prior to planting to improve the soil's water-holding

capacity and plant with the rootball about 30cm (12in) away from the wall or fence to avoid the driest zone. Water regularly until the plants are well established, and during dry spells.

Care and maintenance
Feeding and watering

Garden plants need relatively little maintenance to keep them in tip-top condition. Feeding is the top priority, particularly in a small space where the planting is likely to be very dense. All plants should be given a dressing of slow-release fertilizer in late winter or early spring, followed by a second application in summer. After applying the fertilizer, rake or hoe the ground lightly to incorporate it into the soil, and water in if rain doesn't fall within a couple of days. Flowering plants such as roses benefit from a

PLANTING A CLIMBER AGAINST A WALL

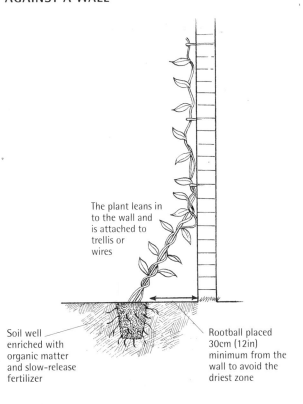

The plant leans in to the wall and is attached to trellis or wires

Soil well enriched with organic matter and slow-release fertilizer

Rootball placed 30cm (12in) minimum from the wall to avoid the driest zone

fertilizer that is high in potash, which promotes flower production.

Watering of established plants may be necessary during long spells of dry weather. Watch out for signs of stress, such as wilting or yellowing of the leaves. Water once or twice a week, giving plants a thorough soaking, rather than little and often which can do more harm than good. The best times to water are early in the morning or in the evening, when less water is lost by evaporation and there is no danger of the sun's rays undergoing a 'magnifying glass' effect via droplets scattered on leaves and flowers and causing damage.

An annual mulch of bulky, nutritious organic matter will improve the condition of the soil, reduce water loss and discourage weeds. Apply a 5cm (2in) layer of material such as garden compost, cocoa shell or well rotted manure, and take care to keep it away from plant stems otherwise rotting could occur.

Pruning

Many gardeners are reluctant to reach for their secateurs, with the result that gardens everywhere are full of overgrown plants that desperately need a good haircut. Certainly, not all plants need regular pruning, but with many shrubs it is necessary after a few years when the plant has become congested, for example, or merely to keep an exuberant variety within bounds.

For those plants that benefit from regular pruning, details are given in the individual entries in the Plant Directory on page 126. The way to tackle overgrown shrubs is covered on page 21. In all cases, it is best to identify your subject first to make sure that, for example, you are not cutting off next season's flowers. A few general guidelines apply to all plants: take out any dead, diseased or damaged growth first, then carry out any formative pruning. Frost-damaged growth should be pruned out in late spring by cutting back to the point where healthy leaves and shoots are being produced.

Pest and disease control

Prevention rather than cure is the key to successful pest and disease control. Plants that are healthy and growing strongly are much more resistant to attack than those which are starved and under stress. Regular inspections should reveal any potential problems in the early stages, when attacks can be nipped in the bud by hand-picking diseased leaves or squashing pests while the infestation is still minor, rather than waiting until it has really taken hold. If there is no visible pest, the damage may be the work of one of the many that operate under cover of darkness, and which can often be identified by an occasional nocturnal inspection under torchlight. If the infestation is more widespread, control with chemicals or a biological agent may be necessary.

When it comes to diseases, fungicides can prevent further spread of the infection, although they cannot cure plant material that is already affected; again, control in the early stages is most effective.

Before embarking on any treatment it is best to identify the pest or disease, as in most cases the chemical or biological control is specific. A good reference book is a vital aid in identifying pest and disease problems and their most effective treatment.

Growing plants in containers
Preparation and planting

Clean out used containers using hot, clean water and a stiff brush, as old debris can harbour pests and diseases. Stone and terracotta containers are porous, so soak them in water for about an hour before planting or they will take water from the compost.

Good drainage is vital to avoid the compost becoming waterlogged, which would deprive the roots of air and eventually kill the plants. Check that your container has drainage holes, and then put a layer of stones, broken crocks or pieces of polystyrene in the base of the pot to prevent the holes becoming blocked and water building up. To be really sure of effective drainage, cover the crocks with coarse leaf mould or fine plastic mesh to prevent compost washing down and clogging up the drainage layer. Finally, raise the container a centimetre or so off the ground so that surplus water can flow away, by placing ornamental pot

feet, stones or old tiles underneath the pot.

Before starting to plant, soak all the plants' rootballs thoroughly in a bucket of water, as a dry rootball is very hard to re-wet after planting. It also helps the plants to withstand the shock of transplanting. Then, put a layer of compost in the container to reach as far as the bottom of the rootball of the largest plant. Aim to leave a 2.5cm (1in) gap between the top of the compost and the edge of the pot for easy watering. Knock the plants gently out of their pots and place them in the container, filling the gaps in between with compost. Firm it gently with your fingers, but take care not to press too hard as it is easy to over-firm composts, particularly the soil-less types. Finally, use a watering can or a hose fitted with a fine rose to water the compost thoroughly but gently. If it settles to leave gaps, top up with extra compost.

PLANTING A PERMANENT PLANT IN A CONTAINER

Top of rootball level with the compost

Tease any circling roots out of the rootball

John Innes No 3 potting compost

Container raised off the ground to prevent drainage holes becoming blocked

Stones or broken pottery over drainage holes to a depth of 6cm (2½in)

Watering

Regular watering is crucial to the success of container plants, as they are totally dependent on you for all their needs. Rain is very rarely adequate as the small area of soil is usually covered by an umbrella of foliage. Pay special attention to hanging baskets, wall pots and other suspended containers: they dry out very rapidly because the whole rootball is exposed to sun and drying breezes. Don't forget to check the need for watering even during wet weather.

The amount of water required by plants in containers varies enormously according to the location, orientation and exposure of each individual site. As a general guide, water hanging containers and small pots at least once and probably twice a day during hot, sunny weather. Aim to keep the soil consistently moist, not allowing it either to dry out or become waterlogged. If possible, water your plants in the early morning or evening, rather than in the heat of the day, when water-splashed growth can become sun-scorched and more water is lost through evaporation.

Feeding

Potting compost contains fertilizer that will last for the first couple of months, but thereafter supplementary feeding becomes essential

---

CHOOSING COMPOST FOR CONTAINERS

A wide selection of potting composts are available which have been formulated specifically for container plants . Never be tempted to skimp and use old compost or to eke it out with garden soil: remember that these plants will be growing in a very confined space and need a really good medium in order to perform to a high standard.

Most composts are soil-less: many are based on peat, while there is an increasing range made from peat alternatives or recycled materials, the choice of which is down to personal preference. One great advantage of these types is their relative lightness, which is essential when growing plants in raised or suspended containers like hanging baskets or window boxes. It is particularly important that soil-less composts are kept evenly moist, as they can be extremely difficult to re-wet once they have dried out completely.

Loam- or soil-based potting composts are much heavier and provide a better buffer against drought. These types should always be used when permanent plants such as shrubs, perennials or climbers are to be grown. Don't use soil-based compost in hanging containers due to its weight.

---

through the growing season to keep plants performing at their best. There are two options: weekly applications of diluted liquid fertilizer, or a one-off application of controlled-release fertilizer. The latter consists of granules coated in temperature-sensitive, slow-dissolving resin, so nutrients are only made available when it is sufficiently warm for plants to grow actively. It goes without saying that this option is ideal for busy gardeners, too.

If a controlled-release fertilizer is used in containers of seasonal summer plants such as annuals and tender perennials, their peak performance can often be extended by applying a high-nitrogen liquid fertilizer in late summer when the original fertilizer is becoming exhausted.

Watering systems

Watering is a time-consuming yet essential job, and it may be worth considering installing a watering system. There are some excellent and reasonably priced systems now available for the ordinary garden. Add a timer to pre-program the watering times and your system becomes fully automatic – ideal for holidays or for busy professionals.

At first glance a watering system can look complex, but it is actually quite straightforward to set up. It consists of a 'mains' pipe to run from your tap around the area to be watered, from which run small 'spaghetti' lines that are pegged on to each container. Each one ends in a little drip head that delivers a litre or so of water per hour. Alternatively, you can set up mini-sprinklers instead of – or as well as – the spaghetti lines.

Before purchasing and setting up a system, first position the containers exactly where you want them in order to measure how much hose

Lots of pots mean a good deal of work, so consider installing a watering system. *Rosa* 'Pretty Polly' is on the left and *Pelargonium* 'Sugar Baby' on the right.

you will need and the number of containers to be watered. If possible, install your system on a warm day as the pipes will be more flexible. First set out the mains pipe in an unobtrusive position, usually along the base of a wall. For hanging baskets, run the pipe in a straight line above the containers – between ground- and first-floor windows, for example. Use joints to fit the pipe snugly around corners.

Frequency of watering will vary depending on the site and weather conditions, and you should experiment to see how long it takes to give your containers a good soaking. In warm summer weather it is usually best to water in the early morning and again in the evening.

Propagation
Trees, shrubs and roses

SEED

A number of tree varieties are produced by grafting and the growing of these is best left to the professionals. However, those that produce seed or berries, such as *Acer grosseri* var. *hersii*, can be raised relatively easily, although it does take a few years to produce a tree of any reasonable size. Species will come true from seed; named hybrids and cultivars tend not to, although it is well worth growing on seedlings of such plants and selecting those which appear promising.

Harvest the seed when ripe, remove it from its outer coating and sow in deep pots filled with potting compost with about one-third of coarse grit mixed in. Cover with a thin layer of grit, label and stand the pots in a cold frame or a sheltered spot outside. Germination can often take several months. With trees that produce berries, split open the fruit and wash the seed clean of the surrounding pulp, then sow as above.

Some shrubs and roses can be propagated from seed in the same way as for trees.

HALF-RIPE CUTTINGS

The most reliable way to propagate the majority of shrubs is by half-ripe cuttings, taken in mid- to late summer from the current year's growth which is just beginning to turn woody. Take cuttings 7.5–10cm (3–4in) long, either from the end part of a shoot or by gently pulling off sideshoots. Trim the base just below a leaf joint. Take off the leaves on the bottom two-thirds of the cutting and dip the base into hormone rooting powder. Put the cuttings in pots of seed and cuttings compost mixed with equal parts of vermiculite, either placing a single cutting in a 7.5cm (3in) pot or several in a larger pot. Cover the pots with polythene or stand them in a propagator until the cuttings have rooted, when signs of new growth will be apparent. The following spring, pot up the rooted cuttings individually and grow them on for planting out later the same year.

Conifers can also be propagated by half-ripe cuttings, taken in late summer. Take care to select only those shoots which have the characteristics of the parent plant that you wish to propagate.

TAKING HALF-RIPE CUTTINGS

Select a shoot 7.5–10cm (3–4in) long and cut just below a leaf joint

Remove the leaves from the bottom two-thirds of the cutting, dip in hormone rooting powder and place several cuttings together in a pot of compost. Cover with polythene until rooted

HARDWOOD CUTTINGS

Trees, shrubs and roses can be propagated by hardwood cuttings, taken in autumn just after leaf-fall and rooted outdoors. Select healthy shots of the current season's growth, preferably of about pencil thickness. Trim the base just below a leaf joint and remove the soft growth from the top to leave a cutting about 23cm (9in) long. Make a narrow trench in the soil to about one spade's depth, then fill it about one-third full with sharp sand. Put the cuttings in the trench, about 15cm (6in) apart, so that their tops are about 10cm (4in) above ground, and firm the soil around them. Rooting usually takes about a year.

LAYERING

This method takes longer but is an excellent way to propagate shrubs such as daphnes, which are difficult to raise from cuttings. In spring or early

LAYERING

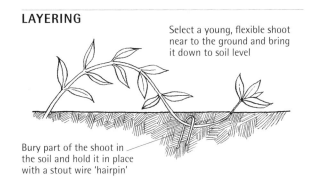

Select a young, flexible shoot near to the ground and bring it down to soil level

Bury part of the shoot in the soil and hold it in place with a stout wire 'hairpin'

summer, select a supple young branch and bend it down to touch the soil. Remove a sliver of bark from the underside at this point. Mix a little potting compost into the soil underneath and firmly peg down the branch. After a year it should have rooted and can be detached, potted up and grown on for 6–12 months until established.

Climbers and wall shrubs

Climbers can be propagated by cuttings or by layering. If the shoots are too high to reach the soil, use the technique of 'air layering' – preparing the shoot in the same way, but wrapping it round with a mixture of potting compost and moss contained within a polythene bag, which is secured using elastic bands. The advantage of this method is that it is easy to see when the layer has rooted.

Herbaceous perennials and ornamental grasses

DIVISION

Division is the easiest method of propagating perennials and grasses that have formed large, established clumps. Ornamental grasses are best divided in early spring, while perennials that flower early in the season should be divided in autumn, and those that flower later do better if divided in early spring.

Dig up the clump using a fork, then split it up into several smaller pieces, either by using two garden forks placed back-to-back in the centre which can be levered apart, or, for fleshy-rooted plants like hostas and *Sedum spectabile*, using a large, old knife to saw up the clump. Aim to discard the old, congested centre of the clump and keep the younger pieces that have been produced near the edges – just make sure that each division has a good portion of root and a few buds. Refresh the ground by digging in plenty of well rotted organic matter and some slow-release fertilizer, then replant the divisions. Keep the plants well watered until established.

BASAL CUTTINGS

Many perennials can be propagated by basal cuttings taken in spring from the new shoots that arise at the base of the plant. When the shoots are about 7.5–10cm (3–4in) long, cut them off as close as possible to the crown of the plant. In some cases, such shoots can be removed with a small amount of root attached, which virtually guarantees success. Put the cuttings into pots of moist compost, cover with polythene and place in a warm, shady spot until rooted.

Annuals and biennials

Most annuals and biennials can be raised from seed with relative ease, although some are much easier to grow than others. Hardy annuals can be sown outside where they are to flower, in autumn or spring, while half-hardy annuals will not tolerate any frost and are best grown under cover in pots from seed sown in early spring.

Biennials are fully hardy and can be sown outside, either where they are to flower if an informal effect is desired or, if destined for use in a bedding scheme, in a nursery bed, for transplanting into their flowering positions in autumn.

Tender perennials

Tender perennials can be raised from cuttings taken at any time from spring to late summer, and in most cases they will root easily. If the intention is to produce small young plants to overwinter under cover, the cuttings should be taken in late summer. Select healthy shoots, non-flowering if possible – although this can be difficult with some very floriferous varieties – and take a cutting about 7.5–10cm (3–4in) long, cutting just below a leaf joint. Remove the leaves on the bottom two-thirds of the shoots, dip the base in hormone rooting powder, and put several cuttings in a medium-sized pot filled with seed and cuttings compost mixed with equal parts of vermiculite. Cover with polythene and stand in a well-lit place out of direct sun until the cuttings have rooted.

Bulbs

Many bulbs increase themselves by forming small offsets around the original bulb, and these offsets can be separated out while the clump is dormant and grown on. They can be potted up or lined out in a nursery bed and grown on for a year or two, at which point they should be transplanted to their final positions.

Plant Directory

WITHIN THIS DIRECTORY
of plants for small gardens, the
plants have been grouped in a
more user-friendly way than the
inaccessible A–Z format usually adopted.
Depending on the type of plant, I have divided
up each group according to their ornamental
merits, making it easier to choose a selection of
varieties to give colour throughout the year. So,
trees, for example, have been listed according to
whether they have flowers, decorative foliage,
fruit or ornamental bark, while shrubs have
been listed under their flowering season or for
attractive foliage. Of course, the reason that
many plants have been selected for inclusion is
that they have more than one attribute, and in
these cases I have placed the plant according to
its most dominant feature.

The sizes given are a guideline to the height
(H) and spread (S) reached after 10 years and
are necessarily approximate, as factors such as
soil fertility and available moisture will
influence the speed of growth. Specific pruning
and/or training requirements are given where
appropriate, and propagation details are
provided for all plants except those best left to
the professional nurserymen.

Cercis siliquastrum (Judas tree)

TREES

The trees described below will grow in most soils and situations.

FOR FLOWERS

Amelanchier lamarckii
SNOWY MESPILUS

H 4.5m (15ft)

Panicles of white flowers are borne in spring among the newly emerged leaves, which are particularly decorative, being silky, rounded and an attractive shade of coppery red. The foliage matures to dark green, and in autumn develops wonderful tints of red and orange. The best autumn colour is produced on lime-free soil, although this round-headed tree will also grow happily in other types of ground ranging from sandy to boggy. Propagate from seed sown in autumn.

Malus
CRAB-APPLE

H 5–6m (16–20ft)

Most varieties of crab-apple make excellent small-garden trees, with spring flowers followed by autumn fruit. Those with the most decorative flowers are listed here, and varieties with fruit that is particularly long-lasting are described on pages 128–9. Occasionally, compact forms are available that have been grown on the dwarfing rootstock M27, which limits their height to around 2.5m (8ft). Grow on fertile, moist but well drained soil. Propagate from seed sown in autumn.

M. floribunda
JAPANESE CRAB

Masses of pretty flowers are borne in mid-spring, which are red in bud and open to white flushed with pale pink. Small red-and-yellow fruits follow in autumn. This variety forms a rounded head of arching branches which looks a little untidy in winter, so it is best grown in a border rather than as a single specimen.

M. × schiedeckeri 'Red Jade'

The spring flowers are red in bud, opening to white or pink-flushed blooms. Small, glossy, bright red fruits are borne in autumn. This variety has a weeping habit and becomes wider than it is high.

M. 'Royal Beauty'

Very compact variety which bears dark red-purple flowers in spring, followed by dark red fruits. The leaves are reddish purple when young, turning dark green with a purple underside. A weeping habit and a height of around 2.5m (8ft) make this variety ideal for a very small space.

M. 'Van Eseltine'

Large, semi-double flowers make a magnificent spring display. They are red in bud, opening to pink flushed with white, and are followed by yellow autumn fruits. An upright, almost columnar shape makes this a good tree where space is very limited.

Malus 'Van Eseltine' (crab-apple)

Prunus
FLOWERING CHERRY

There is a vast range of flowering cherries, most of which bloom during early to late spring and give a spectacular show of blossom. The chief exception is the autumn cherry, *P. × subhirtella* 'Autumnalis', which flowers from autumn to spring. Many flowering cherries are, however, best avoided in a small garden

as they either grow too large or bloom for a very short space of time. Grow on any moist, well drained soil.

P. 'Amanogawa'
LOMBARDY CHERRY

H 3m (10ft)

Large, shell-pink, semi-double flowers are borne in profusion from mid- to late spring. The foliage also develops colourful autumn tints of red and yellow. The overall shape is very narrow and columnar when young, broadening with age.

P. × blireana

H 4m (13ft)

Double pink flowers are borne singly and before the leaves appear in early to mid-spring. A neat, small tree with a spreading habit.

P. 'Kiku-shidare-zakura', syn. *P.* 'Cheal's Weeping'

H 3m (10ft)

Popular weeping tree that bears dense clusters of large, fully double, bright pink flowers in mid- to late spring. This variety is often available in two different forms: 'top-worked' trees have been grafted on to a stem about 1.8m (6ft) high to create a tree that forms an umbrella-shape of weeping branches, while 'bottom-worked' trees have been grafted at the base so that the whole stem is furnished with branches.

P. 'Okame'

H 6m (20ft)

Profuse quantities of cup-shaped, carmine-pink flowers are borne in clusters in early spring. The toothed, dark green leaves turn orange and red in autumn. Forms a rounded, bushy head of branches.

P. × subhirtella 'Autumnalis'
AUTUMN CHERRY

H 6m (20ft)

Small clusters of dainty, semi-double white flowers are produced from midwinter through to early spring.

Flowering may be intermittent, depending on the weather. Sprigs can be cut in bud to bloom indoors. Plant in a spot sheltered from strong winter winds. 'Autumnalis Rosea' is the same, but with blush-pink flowers.

P. × *yedoensis* 'Shidare-yoshino'
YOSHINO CHERRY

H 6m (20ft)

Masses of pale pink to white flowers are borne in dense racemes in early spring, before the leaves appear. This variety has a weeping habit with branches that arch to the ground.

ATTRACTIVE FOLIAGE

Acer negundo
BOX ELDER

H 6m (20ft)

The variegated forms make handsome garden trees, bearing small, decorative pinnate leaves with variegations that are more pronounced in spring when the leaves first appear. The overall habit is upright. Summer pruning will encourage greater production of shoots with attractive young foliage, and it is possible to grow these varieties as bushy shrubs by hard annual pruning. 'Flamingo' has glaucous shoots and leaves that are broadly margined with pink when young, turning white in summer. Grow on fertile, moist but well drained soil.

Cercis siliquastrum
JUDAS TREE

H 5m (15ft)

Attractive in both foliage and flower, this tree has rounded green leaves that are bronze when young and turn yellow in autumn, and produces clusters of magenta-pink flowers in spring and early summer. A rounded, spreading tree that can be grown as a single- or multi-stemmed specimen. Grow on fertile, moist but well-drained soil. Propagate from seed sown in autumn.

Fagus sylvatica 'Purpurea Pendula'
WEEPING PURPLE BEECH

H to 3m (10ft)

Deep purple-black leaves are borne on a mushroom-shaped tree, forming a neat mound that becomes almost as wide as it is high. One of the few beeches that is suitable for a small space. Grow on any well drained soil.

Gleditsia triacanthos 'Sunburst'
HONEY LOCUST

H to 10m (33ft)

Attractive, fern-like leaves appear in late spring and are golden yellow, eventually becoming light green, then turning yellow again in autumn. Although fairly large with a broadly conical shape, the open and comparatively sparse growth creates a light canopy, under which is it possible to grow a wide range of plants. Prefers well drained soil.

Pyrus salicifolia 'Pendula' (weeping willow-leaved pear)

Pyrus salicifolia 'Pendula'
WEEPING PEAR

H 5m (16ft)

The narrow, willow-like leaves of this weeping tree are silvery in colour. Small creamy-white flowers are borne in spring, followed by pear-shaped green fruit. The branches weep stiffly to the ground, and although the overall shape may

look a little untidy in winter, annual trimming can be carried out to ensure a neat dome shape. Grow on fertile, moist but well drained soil.

Salix caprea 'Kilmarnock', syn *S. c. pendula*
KILMARNOCK WILLOW

H 1.8m (6ft) approx

Masses of small, silvery-grey 'pussy willow' catkins are borne in spring all along the branches of this small tree. It has a neat habit, forming a 'mushroom' of weeping branches. The overall size can vary according to the height at which the tree was grafted. The leaves are green and rounded. Prefers moist soil.

Salix purpurea 'Pendula'
WEEPING PURPLE WILLOW

H 1.8m (6ft)

Attractive weeping tree that has long, slender, dark green leaves and reddish-purple stems. Small purple-green catkins are borne in early spring. Prefers moist soil.

DECORATIVE FRUIT

Cotoneaster frigidus 'Cornubia'
H 4.5m (14ft)

Cotoneasters are excellent for attracting wildlife, with flowers that are popular with bees and fruit which is a firm favourite with birds. This variety forms a rounded head of arching branches. Narrow, dark green leaves remain through winter unless the weather is severe. Propagate from seed sown in autumn. Grows on all except moist soils.

Malus
CRAB-APPLE

H 5–6m (16–20ft)

All the following crab-apples are noted for their fruit, which is either particularly colourful or remains on the tree for a long period. All bear attractive flowers in spring (see also page 127). Propagate from seed sown in autumn.

M. 'Crittenden'

Bright scarlet autumn fruits are held on the tree from autumn until well into winter. Pink-flushed white flowers are borne in late spring. The habit is compact and spreading.

M. 'Evereste'

Many red-flushed, orange-yellow fruits are borne in autumn. The spring flowers are red in bud, opening to white. This variety has a neat, conical shape.

M. 'John Downie'

The best fruiting crab, bearing heavy crops of orange-and-yellow fruits which are larger than those of most others. This is the best variety for making crab-apple jelly. White flowers are borne in spring. The branches grow in an upright manner to form a broadly columnar shape.

M. × robusta 'Red Sentinel'

Masses of glossy fruit are borne in autumn, yellow flushed with red at first, later turning dark red. The fruits may remain on the tree right through winter, birds permitting. White flowers are produced in late spring. This variety is broadly pyramidal in shape.

M. × zumi 'Golden Hornet'

Bright golden-yellow fruits are borne in autumn and remain for months, making this one of the best trees for winter colour. Flowers are produced in late spring, pink in bud, opening to white. The overall shape is rounded.

Sorbus
H 4–6m (13–20ft)

These valuable ornamental trees give interest with flowers and foliage, and particularly with colourful berries produced in late summer and autumn. Red and orange berries are popular with birds, while white, pink and yellow berries tend to remain well into winter. Propagate from seed sown in autumn. Prefers moist but well drained, acid to neutral soil.

S. americana
AMERICAN MOUNTAIN ASH

Pinnate, light green leaves are divided into as many as 15 leaflets, and turn yellow and red in autumn. Dense clusters of white flowers are borne in late spring and early summer, followed by red autumn berries. Forms a rounded head of branches.

S. aucuparia 'Fastigiata'
MOUNTAIN ASH, ROWAN

Clusters of white flowers in late spring are followed by dark red

Sorbus aucuparia (rowan or mountain ash)

autumn berries. The mid-green leaves are composed of up to 12 toothed leaflets and turn red or yellow in autumn. A small, densely growing columnar tree with upright branches, becoming more conical with age.

S. aucuparia 'Sheerwater Seedling'

The flowers, fruit and foliage are similar to those of S. a. 'Fastigiata'.

The shape is more open but still narrowly upright.

S. cashmiriana
KASHMIR SORBUS

Large clusters of white or pale pink flowers are borne in late spring among leaves that are finely divided and fern-like in appearance. Clusters of white, pink-tinged berries appear in autumn and remain on the tree for months. This variety forms a rounded, slightly spreading head of open branches.

S. 'Chinese Lace'

The foliage of this variety is particularly attractive, being very finely divided. White spring flowers are followed by orange-red autumn berries. The habit is upright.

S. 'Joseph Rock'

Finely divided leaves turn shades of red, orange and purple in autumn. White flowers in late spring are followed by yellow-orange autumn berries. Forms a broadly upright head of branches.

ORNAMENTAL BARK

Acer grosseri var. hersii
SNAKE-BARK MAPLE
H 6m (20ft)

So called for its attractive bark, which is patterned and streaked with green and white, in a similar way to a snake's skin. Large, three-lobed green leaves turn orange to yellow in autumn. Forms a spreading head of branches. Grow on fertile, well drained soil. Propagate from seed sown in autumn. (See also *Acer palmatum* 'Senkaki' on pages 135–6.)

Betula
BIRCH
H 10–12m (33–40ft)

The birches generally attain a greater size than the other trees described here. However, they still make good small-garden trees due to their sparse and open canopy of foliage that casts a light, dappled shade in which a great many plants can be grown. Birches prefer well drained soil.

B. albosinensis var. *septentrionalis*
CHINESE RED BIRCH

Peeling orange-brown bark is cream when first exposed. Yellow-brown catkins appear with the first leaves in spring, and the pale green leaves turn yellow before falling. Forms an upright, conical tree.

B. pendula
SILVER BIRCH

Another of its common names, 'lady of the woods', gives some indication of the graceful shape formed by this tree, which looks attractive at every season of the year. Peeling white bark becomes marked with dark cracks with age. Yellowish catkins are borne in early spring, and the diamond-shaped, toothed green leaves turn a lovely shade of butter-yellow in autumn. Forms a narrowly conical head of branches. Propagate from seed sown in autumn.

B. utilis var. *jacquemontii*
HIMALAYAN BIRCH
H 10m (33ft)

Dazzling white bark looks particularly striking in winter when the tree is bare of leaves. Yellow-brown catkins appear in spring and the tapered, dark green leaves turn yellow in autumn. Forms a widely conical head of branches.

Prunus serrula
TIBETAN CHERRY
H 6m (20ft)

Glossy, mahogany-red bark looks good all year but is particularly appreciated in winter. Bowl-shaped white flowers are borne singly or in small clusters in late spring and the dark green leaves turn yellow in autumn. Forms a rounded head of branches.

SHRUBS

Yucca filamentosa 'Variegata' (Adam's needle).

FOR FLOWERS
SPRING

Daphne laureola
SPURGE LAUREL
H 0.9cm (3ft), S to 1.2m (4ft)
Part or full shade

Bushy, spreading shrub with leathery, glossy, very dark green evergreen leaves. Clusters of fragrant, pale green or yellowish-green flowers are borne in late winter and early spring, followed by black berries. *D. l.* subsp. *philippi* is similar but more compact. Tolerates any reasonable soil. Propagate from seed sown as soon as ripe.

Daphne odora 'Aureomarginata'
H&S 0.9m (3ft)
Sun or part shade

Forms a rounded and attractive mound of leathery, glossy, mid-green evergreen leaves narrowly edged with cream. In late winter and early spring, this shrub produces clusters of richly scented flowers which are red-purple outside and pale pink to white inside. Prefers humus-rich soil that is well drained but not dry. Propagate from cuttings taken in midsummer or by layering in spring.

Osmanthus × burkwoodii
H&S 1.8m (6ft)
Sun or part shade

Small-leaved evergreen that forms a rounded bush of oval, glossy, dark green leaves. Many clusters of small, tubular white flowers, which are exceptionally fragrant, are borne in mid- to late spring. Grow in any fairly fertile, well drained soil. Tolerates hard pruning immediately after flowering. Propagate from cuttings taken in midsummer.

Rhododendron yakushimanum hybrids
H&S 0.9m (3ft)
Sun or part shade

Unlike many dwarf rhododendrons, this species has large, attractive evergreen leaves which are often coated with a reddish-brown 'woolly' layer, called indumentum, and look handsome all year. Forms an upright dome shape. Trusses of 5–10 large, funnel-shaped flowers are produced in mid-spring. There is a good range of attractive colours available, including 'Dusty Miller' (pale pink, flushed red, fading to cream), 'Grumpy' (cream tinged with pink, spotted inside), 'Surrey Heath' (pale rose-pink, darker edges), and 'Titian

Beauty' (red). Rhododendrons must have an acid soil and prefer one that is humus-rich, moist and well drained, and a site sheltered from strong winds. Their root system is shallow, growing close to the soil's surface, so take care to avoid deep planting and mulch the surface annually to protect from extremes of temperature.

Syringa meyeri var. spontanea 'Palibin'
H 1.2m (4ft), S 0.9m (3ft)

Sun

Unlike most lilacs, which can reach tree-like proportions, this variety is very compact in habit and forms an upright, slightly spreading bush with oval, mid-green leaves. Dense panicles of scented, lavender-pink

Syringa meyeri 'Palibin' (lilac).

flowers are borne in late spring and early summer. Prefers fertile, well drained soil. Propagate from cuttings taken in early summer or by layering in spring.

Viburnum × juddii
H&S 1.2m (4ft)

Sun or part shade

Rounded shrub with oval, dark green leaves, and the most compact of the spring-flowering viburnums that bear large, rounded heads of deliciously fragrant flowers. The blooms are pink in bud, opening to white

tinged with pink. Grows in any reasonably fertile, well drained soil. Propagate from cuttings taken in summer.

SUMMER/AUTUMN

Calluna vulgaris
HEATHER

H 30–60cm (12–24in), S 60–90cm (24–36in)

Sun

The bud-blooming varieties of heather are particularly decorative as their flower buds, which form in summer, never open and so remain colourful through autumn and even into winter. Varieties include 'Alexandra' (deep purple), 'Annette' (pink and white), 'Marleen' (pink) and 'Melanie' (white). These evergreen shrubs need a lime-free (acid) soil that is neither excessively wet nor dry. Trim in early spring to maintain a bushy shape. Propagate from cuttings taken in midsummer or by layering in spring.

Caryopteris × clandonensis
H&S 0.9–1.2m (3–4ft)

Sun

Neat shrub that forms an upright mound of small, toothed, grey-green leaves. Clusters of spiky, deep blue flowers are borne in late summer, in such profusion that the whole shrub appears as a haze of blue. The flowers are attractive to bees. Varieties include 'Heavenly Blue' (extremely dark blue) 'Kew Blue' (deep blue) and 'Worcester Gold' (lavender-blue, yellow leaves). Requires light, well drained soil. Propagate from cuttings taken in midsummer.

Ceratostigma willmottianum 'Forest Blue'
H 45cm (18in), S 60cm (24in)

Sun

Compact variety of this spreading shrub, which has slender stems clad with dark green, purple-tinged leaves that turn deep red in autumn before falling. Clusters of brilliant

blue flowers are borne from late summer through autumn. Requires light, moist but well drained soil and a sheltered site. Propagate from cuttings taken in midsummer or by layering in autumn.

Convolvulus cneorum
H&S 45–60cm (18–24in)

Sun

Compact, mound-forming shrub with satin-textured, evergreen, silvery leaves. The flowers are pink in bud, opening to white tinged with pink and with yellow centres,

Convolvulus cneorum.

and are borne from late spring to summer. Requires well drained soil. Propagate from cuttings taken in early to midsummer.

Hebe
H&S 0.3–1.2m (1–4ft)

Sun

Invaluable group of long-flowering, evergreen shrubs which bloom through summer. Many species and hybrids are available, in sizes ranging from compact dwarves to medium-sized shrubs. As a general guide, those with large leaves tend to be less hardy than small-leaved types. Good varieties include 'Autumn Glory' (violet-blue, small), 'Baby Marie' (pale lilac, dwarf), 'Caledonia' (violet flowers, red stems, small), 'Great Orme' (long racemes of bright pink flowers, medium), 'Mrs Winder' (violet-blue, red-purple young foliage, medium), 'Purple Pixie' (masses of small purple flowers, small) and 'Wiri Splash' (lilac, dwarf). Grow in any reasonable, well drained soil. Propagate from cuttings taken in summer. (See also pages 133–4.)

Lavandula angustifolia
LAVENDER
H&S 30–60cm (12–24in)
Sun

Old garden favourite with slender, aromatic, evergreen grey-green leaves and spikes of fragrant flowers in shades of blue, pink or white that are popular with bees and butterflies. Varieties include 'Alba' (white), 'Hidcote' (violet-blue), 'Loddon Pink' (pale pink), and 'Munstead' and 'Twickel Purple' (blue-purple). Lavenders require light, well drained soil. Trim off dead flower stems and clip new growth lightly after flowering, and prune in spring by cutting flowered shoots back to within a few centimetres of last year's growth. Do not cut into old wood. Propagate from cuttings taken in summer.

Lavatera hybrids
TREE MALLOW
H 1.8m (6ft), S 1.2–1.5m (4–5ft)
Sun

Exceptionally long-flowering shrub that produces many showy, hollyhock-like blooms from early summer right through to autumn. Good hybrids include 'Barnsley' (white with a red eye), 'Burgundy Wine' (rich pink with darker veins), 'Rosea' (dark pink) and *L. thuringiaca* 'Ice Cool' (pure white). Grow in well drained soil and prune hard in mid-spring by cutting all the previous year's flowered stems as near to ground level as possible. Left unpruned, the plant becomes large and straggly, the stems often breaking under their own weight. Can be short-lived, but new plants are grown easily from cuttings taken in summer.

Lotus hirsutus, syn. Dorycnium hirsutum
CANARY CLOVER
H&S 60cm (24in)
Sun

Dainty, spreading plant that forms a lax mound of stems clad with tiny, silvery-grey leaves. Evergreen in mild winters. Clusters of creamy-white, pink-tinged flowers are borne in late summer, followed by reddish seed pods. Requires well drained soil. Propagate from cuttings taken in summer.

Parahebe catarractae
H&S 30cm (12in)
Sun

Long-flowering, dwarf evergreen shrub that forms a compact, spreading mound of small, glossy, dark green leaves. Open racemes of pale purple, white-tinged flowers are borne through summer. 'Miss Willmott' has pure white flowers. Requires well drained soil. Propagate from cuttings taken in summer.

Philadelphus 'Manteau d'Hermine'
MOCK ORANGE
H 0.9–1.2m (3–4ft), S 60–90cm (24–36in)
Sun or part shade

Old garden favourite with sweetly scented flowers. Unlike most philadelphus, this variety is compact, with toothed green leaves and many double white flowers in midsummer. Forms a rounded, twiggy bush. Tolerates most soils including poor ones. Propagate from cuttings taken in summer.

Phygelius
CAPE FIGWORT
H 0.9–1.8m (3–6ft), S 60cm (24in)
Sun

Versatile shrub that can either be grown against a wall, where it will attain the upper height in the range, or mid-border, where it can be treated as an herbaceous plant and cut back hard in spring. Tall stems bear exotic-looking tubular flowers from summer into autumn. Varieties

Phygelius aequalis 'Yellow Trumpet'.

include *P. capensis coccineus* (orange-red), *P. aequalis* 'Yellow Trumpet' (creamy yellow), *P. × rectus* 'African Queen' (orange-red with a yellow mouth) and 'Winchester Fanfare' (reddish pink). They require a sheltered site and well drained soil. Propagate from cuttings taken from early to midsummer.

Potentilla fruticosa
H to 0.9m (3ft), S to 1.2m (4ft)
Sun

Long-flowering, easily grown shrub that bears colourful, saucer-shaped flowers from as early as late spring, through to mid-autumn. The fern-like foliage is green or grey-green. Many varieties are available; the following represent the colour range on offer: 'Abbotswood' (white), 'Beesii' (golden-yellow flowers, silver foliage), 'Daydawn' (creamy yellow flushed orange-pink), 'Floppy Disc' (pink, semi-double), 'Gold Drop' (golden yellow), 'Pretty Polly' (pale pink), 'Princess' (pale pink to white), 'Red Robin' (red) and 'Tangerine' (coppery orange). Potentillas prefer well drained soil that is not too rich. Propagate from cuttings taken in summer.

Rosmarinus officinalis 'Miss Jessopp's Upright'
ROSEMARY
H 1.5m (5ft), S 60–75cm (24–30in)
Sun

This rosemary forms a neat, upright bush of dense, spiky, dark evergreen foliage and in early summer is smothered with tiny mid-blue flowers that are popular with bees. Can be used for culinary purposes. Prefers well drained soil and tolerates drought. Propagate from cuttings taken in summer.

WINTER

Erica carnea
WINTER-FLOWERING HEATHER
H 15–30cm (6–12in), S 30–45cm (12–18in)
Sun or part shade

Useful ground-covering evergreen that bears many spikes of small, urn-shaped, colourful flowers from mid-winter to early spring. Unlike many heathers which need acid soil, this species tolerates a mildly alkaline soil and some shade. Good varieties include 'December Red' (purplish pink), 'Foxhollow' (pink flowers, yellow foliage deepening to bronze in winter), 'Myretoun Ruby' (pink ageing to crimson), 'Springwood Pink' (pale pink darkening with age), 'Springwood White' (pure white) and 'Vivellii (purplish pink, bronze leaves). Grow in retentive but well drained soil; avoid rich ground and excessive fertilizer. Keep neat by trimming off the dead flowers and shoot tips in spring. Propagate from cuttings taken in mid- to late summer or by layering in spring.

Mahonia aquifolium 'Smaragd'
H 60cm (24in), S to 90cm (36in)
Part or full shade

Handsome evergreen shrub with pinnate, glossy, mid- to dark green leaves, usually spiny-margined. Clusters of bright yellow, fragrant flowers are borne in late winter and early spring. One of the most compact mahonias, although there are a number of much larger varieties such as *M.* × *media* 'Charity', which can be useful to provide architectural impact. Grows on any reasonable soil. Propagate from cuttings taken in mid- to late summer.

Sarcococca hookeriana var. *digyna*
CHRISTMAS BOX
H&S 60cm (24in)
Sun or shade

Compact evergreen shrub that forms a neat, spreading mound of slender, dark green leaves. Many small, tassel-like clusters of very strongly scented, creamy-white flowers are borne from mid- to late winter. Prefers moist, well drained soil, particularly if grown in sun, but tolerates most conditions. Propagate from cuttings taken in early to midsummer, or detach rooted suckers in late winter.

Skimmia japonica 'Rubella'
H&S 60cm (24in)
Part or full shade

Neat, mound-forming evergreen shrub with oval, dark green leaves. One of the most decorative skimmias, with red-margined leaves and showy clusters of red flower buds that appear in autumn and last on the plant until spring, when they open to fragrant white flowers. Prefers humus-rich, moist but well drained soil, ideally acid to neutral. Feed with sequestered iron if yellowing of the leaves occurs. Propagate from cuttings taken in late summer.

Viburnum tinus 'Eve Price'
LAURUSTINUS
H to 1.8m (6ft), S 1.2m (4ft)
Sun or part shade

Compact form of the popular evergreen laurustinus, with narrowly

Viburnum tinus 'Eve Price' (laurustinus).

oval, dark green leaves and many flattened heads of small white flowers borne over a long period in winter and early spring. Grows in any retentive, well drained soil and tolerates hard pruning if overgrown, carried out in spring after flowering. Propagate from cuttings taken in mid- to late summer.

DECORATIVE EVERGREEN FOLIAGE

Aucuba japonica 'Crotonifolia'
SPOTTED LAUREL
H&S to 1.5m (5ft)
Part shade

Showy shrub with large, pointed, glossy leaves that are green, boldly splashed with yellow. Bright red berries may be sparsely borne in autumn. Can be grown in sun, but ideally with shade from the strongest midday rays which can cause unsightly scorching. This variety is the brightest and most reliable: 'Picturata' is similar but more likely to revert to plain green. Grows in all but very moist soils. Propagate from cuttings taken in summer.

Buxus sempervirens
BOX
H to 3m (10ft), S to 1.8m (6ft)
Sun or part shade

Useful shrub with tiny, rounded, glossy dark green leaves. Left untrimmed, it will slowly attain the size given, but this plant is very useful for its tolerance to trimming into all sorts of shapes. Clipping is best carried out in spring and summer; hard renovation pruning can be done in late spring. 'Suffruticosa' is very compact and slow-growing, excellent for a low hedge. Several varieties with variegated foliage are also available: 'Aureovariegata' has yellow-edged leaves, 'Argenteovariegata' and 'Elegantissima' are edged with white. Grow in any reasonable soil. Propagate from cuttings taken in summer.

Choisya ternata 'Sundance'
MEXICAN ORANGE BLOSSOM

H 1.5m (5ft), S 1.2m (4ft)

Sun or light shade

Upright, dome-shaped shrub with glossy, bright yellow leaves. A little shade is beneficial to prevent scorching of the young growth, although too much will result in yellow-green foliage. Clusters of white, fragrant flowers are borne in summer. Prefers a sheltered site and fertile, well drained soil. Propagate from cuttings taken in summer.

Cordyline australis
CABBAGE TREE

H to 3m (10ft), S 1.2m (4ft)

Sun

Spiky-leaved shrub with leathery, pointed leaves, that slowly grows to develop a clear stem and becomes palm tree-like in appearance. A number of varieties have coloured leaves and these are the most decorative and more compact. They include 'Albertii' (green striped with red, cream and pink), 'Sundance' (stained red at the base), 'Torbay Dazzler' (boldly striped and margined with cream) and 'Torbay Red' (deep red). Prefers fertile, well drained soil and a sheltered site. Propagate by detaching well rooted suckers in spring.

Euonymus fortunei
H to 60cm (24in), S to 0.9m (3ft)

Sun or shade

Easily grown shrubs that make excellent ground cover with their spreading stems clad with oval leaves. A number of varieties are available, including 'Dart's Blanket' (dark green turning bronze-red in autumn and winter), Emerald Gaiety (white-edged green, tinged pink in winter), Emerald 'n' Gold (green edged with bright yellow), 'Gold Tip' (dark green tipped gold when young) and 'Harlequin' (mid-green strongly splashed with white and yellow-green). Grow in any reasonably well drained soil. Propagate from cuttings taken in summer.

Hebe
H&S 30–60cm (12–24in)

Sun

In addition to the many flowering hebes (see page 131), a number of varieties are grown for their attractive foliage – summer flowers are produced but are of secondary importance. They include *H. ochracea* 'James Stirling' (unusual rich yellow-ochre 'whipcord' foliage, white flowers), *H. pimeleoides* 'Quicksilver' (tiny pewter-grey leaves, lilac flowers on a spreading plant), *H. pinguifolia* 'Pagei' (small, rounded, blue-grey leaves, white flowers, semi-prostrate), *H. rakaiensis* (bright green leaves, white flowers) and 'Red Edge' (grey-green leaves, red-tinted young growth intensifying in winter). Hebes prefer retentive but well drained soil, and shelter from cold winds. Propagate from cuttings taken in summer.

Ilex
HOLLY

H to 8m (25ft), S to 5m (15ft)

Sun or part shade

Excellent specimen shrubs with glossy, usually spiny leaves. They respond well to clipping and shaping and, if left untrimmed, will grow into trees. Both male and female plants are required if the females are to produce berries in autumn. Many varieties have attractively shaped or coloured foliage. Hollies prefer moderately fertile, well drained soil: the variegated forms colour best in sun. Trim hedges in spring, and clip formal specimens in summer. Propagate from cuttings taken from late summer to early autumn.

I. × altaclerensis
Varieties include 'Camelliifolia' (dark green, often spineless leaves, red berries), 'Golden King' (grey-green with wide bright gold margins, red berries which are rarely produced in quantity) and 'Lawsoniana' (light green leaves splashed with gold, red berries).

I. aquifolium
COMMON HOLLY, ENGLISH HOLLY

Dark green-leaved species with red berries which is excellent for hedging. Varieties include 'Ferox Argentea' ('hedgehog holly' – green, cream-edged leaves covered with spines, male), 'Handsworth New Silver' (mid-green, spiny leaves with cream margins, red berries), 'Madame Briot' (large, dark green leaves, scarlet berries) and 'Silver Queen' (green leaves with broad creamy margins, male).

Laurus nobilis
BAY LAUREL, SWEET BAY

H to 10m (30ft), S 6m (20ft)

Sun or part shade

Although attaining tree size if left untrimmed, bay is most popular when grown in shapes such as lollipops or pyramids and kept at a height of around 1.8m (6ft). The glossy, pointed, dark green leaves are aromatic when crushed and useful for cooking. Requires a site sheltered from cold winds and fertile, moist but well drained soil. In cold areas, grow in a large container and move under cover in winter. Trim trained specimens twice during early and late summer. Propagate from seed sown in autumn or from cuttings taken in midsummer.

Ligustrum ovalifolium 'Aureum'
GOLDEN PRIVET

H&S to 3m (10ft)

Sun or part shade

Vigorous, tough, easily grown shrub which responds well to trimming and shaping, so makes a good specimen shrub to create a formal shape or a quick-growing hedge. Left untrimmed, it quickly becomes a large and graceful mass of billowing foliage. The oval leaves are rich green with wide, bright yellow edges. Grows in any reasonably well drained soil. Trim twice during summer if required. Propagate from cuttings taken in summer.

Lonicera nitida 'Baggesen's Gold'

H 1.5m (5ft), S 1.2m (4ft)

Sun or shade

Bushy shrub with arching branches covered in tiny, bright yellow leaves. In shade, the colour becomes an attractive shade of light green. Responds well to trimming in summer. Makes a good low hedge – the green-leaved species is faster-growing. Grows in any reasonable soil, but dislikes wet ground. Propagate from cuttings taken in summer.

Phormium

NEW ZEALAND FLAX

H to 1.8m (6ft), S 1.2m (4ft)

Sun

Architectural plants with long, sword-shaped leaves, many varieties having attractively coloured or variegated foliage. Good varieties include 'Maori Sunrise' (striped apricot and pink); 'Bronze Baby' (bronze, compact to 60cm (24in) tall), 'Dazzler' (bronze striped with pink, orange and red), 'Yellow Wave' (yellow-green striped with paler green) and *P. cookianum* subsp. *hookeri* 'Cream Delight' (green broadly striped with cream). Phormiums prefer fertile, moisture-retentive soil. In cold areas, grow in containers and move under cover for the winter. Propagate by division in spring.

Rhamnus alaternus 'Argenteovariegata'

ITALIAN BUCKTHORN

H to 4m (12ft), S to 2.4m (8ft)

Sun or part shade

Fast-growing shrub which responds well to trimming, with small leaves that are grey-green broadly edged with white. Clusters of yellow-green flowers are borne in summer, followed by red berries that ripen to black. Prefers well drained soil, and a sheltered site in cold areas. Trim in late spring. Any green-leaved shoots should be removed when seen. Propagate from cuttings taken in summer.

Viburnum davidii

H&S 0.9m (3ft)

Sun or part shade

Compact, mound-forming shrub with large, oval, dark green leaves that are distinctively ridged. Female plants produce egg-shaped, turquoise-blue fruit: although both male and female plants are required for this, there is no reliable way of identifying a plant's sex. Tolerates all but the most extreme soils. Propagate from cuttings taken in summer.

Vinca minor

LESSER PERIWINKLE

H 10cm (4in), S 60–90cm (24–36in)

Sun or shade

Easily grown plant that makes a wonderful ground-covering carpet of glossy, pointed, dark green leaves, the shoots rooting as they spread. Pale to mid-blue flowers are borne over a long period from mid-spring to autumn. There are many variations in flower and foliage colour, including 'Alba Variegata' (white flowers, pale yellow leaf margins), 'Argenteovariegata' (blue flowers, creamy-white leaf margins), 'Atropurpurea' (plum-purple flowers), 'Aureovariegata' (green-and-gold leaves), 'Gertrude Jekyll' (pure white flowers) and 'Multiplex' (double, dark purple flowers). Grows in all but very dry soil. Do not confuse with the rampant *V. major* (greater periwinkle). Propagate from cuttings taken in summer, or by division from autumn to spring.

Yucca

H 75cm (30in), S to 1.2m (4ft)

Sun

Bold, architectural plants that form a clump of sword-like, sharp-tipped, fleshy leaves. Varieties with green leaves attractively edged with yellow are *Y. filamentosa* 'Bright Edge', *Y. flaccida* 'Golden Sword' and *Y. gloriosa* 'Variegata'. Large, upright panicles of creamy white flowers may be borne if the season has been hot. The species have green leaves,

although they grow considerably larger than the sizes detailed above. Yuccas need well drained soil and a sheltered site. In cold areas, grow in containers and move under cover for the winter. Propagate by detaching rooted suckers in spring.

FOLIAGE INTEREST

Acer palmatum

JAPANESE MAPLE

H 0.9–2.4m (3–8ft), S 0.9–1.8m (3–6ft)

Part shade

Attractive shrubs with delicate, five- to nine-lobed leaves that come in a wide variety of colours, including many shades of green, red and purple, and variegations. All develop attractive autumn colour in shades of orange, red or yellow. Japanese maples broadly divide into two types: those which have upright, spreading branches and grow slowly into large shrubs or small trees, and the mound-forming *A. p.* 'Dissectum' varieties which form a spreading 'mushroom' shape, remaining at the lower end of the size range. Numerous varieties are available, of which the following is a selection of the most popular.

Upright varieties include 'Burgundy Lace' (deeply cut, five-lobed, dark reddish purple), 'Butterfly' (small, five-lobed, grey-green, edged with white and pink), 'Crimson Queen' (similar to 'Burgundy Lace' but brighter red-purple) and

Acer palmatum 'Senkaki' (Japanese maple).

'Senkaki' (deeply cut, five-lobed, opening orange-yellow and ageing to pale green, bright coral-red shoots in winter).

Mound-forming varieties: 'Dissectum' (finely cut, pale green leaves), 'Dissectum Atropurpureum' (similar but red-purple) and 'Dissectum Nigrum' (dark red-purple). Japanese maples require fertile, moist but well drained soil, and shelter from cold winds, late frosts and strong sunlight, all of which can damage the leaves. Seed can be sown in autumn but the resulting seedlings will vary in appearance.

Artemisia 'Powis Castle'
H 60cm (24in), S to 90cm (36in)
Sun

Forms a low, spreading mound of dainty, silver filigree foliage which is aromatic when crushed. Prefers well drained, fertile soil. If the plant becomes leggy, cut back hard in spring. Propagate from cuttings taken in summer.

Bamboos
Part or full shade

Bamboos are easy to grow, tolerating all soils except waterlogged ground, but do best in light soils which are moist and well drained, with shelter from cold winds. Cut out dead stems in late winter and thin out overgrown clumps. Propagate by dividing established clumps in spring.

The names of many bamboos have undergone recent changes, so they are listed here under the name by which they are still widely known, with the now-correct name afterwards. All the following are evergreen.

Arundinaria murieliae, syn. Fargesia murieliae
H to 3m (10 ft), S 1.2m (4ft)

Forms a tall clump of yellow-green stems which are topped with lance-shaped bright green leaves. A useful tall specimen to create impact.

'Simba' is more compact, growing to about 1.8m (6ft).

A. nitida, syn.. Fargesia nitida
H 3–4m (10–12 ft), S 1.5m (5ft)

Useful large specimen for rapid height. Can be invasive, so grow in a sunken container to restrict growth. Purple-green stems produce cascades of narrow, dark green leaves.

A. viridistriata, syn. Pleioblastus auricomus
H 45cm (18in), S 0.9m (3ft)

Forms a neat clump of showy leaves which are green striped with bright gold. Requires some sun to colour well.

Phyllostachys nigra
BLACK BAMBOO
H 1.8–3m (6–10ft), S to 1.2m (4ft)

Handsome large specimen with slender green canes that age to shiny black, and slender, dark green leaves. Forms a compact clump in cool climates, but may be invasive in warmer areas.

Shibataea kumasasa
H 90cm (36in), S 60cm (24in)

Forms a neat, rounded clump of broadly lance-shaped, rich green leaves.

Berberis thunbergii
H&S to 1.2m (4ft)
Sun or part shade

Easily grown species with leaves that are brightly coloured, usually with gold or purple. Good varieties include 'Aurea' (bright yellow when young, ageing to greeny gold, prefers partial shade to avoid sun scorch) 'Bonanza Gold' (brighter yellow, more compact), 'Dart's Red Lady' (dark red-purple), 'Helmond Pillar' (red-purple, forms a narrow, upright bush) and 'Rose Glow' (red-purple strongly flecked with white). These berberis tolerate most reasonably well drained soils. Propagate from cuttings taken in summer.

Ceanothus 'Diamond Heights'
H 45cm (18in), S 90cm (36in)
Sun

Low-growing, spreading evergreen shrub with leaves attractively mottled green and gold. Clusters of deep blue flowers are borne in summer, contrasting well with the foliage. Requires well drained soil and a sheltered site. Propagate from cuttings taken in summer.

Cornus alba
RED-STEMMED DOGWOOD
H&S to 1.8m (6ft)
Sun or part shade

Shrub with coloured stems that provide good winter interest, and several varieties have variegated or coloured

Cornus alba 'Sibirica' (dogwood).

foliage including 'Aurea' (bright yellow), 'Elegantissima' (grey-green edged with white), and 'Spaethii' (yellow-variegated). Prune hard in late winter or early spring, cutting all stems back to within 10cm (4in) of the base. Dogwoods tolerate most soils, including wet ground. Propagate from cuttings taken in summer or by layering in spring.

Helichrysum italicum subsp. serotinum
CURRY PLANT
H 45cm (18in), S 75cm (30in)
Sun

Silver-leaved, bushy, spreading evergreen shrub with narrow leaves that smell strongly of curry. Heads of dark yellow flowers are borne from summer to autumn. Requires a well drained soil and a site sheltered from cold winds. Prune in spring by cutting back shoots to within 2.5–5cm (1–2in) of the previous year's growth. Propagate from cuttings taken in summer.

Physocarpus opulifolius
H&S 1.5m (5ft)
Sun or part shade

Rounded shrub with three-lobed, toothed leaves that are gold or purple. Good varieties include 'Dart's Gold' (bright yellow when young, ageing to greeny gold) and 'Diablo' (dark purple). Prefers acid, well drained soil. Prune in early spring by thinning out several of the oldest branches. Propagate from cuttings taken in summer.

Ruta graveolens 'Jackman's Blue'
RUE
H 60cm (24in), S 45cm (18in)
Sun or part shade

Rounded evergreen shrub with upright stems clad with divided, blue-green leaves that have a strong, pungent smell when crushed. Flat heads of yellow flowers are borne in summer. Contact with the skin in bright sunlight can cause irritation. Needs a very well drained soil and will tolerate hot, dry conditions. Trim in spring to encourage bushy growth. Propagate from cuttings taken in summer.

Salvia officinalis
COMMON SAGE
H&S 45cm (18in)
Sun

Spreading evergreen shrub with long, woolly leaves in a range of colours. Aromatic when crushed, these can be used in cooking. Spikes of blue or mauve flowers are borne in summer. Varieties include 'Aurea' (yellow), 'Icterina' (variegated yellow and green), Purpurascens Group (purple young leaves ageing to

greeny purple) and 'Tricolor' (grey-green marked with cream, pink and purple). Requires light, well drained soil. Propagate from cuttings taken in summer.

Sambucus racemosa 'Plumosa Aurea'
GOLDEN ELDER
H&S to 2.5m (8ft)
Sun or part shade

Bushy shrub with large, very decorative leaves with finely cut leaflets that are bronze when young and then turn golden yellow. Grow in any reasonably moist but well drained soil. Tolerates sun in cool areas, but otherwise site in part shade to prevent leaf scorch. Cut back hard in early spring, to within two or three buds of the base, to keep the plant compact and encourage brightly coloured foliage. Propagate from cuttings taken in summer.

Santolina
COTTON LAVENDER
H&S 45–60cm (18–24in)
Sun

Low-growing evergreen shrub with finely divided leaves in grey or green, aromatic when crushed. Button-like flowerheads are borne on individual stems in summer. The range includes *S.chamaecyparissus*, syn. *S. incana* (woolly, grey-white foliage, bright yellow flowers), *S. pinnata* subsp. *neapolitana* (very finely divided, silver-grey foliage, yellow flowers) and *S. rosmarinifolia* subsp. *rosmarinifolia* 'Primrose Gem' (bright green leaves, soft yellow flowers). Requires a well drained soil. Cut back the previous year's growth to 2.5–5cm (1–2 in) in spring. Propagate from cuttings taken in summer.

DECORATIVE BERRIES

Cotoneaster dammeri
H 20cm (8in), S to 1.2m (4ft)
Sun or shade

Vigorous, ground-covering evergreen shrub with pointed, dark green

leaves. Small white flowers are borne singly or in small clusters in spring, followed in autumn by red berries. Grows in any reasonable soil and tolerates dry conditions. Propagate from seed sown in autumn or from cuttings taken in summer.

Gaultheria procumbens
CHECKERBERRY, WINTERGREEN
H 15cm (6in), S 60cm (24in)
Part shade

Low-growing, spreading evergreen shrub with pointed, dark green leaves that are strongly aromatic when crushed. Small urn-shaped, white or pale pink flowers are borne in summer, followed in autumn by showy scarlet berries that often last through to spring. Requires acid or neutral, moist soil. Tolerates sun if the soil is reliably moist. Propagate from seed sown in autumn or from cuttings taken in summer.

Skimmia japonica subsp. reevesiana
H 60cm (24in), S 90cm (36in)
Part to full shade

Unlike most skimmias, this variety is hermaphrodite (male and female flowers on the same plant), so reliably produces berries on its own. It forms a low, spreading mound of dark green, slender, pointed evergreen leaves, and in autumn bears showy clusters of red berries which often persist through to spring. Requires a humus-rich, moist but well drained soil. Propagate from cuttings taken in late summer.

Viburnum opulus 'Compactum'
GUELDER ROSE
H&S 1.2m (4ft)
Sun or part shade

Rounded shrub with maple-like dark green leaves that turn red in autumn. Heads of white flowers in early summer are followed by showy clusters of shiny, bright red fruit. Grows on any reasonable soil that is not too dry. Propagate from cuttings taken in early to mid-summer.

CLIMBERS AND WALL SHRUBS

Many climbers and wall shrubs require pruning and/or training to keep them growing neatly against their support and/or flowering well. Details are given in the individual descriptions.

Clematis 'Countess of Lovelace' with *Rosa* x *odorata* 'Mutabilis'.

FOR FLOWERS

Akebia quinata
H up to 5m (16ft)
Sun or part shade

Rich, reddish-purple flowers are borne in spring among a mass of five-lobed, fresh green leaves on slender, twining stems. The flowers have a wonderful chocolate scent. Usually deciduous, although semi-evergreen in mild winters. Prefers a sheltered spot and reasonably retentive soil. Propagate from cuttings taken in summer or by layering in winter.

Chaenomeles speciosa, C. × superba
FLOWERING QUINCE
H 1.8m (6ft)
Sun or shade

Profuse quantities of colourful, saucer-shaped flowers are borne along the prickly stems in spring, before the leaves appear. A wide range of varieties is available in colours including white, pink, red and orange. In autumn, edible fruits are produced which can be used in preserves. These easily grown wall shrubs thrive on all soils except chalk. Train by pruning back outward-growing shoots to two buds immediately after flowering, and tying in others. Propagate from cuttings taken in summer or by layering in autumn.

Clematis

Justifiably known as the 'queen of climbers', clematis are the most varied and versatile of all climbing plants. They divide broadly into two main groups: the large-flowered hybrids with substantial blooms, and a number of different species and their hybrids which, although their flowers are smaller, more than make up for this by producing them in larger numbers and often over a longer period.

Large-flowered hybrids
Large, sumptuous blooms up to 20cm (8in) across are borne from early to late summer, depending on variety. This group needs good growing conditions in order to give of their best. An ideal site should be sheltered from strong winds, with the roots in shade and the 'heads' in sun. If necessary, shade the roots with large stones or ground-cover plants. The soil should be deep and moisture-retentive, rich in organic matter, and neutral or alkaline (limy) rather than acid. If conditions are less than ideal, opt for species clematis. Propagate from internodal cuttings taken in summer or by layering in spring.

The following varieties are a selection of the most popular from the considerable range available. Note that with double-flowered varieties, it is not unusual for single blooms to be produced, particularly during the latter part of the season and when the plant is young.

SMALL   = 1.8–2.5m (6–8ft)
MEDIUM = 2.5–4m (8–12ft)
LARGE   = 4–5m (12–16ft)

'**Arctic Queen**' has double, pure white blooms. Small.
'**Blue Moon**' has pale blue-mauve flowers and wavy-edged sepals. Medium.
'**Comtesse de Bouchaud**' is a soft pinky mauve. Medium.
'**Countess of Lovelace**' has double, bluish-lilac flowers. Small.
'**Duchess of Edinburgh**' has double flowers which are white with yellow stamens. Small.

'Ernest Markham' is deep petunia-red. Large.

'Fireworks' has bluish-purple sepals with a red stripe. The sepals are slightly twisted to give a spinning effect, hence the name. Medium.

'Guernsey Cream' is creamy yellow. Small.

'Haku-ôkan' is violet-blue with contrasting white stamens. Small.

'H. F. Young' is wedgewood-blue with cream stamens. Small.

'Jackmanii Superba' is darkest of all, with rich royal-purple blooms. Large.

'John Huxtable' is white with cream stamens. Medium.

'Lasurstern' has rich lavender-blue flowers. Medium.

'Marie Boisselot', syn. 'Madame le Coultre', is one of the best and most reliable varieties, with pure white flowers. Large.

'Mrs N. Thompson' is deep violet with a bright pink bar. Small.

'Nelly Moser' is an old favourite, with pale mauve-pink flowers that have a deep pink bar. Medium.

'Niobe' is rich ruby-red. Medium.

'Perle d'Azur' is a beautiful sky-blue. Large.

'Pink Champagne', syn. 'Kakio', is deep pink with a pale bar. Medium.

'Pink Fantasy' is deep pink with a slightly deeper bar. Medium.

'Royalty' has double, purple-mauve flowers. Small.

'Silver Moon' is an unusual shade of pearly grey. Small.

'The President' is purple-blue. Medium.

'Ville de Lyon' has deep carmine-red flowers. Medium.

'Vyvyan Pennell' has double, violet-blue blooms. Medium.

'William Kennett' is lavender-blue. Large.

Clematis wilt

Only the large-flowered hybrids tend to be susceptible to this disease. All or part of a plant will suddenly wilt and collapse, as though suffering from lack of water, but the affected parts will eventually die.

There is no cure, but measures can be taken to give a good chance of recovery. Plant with the top of the rootball around 8cm (3in) lower than it was growing previously, so that the plant will produce stems from below ground. Should it become affected, growth can be cut back to ground level and fresh stems may well be produced.

Be patient, as new shoots may not be produced for six months or more. Healthy plants are much more resistant to attack, so pay attention to good ground preparation, regular feeding and watering, plus an annual mulch of organic matter, to keep the plant growing strongly.

Species

Most clematis species are a lot tougher and more tolerant of adverse conditions than the large-flowered hybrids. Small blooms are produced in profusion at various seasons, so careful selection of a succession of varieties will ensure colour for a good part of the year.

C. alpina, C. macropetala
H 2.5m (8ft)
Sun or shade

Many nodding flowers are borne in early spring among divided, fresh green leaves. The flowers are usually blue, as in *C. alpina* 'Pamela Jackman' and 'Frances Rivis', although there are pink and white forms as well. These species have slender stems and are not over-vigorous, so are ideal for small gardens and for partnering with other plants. Propagate from seed sown as soon as ripe.

C. armandii
H 4–5m (12–15ft)
Sun

One of the few evergreen clematis with large, glossy, dark green leaves, that make a perfect foil for the clusters of pale, fragrant flowers in spring. 'Apple Blossom' is white flushed with pink. In colder areas, plant against a sheltered wall to avoid frost damage. Propagate by layering in early spring.

C. cirrhosa
H 4–5m (12–15ft)
Sun

Another evergreen, with small, deeply cut, attractive leaves that become tinged with bronze in winter. Bell-shaped blooms are borne in winter and early spring. Varieties include *C. c.* var. *balearica* (fern-leaved clematis – very divided leaves, ivory-white flowers splashed red inside), 'Freckles' (more strongly splashed and spotted with red) and 'Wisley Cream' (pure ivory-white). Plant against a sheltered wall in all but the mildest areas, in well drained soil. Propagate by layering in early spring or from cuttings taken in early summer.

C. × durandii
H 1.2–1.8m (4–6ft)
Sun or shade

Semi-herbaceous in habit, this species does not grow well if unsupported, but its slender stems are perfect to grow through a small shrub or to sprawl over a low, ground-covering plant. Deep wedgewood-blue flowers are borne in midsummer. Propagate by layering in early spring.

C. montana
H 6–10m (20–30ft)
Sun or shade

Most rampant of all the clematis described here, this plant needs a large tree or shed or a long fence as its support. Masses of four-petalled, pure white blooms are borne in late spring among bronzed and divided foliage. Varieties include 'Alexander' (fragrant, slightly larger white flowers), 'Elizabeth' (pale pink), *C. m.* var. *rubens* (deep pink) and 'Tetrarose' (lilac-pink). Prune if necessary to contain growth immediately after flowering. Propagate from cuttings taken in summer or by layering in early spring.

C. orientalis, C. tangutica
H 2.5–3m (8–10ft)
Sun or shade

Yellow, lantern-shaped flowers are borne among divided, sea-green leaves in late summer and early autumn. These are followed by attractive, fluffy seed heads that, as the flowers are borne over a number of weeks, are joined by the blooms that appear towards the end of the season. If the plant has grown out of hand, hard prune to within 60cm (24in) of the ground in late winter or early spring. Propagate from seed sown as soon as ripe.

Clematis tangutica.

C. texensis
H 1.8–3m (6–10ft)
Sun

Charming bell-shaped flowers are borne in late summer, in a variety of richly coloured shades including 'Duchess of Albany' (deep pink with a red band), 'Etoile Rose' (deep pink edged with silvery pink) and 'Gravetye Beauty' (ruby-red blooms that expand outwards to form a star shape). In cold areas, the plants will need the protection of a warm,

sheltered wall. Propagate from cuttings taken in summer.

C. viticella and hybrids
H 3m (10ft)
Sun or part shade

Masses of flowers are borne over a long period from mid- to late summer and into autumn. Flower shapes vary from an open flower of four petals to a nodding bell shape with the petals reflexed and curving back at the tips. Good varieties include 'Purpurea Plena Elegans' (double flowers that form little violet-purple rosettes) and the hybrids 'Abundance' (rose-pink), 'Alba Luxurians' (white tinted with green), 'Etiole Violette' (dark violet), 'Madame Julia Correvon' (wine-red), 'Minuet' (white veined with mauve) and 'Polish Spirit' (bright red). Most versatile of all the species clematis – due to the speedy production of slender stems, which enable varieties to be grown through and over lots of different plants, and also because they benefit from annual hard pruning. Cut back the whole plant to within 45cm (18in) of the ground in late winter or early spring. Propagate from cuttings taken in summer or by layering in early spring.

Pruning

The pruning of clematis can cause confusion, although it is quite straightforward so long as you check when your plant flowers. If in doubt, leave unpruned until it flowers and you can identify the variety or species. GROUP 1 clematis flower in spring and early summer, so the flowers are borne on growth that was made the previous summer. This group includes *C. alpina*, *C. macropetala* and *C. montana*, as well as a number of early-blooming large-flowered hybrids. Little pruning is needed apart from the removal of dead and weak stems after flowering. Overgrown plants can be pruned hard at the same time if you need to contain growth. GROUP 2 clematis flower from early

to midsummer, also on the previous year's growth. This group includes many of the large-flowered hybrids. Cut out dead and weak stems after flowering, and prune the remainder back to a strong pair of buds. GROUP 3 clematis flower late in the season on growth produced in the current spring and summer. This group includes clematis species such as *C. orientalis* and *C. viticella*, and vigorous large-flowered hybrids such as 'Gipsy Queen' and 'Jackmanii Superba'. In very early spring, cut all growth back to about 30–45cm (12–18in) from ground level.

Eccremocarpus scaber
CHILEAN GLORY FLOWER
H 1.8m (6ft)
Sun

Exotic, tubular, brightly coloured flowers, usually orange but sometimes red and yellow, are borne from midsummer onwards. This fast-growing plant scrambles up by means of tendrils. It grows readily from spring-sown seed and tends to flower well in its first year, so in very cold areas can be treated as an annual. It keeps its foliage in warmer areas but tends to die back to the ground if hard frosts occur. Prefers well drained soil. Propagate from seed sown in spring (light is required for germination).

Hydrangea anomala subsp. petiolaris
CLIMBING HYDRANGEA
H 3m (10ft)
Shade

Large 'lacecap' heads of cool white flowers are borne in summer. A mass of fresh green leaves provides an ideal background, and in autumn these turn butter-yellow before falling. A slow starter, this plant can take several years to become established and begin growing strongly. It will grow in most reasonable soils and is self-clinging, although it may need some initial training. Propagate from cuttings taken in early summer.

Jasminum nudiflorum
WINTER JASMINE
H 1.8m (6ft)
Sun or shade

Numerous starry, bright yellow flowers are produced all along the leafless branches from early to late winter. Although this tough, easily grown wall shrub will naturally form a mound against a support, training and pruning will produce a much neater and more free-flowering plant. Grows in most reasonable soils. Prune immediately after flowering by cutting all flowered shoots back to two or three buds from the main stem. Propagate by layering in spring (the plant also readily layers itself).

Jasminum officinale
COMMON JASMINE, POET'S JASMINE
H 4.2m (13ft)
Sun or shade

Clusters of white flowers are borne from early summer through until autumn against a background of small, dark green, deciduous leaves. One of the best plants of all for fragrance, giving off a delicious scent that is strongest in the evening. Flowers tend to be more freely produced in a sunny site. Grows in most reasonable soils. Prune in late winter by thinning out entire branches, but do not shorten branches as lots of thin, shoots may then be produced. Propagate by layering in spring or summer.

Lathyrus latifolius
PERENNIAL PEA
H 1.8–2.5m (6–8ft)
Sun

Stems of bright pink flowers are produced in profusion in mid- to late summer. Two paler forms are available: 'Rosa Perle', syn. 'Pink Pearl' (soft pink) and 'White Pearl' (pure white). Unlike annual sweet peas, this species has no scent. The perennial pea climbs by means of tendrils and can be grown up wire mesh or pea sticks and through other plants, or even left unsupported to tumble down a sunny bank. It is herbaceous in habit, dying back to the ground in autumn. Prefers well drained soil. Propagate by division in early spring.

Lonicera
HONEYSUCKLE
H up to 4.2m (13ft)
Sun or part shade

Most varieties are notable for their clusters of sweetly scented flowers produced from early summer onwards, although a couple are handsome but scentless. Ideal for most sites, honeysuckles prefer a fertile, well drained soil, with their roots in the shade and heads in the sun. Propagate from cuttings taken in summer. Some also readily layer themselves.

Choose from a wide range of species and cultivars; all are twiners.

L. × brownii 'Dropmore Scarlet'
Showy form with glowing orange-red flowers. Unscented.

L × heckrottii 'Gold Flame'
Showy variety with large clusters of rich deep yellow flowers flushed with orange, which are borne from early summer through into autumn.

L. × italica, syn. L. × americana
Bears large heads of flowers which are rich rose-pink outside and pale yellow inside, in late summer and into autumn. The leaves of 'Harlequin' are prettily variegated in cream, pink and green.

L. japonica 'Halliana'
JAPANESE HONEYSUCKLE
Vigorous plant with semi-evergreen leaves that is ideal for covering or screening ugly objects and wire fences. Many small clusters of sweetly scented, white-and-yellow flowers are borne from early summer to autumn. L. j. 'Aureoreticulata' is much more compact and is grown more for its golden-variegated leaves than its flowers. This particular variety is best in a sheltered site on good soil.

L. periclymenum 'Belgica'
EARLY DUTCH HONEYSUCKLE

Flowers in late spring and early summer, bearing clusters of reddish-purple and white flowers which fade to yellow. L. p. 'Serotina' (late Dutch honeysuckle) bears similar flowers from midsummer to autumn; L. p. 'Graham Thomas' has white flowers that later change to yellow.

L. × tellmanniana
Has exceptionally handsome rich yellow flowers, flushed red in bud, borne in a massive display in early to midsummer. Unscented.

Passiflora caerulea
PASSION FLOWER
H 5m (16ft)
Sun

Large, unusually shaped blue-and-white flowers are borne sporadically through summer against attractive lobed, dark green leaves. After long spells of hot weather, egg-shaped orange fruits may be produced, the seeds and pulp being edible. The plant is vigorous, quickly scrambling up by means of tendrils. 'Constance Elliott' has beautiful, pure ivory-white flowers. Prefers a well drained soil. Hardy in all but the most severe winters; sometimes cut to ground level by hard frosts but usually regrows swiftly in spring. Mulch the base with straw in cold areas to give winter protection. Prune in spring if necessary to contain growth. Propagate from cuttings taken in summer or by layering in spring.

Piptanthus nepalensis
EVERGREEN LABURNUM
H 2.5m (8ft)
Sun

Spikes of bright yellow flowers are produced in early summer, and are shown off well against the glossy, three-lobed, dark green leaves. In cold areas, this attractive evergreen wall shrub benefits from a sheltered site. It prefers fertile, well drained soil. Prune immediately after flowering only if necessary. Propagate from seed sown in spring or autumn.

Pyracantha
FIRETHORN
H up to 4m (12ft)
Sun or shade

Clusters of white flowers in late spring are followed in autumn by colourful fruits which can be yellow, orange or red, depending on variety. A wide selection is available: the Saphyr Series are resistant to scab, from which many varieties suffer. These vigorous, evergreen wall shrubs grow well on any soil and respond well to pruning and training to create a formal screen or wall covering. Cut back outward-growing shoots to two or three buds immediately after flowering. Propagate from cuttings taken in summer or from seed sown in autumn.

Solanum jasminoides 'Album'
H 3m (10ft)
Sun

Clusters of elegant, white flowers with a central sheaf of golden stamens are borne from early summer until autumn, against a background of glossy, dark green leaves. Climbs by twining stems. Prefers well drained soil and a sheltered spot. Propagate from cuttings taken from summer to early autumn.

Trachelospermum asiaticum
H 2.5–3m (8–10ft)
Sun

Flowers are jasmine-like but creamy white and yellow-centred, ageing to yellow all over, and are borne from mid- to late summer. A choice and lovely plant which is deliciously fragrant and neat in habit, with self-clinging stems clothed with small, glossy, evergreen leaves. Needs the protection of a sunny, sheltered wall to come through the winter unscathed in all but mild areas, although it is hardier than the similar *T. jasminoides*.

Prefers well drained soil. Prune in spring if necessary to contain growth. Propagate from cuttings taken in summer or by layering in autumn.

Wisteria floribunda
H 4.2–5m (13–16ft)
Sun

Showy, dangling racemes of highly scented flowers are borne in late spring and early summer, and the large, pinnate leaves bring an oriental air to the garden. However, wisteria takes a few years to become sufficiently well established to produce a good show. This species is more com-

Wisteria floribunda 'Multijuga' (Japanese wisteria).

pact than *W. sinensis* (Chinese wisteria). Blue-flowered varieties like 'Multijuga' are the most popular, although there are white- and pink-flowered forms, too. In colder areas, plant wisteria against a sheltered wall and train it in tightly, as the buds can be damaged by late spring frosts. To encourage flower production, prune wisteria twice a year. In summer, thin out overcrowded sideshoots and cut the remainder back to about 15cm (6in). Then in midwinter, cut these same shoots back again, this time to two or three buds. Feeding with sulphate of potash in late winter also helps to boost flowering. Avoid wet soils and high-nitrogen fertilizer, which encourages leafy growth at the expense of flowers. Propagate from

cuttings taken in summer or by layering in autumn. However, the resulting plants can take a number of years to flower – for guaranteed results, buy grafted plants.

Actinidia kolomikta
H 3–4.2m (10–13ft)
Sun

A real stunner for unusual foliage colour, with slender, twining stems covered in heart-shaped green leaves that are tipped with cream and pink, rather like a painter's palette. Protect young plants with netting if there are cats around as they tend to nibble at it. Prefers a moist yet well drained soil. Propagate from cuttings taken in late summer.

Ampelopsis glandulosa var. brevipedunculata 'Elegans'
H 1.5m (5ft)
Sun or light shade

Handsome plant with lobed leaves that are heavily mottled white and tinged with pink. Climbs by means of tendrils and is a slow, compact grower. Grows well on any reasonable soil. Propagate from cuttings taken in summer.

Euonymus fortunei 'Silver Queen'
H to 2.5m (8ft)
Sun or shade

Given support, this shrub will clamber upwards to provide useful all-year interest with its evergreen foliage. The leaves are dark green edged with white, the margins of which become tinted pink with age. Grows well on any reasonable soil. Propagate from cuttings taken in summer.

Hedera colchica
PERSIAN IVY
H to 5m (16ft)
Sun or shade

Vigorous, large-leaved evergreen ivy. The two attractively variegated cultivars are 'Dentata Variegata' (green leaves strikingly edged with creamy white) and 'Sulphur Heart', syn. 'Paddy's Pride' (dark green leaves with a bold central splash of pale lime-green). Grows well on any soil. Propagate from cuttings taken in summer or by layering in spring.

Hedera helix
SMALL-LEAVED IVY
H to 3m (10ft)
Sun or shade

Handsome evergreens with small, glossy, lobed leaves, and tolerant of almost any position and soil type. Ivy is self-clinging by means of aerial roots; this is no problem on walls where brickwork is sound, but avoid old walls where the mortar may be starting to crumble. Keep growth trimmed away from window frames and any other painted wood. Propagate from cuttings taken in summer or by layering in spring.

There are many cultivars available with a huge range of leaf shapes and colours, of which the following is just a very small selection. Those which are completely green are the fastest-growing – the more variegation there is, the slower the rate of growth. **'Buttercup'** is lime-yellow to gold, brighter in sun than shade. **'Glacier'** has greyish-green leaves marked with white. **'Goldheart'** (now unfortunately renamed 'Ori di Bogliasco') is dark green splashed with yellow. **'Green Ripple'** has small, jagged-edged leaves. **'Luzii'** is yellow marbled with green. **'Parsley Crested'**, syn. 'Cristata', has rounded leaves that are crinkled at the edges.

Humulus lupulus 'Aureus'
GOLDEN HOP
H to 5m (16ft)
Sun or part shade

Excellent foliage plant with large, lobed, yellow-green leaves, which by late summer are strongly suffused with green. Female plants bear large,

Humulus lupulus 'Aureus' (golden hop).

decorative seed heads that give off a rich, beery aroma when crushed. Although herbaceous in habit, dying back completely to the ground in autumn, it regrows with great speed in spring. Happy in any reasonable soil. Propagate by division in spring.

Jasminum officinale varieties
SUMMER JASMINE
H 2.5m (8ft)
Sun

Several cultivars of summer jasmine are grown for their attractive foliage. These are 'Aureum' (green and gold), 'Argenteovariegatum' (green and white) and 'Fiona Sunrise' (leaves completely suffused with gold). Although white flowers are produced in summer, they are less profuse than those borne by the green-leaved species (see page 141). Prefers a reasonably moisture-retentive soil. Propagate from cuttings taken in summer or by layering in spring.

Parthenocissus henryana
H to 6m (20ft)
Sun or part shade

Outstanding for fiery autumn colour. A vigorous, deciduous plant with three- to five-lobed dark green leaves on which the veins are traced in silver. Although eventually self-clinging, some initial training may

be required. Keep foliage trimmed away from gutters or paintwork, and carry out any necessary pruning in spring. Prefers a well drained, fertile soil. Propagate from cuttings taken in summer.

Teucrium fruticans
SHRUBBY GERMANDER
H 1.5m (5ft)
Sun

Wall shrub that has attractive foliage as well as flowers. The slender, grey-green leaves are evergreen and make a good backdrop for the pale blue flowers that are borne in summer. Prefers well drained soil and a sheltered site. Propagate from cuttings taken in summer.

Vitis coignetiae
ORNAMENTAL VINE
H 5–6m (16–20ft)
Sun or part shade

Vigorous, deciduous climber with decorative heart-shaped leaves up to 30cm (12in) long, which develop vivid autumn tints of crimson and scarlet. 'Claret Cloak' has young leaves that are coppery purple right through the season. Cut back surplus growth and thin out dense masses of stems in spring. Prefers a good, fertile soil. Propagate by layering in autumn.

ROSES

As there are hundreds of different roses, this section necessarily presents an extremely select list of varieties. It is in no way intended as a comprehensive list of all the roses that are suitable for a small garden. Most of the varieties detailed below produce repeated flushes of flowers through the summer – if you are considering choosing any other roses, it is worth bearing in mind that many of the true old-fashioned types flower only once in the season, although their single display is very spectacular.

Not included here are miniature bush roses and patio roses as they are all suitable for a small garden, growing to 30–60cm (12–24in) high and wide. I have also left out hybrid tea and floribunda roses entirely, as they prefer to be grown in a border on their own. Instead I have concentrated on shrub roses, which do well as part of a mixed border.

CULTIVATION

Roses do best in an open, sunny site, although there a few climbers that tolerate part or full shade. Unless otherwise indicated, all the roses below prefer full sun. They are hungry plants, so prepare the soil before planting by digging in quantities of organic matter such as well rotted manure or garden compost, plus some slow-release fertilizer. Mulch the surface of the ground each spring with more of the same to keep the soil in good heart. Do not plant in soil where roses have been growing previously, as specific diseases tend to build up and the new plants will be much less likely to thrive.

All roses are propagated professionally by budding. In the garden, propagate by hardwood cuttings (see page 124).

DISEASES

Some rose varieties are very prone to disease, others have good natural resistance and it is these which I

Rosa 'Pink Perpétué'.

have chosen in the main. Keeping plants in good health by good planting and maintenance, and watering during dry spells, will greatly increase their ability to resist disease. Good garden hygiene – removing and disposing of (not composting) any affected parts – helps to prevent re-infection.

PESTS

Several pests can be troublesome, such as aphids and rose sawfly. Roses are less susceptible to attack when grown in a mixed border among different types of plants, rather than in an old-style rose bed where a large number of roses are planted by themselves, providing a substantial feast for pests. Again, keeping plants in

good health will help them to withstand any attack. Otherwise, the response varies according to whether you prefer to garden with or without chemicals. My personal preference is not to spray and to encourage natural predators like hoverflies and ladybirds to do the job for me. That, coupled with regular inspections and hand-squashing of any early pest infestations, has always worked exceptionally well in my own garden. If you decide to go for the chemical option, sprays are best applied in the early stages before the pest has had a good chance to breed and build up a large population. Take great care when handling chemicals and always follow the manufacturers' instructions.

CLIMBERS

Climbing roses do best when trained on walls and fences, as they form a framework of permanent branches from which come the lateral sideshoots that produce flowers.

MINIATURE/PATIO CLIMBERS
H 1.8m (6ft), S 0.9–1.2m (3–4ft)

An immensely useful group of new varieties which are more compact in habit than any other climbing roses previously available. Miniature climbers are long-flowering, from midsummer often right through the autumn. They can be grown in a large container such as a wooden half-barrel as well as in the open ground.

'Captain Scarlet' bears masses of bright red flowers.

'Lady Penelope' has double flowers of salmon-pink.

'Laura Ford' has small, well formed blooms of golden yellow, sometimes shaded with salmon, darkening to amber-yellow later in the season.

'Little Rambler' bears large clusters of small blooms, which are very pale pink with a strong fragrance. The stems are pliant and easy to train, typical of a larger rambler.

'Nice Day' has fully double blooms that are soft salmon-pink in colour and sweetly scented.

'Open Arms' is very much like a miniature rambler in appearance, with single, pale pink blooms that have a prominent cluster of yellow stamens.

'Rosalie Coral' produces clear orange, double blooms that open to reveal a yellow 'eye'.

'Warm Welcome' has neat, well formed, fragrant flowers which are orange-red and are set off well by the coppery-red foliage.

MODERN CLIMBERS
H to 3m (10ft)

These varieties bear large flowers, singly or in small clusters, and repeat flower extremely well. They have a reasonably compact habit and are also suitable for training on pillars.

'Compassion' bears flowers which are salmon-pink tinted with orange and very fragrant.

'Danse de Feu' bears semi-double, orange-scarlet blooms. Tolerates shade.

'Golden Showers' has flat, semi-double, golden-yellow blooms. Tolerates shade.

'Handel' has semi-double, creamy-white flowers edged with bright pink.

'New Dawn' bears clusters of double, pale pink, scented flowers. Tolerates part shade.

'Pink Perpétué' is fully double, rich pink in colour, and scented.

'Schoolgirl' is a beautiful shade of apricot-orange tinted with pink, and fragrant.

OTHER CLIMBERS

'Aloha' has large, double, coral-pink flowers which are heavily shaded with orange when young. Very compact in habit, and fragrant. Tolerates shade. H 1.8m (6ft).

'Gloire de Dijon' has beautiful old-fashioned flowers which are buff-yellow tinted with pink, and richly scented. Tolerates shade. H 5m (15ft).

'Madame Alfred Carrière' is a favourite old-fashioned variety which bears small, rounded flowers that are white tinted with pink, and very fragrant. Tolerates shade. H to 6m (20ft).

'Maigold' bears semi-double, bronze-yellow flowers, mostly in early summer but with a second flush towards autumn. The stems are extremely prickly. H 4m (12ft).

'Parkdirektor Riggers' has single flowers which are dark crimson. Tolerates shade. H 3m (10ft).

'Zéphirine Drouhin' bears carmine-pink blooms that are very sweetly scented. The stems are virtually thornless. Susceptible to mildew and may need preventative spraying with a fungicide. H 4m (12ft).

PRUNING

The main stems of climbing roses form a permanent framework of branches from which come the sideshoots that bear the flowers. In late winter or early spring, shorten these sideshoots to two or three buds. With overgrown plants you can remove several of the oldest branches

Rosa 'Compassion'

if necessary. After pruning, tie in the stems, pulling them down to a horizontal position if the site allows, as this will restrict the flow of sap and boost flower production.

RAMBLERS
H 3–6m (10–20ft)

Rambler roses produce masses of tiny flowers in large clusters, over a shorter period than climbing varieties but in greater profusion. Ramblers have long, quick-growing, flexible stems, and as such do best when trained over arches, arbours, pergolas and other structures.

'**Albertine**' has flowers that are coppery-red in bud, opening to large, soft salmon-pink, almost double blooms. Fragrant.

'**Crimson Shower**' bears clusters of deep crimson flowers against dark green, shiny foliage.

'**Emily Gray**' bears small clusters of semi-double, buff-yellow blooms which age to pale yellow. Scented.

'**Félicité Perpétue**' is a vigorous grower that bears large clusters of small, very double, creamy-white flowers.

'**Goldfinch**' bears masses of small, rosette-shaped, double blooms which open to deep yellow and fade to creamy white. Scented.

'**Sanders' White**' produces sprays of many small, double, scented, pure white flowers.

PRUNING

In late summer after flowering, or in late winter the following year, cut back entire branches which have flowered, as near to the ground as possible. After pruning has been completed, tie in the new stems. If there aren't many new stems, keep a few of the old ones but cut their sideshoots back to two or three buds.

SHRUB ROSES
H&S 0.9–1.2m (3–4ft)

Again, of the numerous varieties available, I am limited to just a

handful, and a browse through a couple of rose specialists' catalogues would reveal a considerably wider selection. Those below include some genuinely old-fashioned varieties as well as several English roses, which are new varieties that have been bred to produce the typical 'old' flower shape and fragrance with the repeat-flowering capabilities and disease resistance of modern hybrids.

'**Cécile Brünner**' is a China rose with well formed miniature blooms in shades of pink. Lightly scented.

'**Comte de Chambord**' is a Portland rose with flat, quartered blooms of warm pink. Repeat flowers well. Fragrant.

'**Cottage Rose**' is an English rose with flowers that form shallow, cupped rosettes of pure, warm pink. Light fragrance. Repeat flowers very well.

'**Happy Child**' is an English rose with broadly cupped flowers of deep yellow and a strong, sweet scent.

'**Little White Pet**' is a Polyantha rose which bears clusters of pompon-like white blooms that have a delicate scent.

'**Perle d'Or**' is a China rose which has perfectly formed miniature blooms of buff-yellow.

'**Sharifa Asma**' is an English rose with blush-pink flowers that are richly scented.

'**The Countryman**' is an English rose with glowing, clear pink, scented flowers.

'**The Fairy**' is a graceful, Dwarf Polyantha rose which is festooned with tiny, pale pink flowers.

× *odorata* '**Mutabilis**' can be grown as a climber if supported, or as a free-standing shrub. Single flowers are light yellow changing to pink.

'**Yesterday**' is a modern shrub which is repeat-flowering. Bears small, semi-double blooms that are shaded rich rose-pink to lilac-pink.

PRUNING

Once plants are well established, prune in late winter by taking out one-quarter to one-third of the oldest branches, as near to the ground as possible. Remaining stems can be shortened by one-third if the plant is outgrowing its site.

GROUND-COVER ROSES
County Series
H 30–60cm (12–24in), S 90cm (36in)

Of recent introduction, the County Series roses are compact in habit, long-flowering – from midsummer right into autumn – and have good disease resistance. A good range of colours is available, including 'Avon' (pale pink in bud, opening to white), 'Gwent' (large, bright yellow blooms), 'Suffolk' (crimson-scarlet

Rosa 'Sharifa Asma'.

with prominent golden stamens), 'Sussex' (double, apricot-buff) and 'Warwickshire' (pale pink shading to rose-pink).

'Flower Carpet'
H 45cm (18in), S 90cm (36in)

Extremely free-flowering variety, bearing bright carmine-pink, semi-double flowers in large trusses, through summer to the end of autumn. Good disease resistance. A white-flowered form, 'White Flower Carpet', is now available.

'Magic Carpet'
H 30cm (12in), S 90cm (36in)

Exceptionally free-flowering variety, bearing many small, semi-double, lilac-mauve flowers through summer and into autumn. Has a strong, spicy scent.

'Snow Carpet'
H 30cm (12in), S 75cm (30in)

Compact variety which bears large quantities of tiny, pure white, double flowers from midsummer into autumn.

PRUNING

Cut back hard in late winter or early spring, removing about two-thirds of the previous year's growth.

Rosa 'Flower Carpet'.

CONIFERS

Juniperus squamata 'Blue Carpet'.

Chamaecyparis lawsoniana 'Gimbornii'
H&S 45–60cm (18–24in)
Sun

Very slow-growing, dwarf conifer that forms a neat, rounded mound of greyish-green foliage. Tolerates most soils, but is best grown on moist but well drained soil, ideally neutral to slightly acid. Propagate from cuttings taken in late summer.

Chamaecyparis obtusa 'Pygmaea'
H&S 0.9m (3ft)
Sun

Rounded conifer with its foliage arranged in attractive fan shapes. The shoots are red-brown and the foliage bright green, becoming tinted with brown over winter. Soil preferences as for *Chamaecyparis lawsoniana* 'Gimbornii'. Propagate from cuttings taken in late summer.

Chamaecyparis thyoides 'Ericoides'
H to 1.2m (4ft), S 45cm (18in)
Sun

Narrowly conical, slow-growing plant with green foliage that develops rich purple tints in winter. Prefers moist but well drained soil. Propagate from cuttings taken in late summer.

Juniperus communis 'Sentinel'
H to 1.2m (4ft), S 45cm (18in)
Sun

Narrow, upright conifer with pointed, deep green to blue-green leaves. Prefers well drained soil. Propagate from cuttings taken in early autumn.

Juniperus × *pfitzeriana* 'Gold Sovereign'

H 45–60cm (18–24in), S to 90cm (36in)

Sun

Compact plant with a spreading habit, and foliage that is bright golden yellow throughout the year. Prefers well drained soil. Propagate from cuttings taken in early autumn.

Juniperus scopulorum 'Skyrocket'

H to 3m (10ft), S 45cm (18in)

Sun

One of the very narrowest conifers, tall yet immensely slender,with glaucous, grey-green leaves. Prefers well drained soil. Propagate from cuttings taken in early autumn.

Juniperus squamata 'Blue Carpet'

H 30cm (12in), S to 1.5m (5ft)

Sun

Prostrate, spreading conifer which forms a wide-spreading carpet of foliage that is intensely silvery-blue in colour. Prefers well drained soil. Propagate from cuttings taken in early autumn.

Picea glauca 'Alberta Blue'

H 45–60cm (18–24in), S 30cm (12in)

Sun or part shade

Forms a narrow, upright bush with foliage that is intensely silvery blue in early summer when the new growth appears, retaining a bluish colour all year. Grows on any reasonable soil. Propagate from cuttings taken in late summer.

Pinus mugo 'Winter Gold'

DWARF MOUNTAIN PINE

H to 0.9m (3ft), S 60cm (24in)

Sun

Neat, compact plant with long, yellow-green needles that turn deep gold in winter. Prefers well drained soil.

Taxus baccata

YEW

H to 10m (30ft), S to 8m (25ft)

Sun or shade

Large, broadly conical tree that responds well to trimming and is therefore excellent for hedging and topiary. The narrow, pointed leaves are dark green and red berries are borne in autumn. All parts are highly poisonous if eaten. Trim in summer and early autumn; it will tolerate hard pruning into old wood if overgrown. Grows on any well drained, fertile soil, and is tolerant of exposed sites. Propagate from cuttings taken from late summer to early autumn.

Taxus baccata 'Standishii'

H to 1.2m (4ft), S 45cm (18in)

Sun or shade

Slow-growing, narrow, columnar conifer with golden-yellow leaves, the colour intensifying slightly in winter. The red autumn berries contrast well with the foliage. Grows in any well drained soil. Propagate from cuttings taken from late summer to early autumn.

Thuja occidentalis 'Rheingold'

H to 1.2m (4ft), S 0.9m (3ft)

Sun

Compact, broadly conical conifer with golden-yellow foliage that turns a rich 'old gold' in winter. Prefers moisture-retentive but well drained soil. Propagate from cuttings taken in late summer.

Thuja occidentalis 'Smaragd'

H to 90cm (36in), S 60cm (24in)

Sun

Forms a neat, compact, conical bush of bright green foliage. Prefers moisture-retentive but well drained soil. Propagate from cuttings taken in late summer.

Thuja plicata 'Atrovirens'

H to 10m (30ft), S to 3m (10ft)

Sun

Tall variety with scale-like, very dark green leaves that are aromatic when bruised. An excellent hedging plant that responds well to trimming. Cut in late spring and late summer for a neat finish, or just once in summer for a more informal look. Prefers deep, moisture-retentive soil. Propagate from cuttings taken in late summer.

Pinus mugo 'Winter Gold'.

HERBACEOUS PERENNIALS

Echinops banaticus (globe thistle).

FOR FLOWERS

WINTER AND SPRING

Bergenia
ELEPHANT'S EARS
H 30–45cm (12–18in), S 45–60cm (12–18in)
Sun or part shade

Useful ground-covering plants for all-year interest. Leaves are large, leathery and rounded, often colouring richly during winter, and showy clusters of white, pink or purple flowers are borne in spring. Good varieties include 'Abenglut', syn. 'Evening Glow' (magenta-crimson), 'Baby Doll' (pale pink), 'Bressingham White' (pure white), *B. ×schmidtii* (rose-pink) and 'Silberlicht' (white ageing to pink). Prefers humus-rich but well drained soil, but tolerates most conditions. Propagate by division in autumn or spring.

Dicentra spectabilis
BLEEDING HEART, LADY-IN-THE-BATH
H 90cm (36in), S 45cm (18in)
Part shade

Handy mid-border plant which dies back by late summer, so useful next to spring-pruned shrubs like lavat-eras. Tall, arching stems are hung with pink-and-white locket-like flowers in spring and early summer. The divided leaves are pale green. Prefers moist, retentive soil. Propagate by division in summer.

Euphorbia amygdaloides var. *robbiae*
H 45cm (18in), S indefinite
Sun or shade

Invaluable ground cover for difficult, shady sites, but very invasive in good conditions. In spring, from dark, glossy, evergreen rosettes of leaves rise stems of bright yellow-green 'bracts', which persist into summer. Cut these out at ground level after flowering. The milky sap can cause skin irritations. Propagate by division in autumn or spring.

Euphorbia myrsinites
H 10cm (4in), S 45cm (18in)
Sun

Semi-prostrate stems form a spreading, evergreen mat of succulent, blue-grey leaves, terminating in clusters of greenish-yellow bracts in spring. Needs well drained soil. Propagate from basal cuttings taken in spring.

Helleborus foetidus
STINKING HELLEBORE
H 60cm (24in), S 45cm (18in)
Part or full shade

Despite the off-putting name, the leaves only smell unpleasant when crushed. Otherwise, a handsome plant forming a clump of dark, evergreen, toothed leaves, from which rise stems with many small, bell-shaped green flowers, from midwinter to mid-spring. Does best in neutral to alkaline soil. Sap can cause skin irritations. Propagate from seed sown as soon as ripe.

Helleborus orientalis and hybrids
LENTEN ROSE
H&S 45cm (18in)
Part shade

From the centre of a clump of toothed, evergreen, dark green leaves come stout stems bearing several saucer-shaped flowers, in colours that range from pure white, through many shades of pink, to darkest purple. The flowers are produced from winter to early spring, and last for a long time. Named hybrids are available if specific colours are required, or buy when in flower. Tolerates most garden conditions. Cut off the previous year's leaves in midwinter so that they do not detract from the flowers. Propagate from seed sown as soon as ripe.

Pulmonaria
LUNGWORT
H 30cm (12in), S 45cm (18in)
Part or full shade

Very early to flower and one of the brightest spots of colour for shade, bearing clusters of funnel-shaped flowers on short stems in late winter or early spring. These include several stunning deep blues, such as *P. angustifolia* subsp. *azurea* and 'Mawson's Blue', as well as pink and white forms. The leaves of *P. saccharata* Argentea Group are particularly ornamental, being silver in colour. Lungworts prefer rich soil that is moist but not waterlogged. Propagate by division after flowering or in autumn.

Viola cornuta
HORNED VIOLET
H 15cm (6in), S 45cm (18in)
Sun or part shade

Spreading, evergreen perennial that bears masses of spurred light blue flowers from spring through into summer. Good ground cover, and will also scramble up through low shrubs. Prefers humus-rich, well drained soil. Propagate by division in spring or autumn.

SUMMER

Anthemis tinctoria 'E. C. Buxton'
GOLDEN MARGUERITE
H 45–60cm (18–24in), S 60cm (24in)
Sun

Superb, long-flowering plant that bears large lemon-yellow, daisy-like flowers on single stems for many weeks in summer. The divided leaves are mid-green to grey. Requires well drained soil. Can be short-lived, but longevity is improved by cutting back hard after flowering. Propagate from basal cuttings taken in spring or late summer.

Anthemis tinctoria 'E.C. Buxton'
(golden marguerite).

Crocosmia
Height 60–75cm (24–30in), S 30cm (12in)
Sun or part shade

Clump-forming plants with upright, narrow leaves that provide good vertical interest. Spikes of brightly coloured flowers are borne from mid- to late summer. Good varieties include 'Bressingham Blaze' (orange-red, yellow throat), 'Emily McKenzie' (orange), 'Lucifer' (red) and 'Solfaterre' (apricot-yellow). Crocosmias prefer moist but well drained soil. In cold areas, plant near a wall for winter protection. Propagate by division in spring.

Dicentra
H&S 30–45cm (12–18in)
Part shade

Several species and hybrids form low, spreading mats of fern-like, divided foliage and bear small, nodding racemes of locket-like flowers from early summer onwards. Those with blue-grey leaves are particularly attractive; they include 'Pearl Drops' (white, pink-tinted flowers) and 'Stuart Boothman' (deep pink). Green-leaved varieties include 'Bacchanal' (crimson), 'Bountiful' (purplish pink), *D. eximia* (rose-pink opening to paler shades) and 'Luxuriant' (red). Dicentras prefer moist, humus-rich soil. Propagate by division in spring.

Echinops bannaticus
GLOBE THISTLE
H 90cm (36in), S 45cm (18in)
Sun

For an excellent perennial for architectural effect, use this imposing plant with rounded, metallic-blue flowerheads borne on tall stems in late summer. The tiny florets open gradually to give a long-lasting display. Popular with bees. The jagged-edged leaves are grey-green on top and grey underneath. Prefers well drained soil but will grow in most sites. Propagate by division from autumn to spring.

Euphorbia characias subsp. wulfenii
H 90–120cm (3–4ft), S 60–90cm (2–3ft)
Sun

Superb evergreen plant for architectural effect. From spring to early summer, large heads composed of many small, yellow-green 'bracts' are borne on tall stems. These should be cut out after flowering, leaving the new shoots which will bear the following year's flowers. Grow in well drained soil. Propagate from basal cuttings taken in spring.

Geranium
H 30–60cm (12–24in), S 45–60cm (18–24in)
Sun or part shade

Herbaceous geraniums are one of the most useful of all perennials. Ideal front-of-the-border plants, they flower profusely in summer, often with a second, smaller flush later on. Many varieties are available, and good ones include 'Johnson's Blue' (lavender-blue), *G.* × *oxonianum* varieties such as 'Wargrave Pink' (salmon-pink), *G. wallichianum* 'Buxton's Variety' (sky-blue, white centre) and *G. renardii* (white to pale blue flowers; velvety, puckered, sage-green leaves). *G. macrorrhizum* (pink flowers, large leaves that colour well in autumn) makes good ground cover for shade. Cut back to the ground after flowering to encourage neat mounds of fresh foliage. Geraniums grow well in any soil. Propagate by division from autumn to spring.

Nepeta × faassenii
CATMINT
H&S 45cm (18in)
Sun or part shade

Clump-forming plant with spreading stems clad with scalloped, silvery-grey leaves that are aromatic when crushed. Small spikes of lavender-blue flowers are borne from early summer to autumn. Irresistible to cats! Enjoys any well drained soil. Cut back hard after flowering to keep neat. Propagate by division from autumn to spring.

Anemone × hybrida
JAPANESE ANEMONE
H 90–120cm (3–4ft), S 60–90cm (2–3ft)
Sun or part shade

From a basal clump of palmate, green leaves rise tall, leafed stems topped with large saucer-shaped flowers, which are single or semi-double. Good varieties include 'Honorine Jobert' (single, white with pink underside to petals), 'Queen Charlotte' (semi-double, rich pink), 'Lady Gilmour' (double, pale pink) and 'Luise Uhink' (semi-double, white). The plants thrive in any soil that contains plenty of organic matter, but dislike poorly drained ground. They tend to spread, but are easily restricted (and propagated) by regular dividing every second or third year, from autumn to spring.

Aster × frikartii 'Mönch'
H 70cm (28in), S 30–45cm (12–18in)
Sun

Upright, long-flowering perennial that bears clear lavender-blue flowers with contrasting orange disc florets, on top of stout stems, in late summer and early autumn. Good disease resistance, unlike many other asters. Thrives in any soil with plenty of organic matter, but dislikes poorly drained ground. Propagate in spring, by division or from basal cuttings.

Aster thomsonii 'Nanus'
H 30–45cm (18in), S 30cm (12in)
Sun or part shade

Flowers are similar to those of A. × frikartii 'Mönch', but are borne on a smaller plant. Prefers a moisture-retentive soil. Propagate by division in spring.

Liriope muscari
LILYTURF
H 30cm (12in), S 45cm (18in)
Part or full shade

Evergreen perennial that forms neat, rounded clumps of narrow, strap-shaped, dark green leaves. From early to late autumn, dense, wand-like spikes of vibrant violet-purple flowers are borne on short stems. Several varieties are available, including 'John Burch' and 'Gold-banded', which have gold-and-green leaves, and 'Monroe White', with pure

Liriope muscari (lilyturf).

white flowers. Prefers light, well drained soil rich in organic matter, and will tolerate drought. Propagate by division in spring.

Schizostylis coccinea
KAFFIR LILY
H 60cm (24in), S 30cm (12in)
Sun

Forms a clump of erect, sword-shaped leaves, and bears spikes of flowers in autumn, each made up of several small, cup-shaped blooms. Flowers may persist into winter, weather permitting. Varieties include S. c. alba (white), 'Major' (red) and 'Mrs Hegarty' (pink). Plant in moist but well drained soil; water well in summer to promote flower production. Propagate by division in spring.

Sedum spectabile
ICE PLANT
H&S 45cm (18in)
Sun

Forms a clump of thick, fleshy, grey-green leaves, and in late summer and autumn produces large, flat heads composed of many tiny blooms which are attractive to bees and butterflies. Good varieties include 'Brilliant' (bright pink) and 'Iceberg' (pure white). Prefers well drained, neutral to alkaline soil. Propagate by division in spring.

FOLIAGE INTEREST

Alchemilla mollis
LADY'S MANTLE
H 45cm (18in), S 75cm (30in)
Sun or part shade

Forms a clump of attractive, scalloped, fresh green leaves. Tiny greenish-yellow flowers are borne in loose clusters in summer. Self-seeds freely, so deadhead immediately after flowering if seedlings are not wanted. Thrives in any reasonable soil. Propagate by division from autumn to spring.

Epimedium
BARRENWORT
H 30cm (12in), S 30–45cm (12–18in)
Part shade

Delicate, heart-shaped leaves form a spreading carpet of foliage, from which rise panicles of tiny, spurred flowers in spring. The leaves are often tinted with red in spring, and colour well in autumn. Prefers humus-rich soil and shelter from cold winds. In late winter, cut off the previous year's foliage so that the new flowers and leaves make a good display. Propagate by division in autumn or after flowering.

Heuchera hybrids

H 45cm (18in), S 30cm (12in)

Sun or part shade

Rounded to heart-shaped leaves form neat, spreading clumps of foliage. A large number of hybrids with attractively coloured leaves are now available, including 'Pewter Moon' (purple leaves mottled with silver), 'Snow Storm' (green mottled with silver) and *H. micrantha* var. *diversifolia* 'Palace Purple' (bronze-red). Heucheras grow well in any reasonable soil. Propagate by division in autumn.

Hosta

H 30–60cm (12–24in), S 60–90cm (24–36in)

Full or part shade

Clump-forming plants with large, lush, ovate to heart-shaped leaves. Leafless stems produce bell-shaped flowers in summer. Numerous species and hybrids are available that offer a wide range of foliage colours – principally grey-blue, green or gold – as well as a considerable range of different variegations. Hostas require moist, fertile soil and shelter from cold winds. Gold-leaved varieties colour best in a little sun. Slugs and snails adore hostas, so take preventative measures. Propagate by division in late summer or early spring.

Houttuynia cordata 'Chameleon'

H 15–30cm (6–12in), S to 60cm (24in)

Sun or part shade

Spreading perennial with heart-shaped, brightly coloured leaves that are unusually variegated in shades of green, yellow and red. Prefers moist, humus-rich soil. Can be invasive and so is best grown in a container. Propagate by division in spring.

Iris foetidissima

GLADDON IRIS, GLADWYN IRIS

H&S 45–60cm (18–24in)

Sun or shade

Glossy, dark green leaves form a clump of evergreen foliage. In early summer, stems topped with purple, yellow-tinged flowers are produced. These are insignificant in appearance, but are followed in autumn by inflated seed pods that split to reveal shiny, bright orange seeds. *I. f.* var. *citrina* has yellow flowers which are larger than those of the species. Tolerates poor soils. Propagate from seed sown in autumn or by division in late summer.

Iris pallida 'Variegata'

H&S 45cm (18in)

Sun or part shade

Forms a small, neat clump of upright leaves which are bright green striped with golden yellow. Leaves are retained all year unless the winter is severe. Stems topped with large, soft blue, yellow-bearded flowers are produced in late spring and early summer. Prefers well drained, neutral to acid soil. Propagate from seed sown in autumn or by division in late summer.

Macleaya cordata

PLUME POPPY

H to 2.4m (8ft), S to 0.9m (3ft)

Sun or part shade

Tall, imposing stems, which rarely need staking, are clad with large, lobed, grey to grey-green leaves. In mid- to late summer, the stems are topped with plume-like panicles of tiny buff flowers. Wonderful for introducing height to a border quickly. Prefers moist, well drained soil, but tolerates most conditions. Propagate by division in late autumn or spring.

Ophiopogon planiscapus 'Nigrescens'

H 20cm (8in), S 30cm (12in)

Sun or part shade

Grass-like, evergreen perennial with narrow, strap-shaped, almost black leaves that form a neat, rounded clump. Small, bell-shaped, purplish-white flowers in summer are followed by rounded, blue-black berries. Prefers retentive, moist but well drained soil. Propagate by division in spring.

Sisyrinchium striatum 'Aunt May', syn. *S. s.* 'Variegatum'

H to 45cm (18in), S 30cm (12in)

Sun

Clump-forming, evergreen perennial with iris-like leaves which are grey-green and attractively striped with creamy yellow. In summer, small, cup-shaped, pale yellow flowers are borne in clusters on upright stems. Requires well drained soil, preferably neutral to slightly alkaline. Propagate by division in spring.

Stachys byzantina, syn. *S. lanata*, *S. olympica*

H 30–45cm (12–18in), S 60cm (24in)

Sun

Mat-forming perennial with lance-shaped, woolly, grey-green foliage. Varieties include 'Primrose Heron' (yellowish-green leaves) and 'Silver Carpet' (white to silver). Prefers well drained soil. Propagate by division in spring.

Macleaya cordata (plume poppy).

ORNAMENTAL GRASSES

The grace and form of ornamental grasses give structure and long-lasting interest to a mixed planting.

Carex comans bronze form
H 30cm (12in), S 60cm (24in)
Sun or part shade

Evergreen grass that forms tussocks of hair-like leaves. Colours vary from reddish brown to bronze. Tolerates most soils, but avoid extremes of wet or dry. Propagate by division from mid-spring to early summer.

Carex hachijoensis 'Evergold'
H&S 30cm (12in)
Sun or part shade

Evergreen grass that forms a neat, low mound of slender leaves which are dark green with a broad, central golden stripe. Prefers fertile, moist but well drained soil. Propagate by division from mid-spring to early summer.

Deschampsia cespitosa 'Goldtau', syn. D. c. 'Golden Dew'
TUFTED HAIR GRASS
H 0.9–1.2m (3–4ft), S to 0.9m (3ft)
Sun or part shade

Tussock-forming, evergreen grass that forms a mound of slender, mid-green leaves. From early to late summer, airy panicles of flowers are produced in a splendid display. They are silvery at first, ageing to golden yellow. Grows on any reasonable soil, although dry ground should be enriched with organic matter. Cut off old flowerheads in spring. Propagate by division from mid-spring to early summer.

Festuca glauca
BLUE FESCUE
H&S 30cm (12in)
Sun

Dense, neat, evergreen grass that forms rounded clumps of fine, blue-grey leaves. Panicles of blue-green flowers are borne in summer. Prefers dry or well drained soil which is poor to moderately fertile. Propagate by division in spring.

Hakonechloa macra 'Aureola'
H 35cm (14in), S 45cm (18in)
Sun or part shade

Showy grass forming a clump of arching leaves, which are bright yellow striped narrowly with green. Small panicles of pale green flowers are borne in late summer. Prefers fertile, moist but well drained soil. Propagate by division in spring.

Miscanthus sinensis
H 1.2–1.5m (4–5ft), S to 0.9m (3ft)
Sun

Tall, bamboo-like grass which forms narrow clumps of upright stems. Long stems topped with dense pani- cles of flowers are borne in late summer and autumn, more profusely after a hot summer. Varieties include 'Gracillimus' (green leaves with white midribs), 'Morning Light' (silver leaf margins) and 'Zebrinus' (zebra grass – leaves banded horizontally with cream or pale yellow). Prefers fertile, moist, well drained soil, but tolerates most conditions. Propagate by division in spring.

Molinia caerulea 'Variegata'
PURPLE MOOR GRASS
H 45–60cm (18–24in), S 30–45cm (12–18in)
Sun or part shade

Compact, tuft-forming grass with dark green leaves striped with cream. From early summer onwards, produces tall yellow stems topped with purple spikelets. Prefers moist but well drained soil, ideally acid to neutral. Propagate by division in spring.

Pennisetum orientale
H 60cm (24in), S 75cm (30in)
Sun

Dense, mound-forming grass with narrow, dark green leaves. Grown mainly for its long-bristled flowerheads, which fountain outwards in mid- to late summer; they resemble bottle brushes or hairy caterpillars. Requires light, well drained soil. Propagate by division from late spring to early summer.

Pennisetum orientale.

ANNUALS

Nigella damascena (love-in-a-mist).

Calendula
POT MARIGOLD

Hardy annual

H&S 30–45cm (12–18in)

Sun or part shade

Easily grown plant that bears profuse quantities of yellow or orange flowers over a long period from early summer to autumn. Flowers best in poor, well drained soil. Sow seed *in situ* from early to mid-spring.

Cobaea scandens
CATHEDRAL BELLS,
CUP-AND-SAUCER PLANT

Treat as half-hardy annual

H 3–4.5m (10–15ft)

Sun

Vigorous climber, perennial in mild areas but usually grown as an annual, that scrambles by means of tendrils. Large, bell-shaped flowers with a 'ruff' at the base are borne from summer to autumn, opening pale green and ageing to purple. Requires a moist, fertile, welldrained soil and a sheltered site. Sow seed at 18°C (64°F) in spring.

Cosmos bipinnatus

Hardy annual

H to 120cm (48in), S 45cm (18in)

Sun

Upright plant with branching stems clothed with finely divided leaves. Single, saucer-shaped flowers in white, pink or crimson, with yellow centres, are borne in quantity through summer and autumn. Prefers moist but well drained soil. Sow seed *in situ* from early to mid-spring.

Eschscholzia californica
CALIFORNIAN POPPY

Hardy annual

H&S 45cm (18in)

Sun

Lax, spreading plant with finely divided grey-green leaves, which bears colourful, papery-petalled flowers in profusion through summer and autumn. Colours include yellow and orange. Prefers a poor, well-drained soil. Sow seed *in situ* from early to mid-spring.

Ipomoea tricolor 'Heavenly Blue'
MORNING GLORY

Half-hardy annual

H to 3m (10ft)

Sun

Fast-growing, twining climber that bears many large, saucer-shaped flowers in summer in an exquisite shade of blue, with a white throat. The blooms open in the morning and fade by the end of the day, but are generally produced in profusion to ensure a plentiful supply. Grow in fertile, well drained soil in a sheltered site. Sow seed at 18°C (64°F) in spring, soaking the seed for 24 hours before sowing.

Lathyrus odoratus
SWEET PEA

Hardy annual

H 1.8m (6ft)

Sun or light shade

Popular climber that bears racemes of fragrant flowers on short stems throughout summer. Numerous varieties are available in a wide range of colours, including single colours, bicolours and picotees. Excellent for cutting, and should not be allowed to set seed as flower production will then dwindle. Requires a rich, moisture-retentive soil. Sow seed in deep pots in autumn or early spring, soaking the seed overnight in tepid water before sowing.

Nicotiana
TOBACCO PLANT

Half-hardy annual

H 30–150cm (12–60in), S to 60cm (24in)

Sun or part shade

Rosette-forming plant that bears racemes of tubular or trumpet-shaped flowers for a long period through summer and sometimes into autumn. Colours include white, lime-green, salmon-pink and red. Some varieties give off a strong, sweet scent in the evening and at night. Many of the modern hybrids are compact, although the white-flowered *N. sylvestris* reaches 1.5m

(5ft). Prefers fertile, moist but well drained soil. Surface-sow seed at 18°C (64°F) in spring.

Nigella damascena
LOVE-IN-A-MIST

Hardy annual

H to 45cm (18in), S 23cm (9in)

Sun

Easily grown plant with feathery, bright green leaves and bearing many saucer-shaped flowers, each surrounded by a 'ruff', in summer. Colours are white, pale pink, pale blue and deep blue. The flowers are followed by decorative, inflated seed pods. Grows in any well drained soil. Sow seed *in situ* from early to mid-spring.

Tropaeolum majus and hybrids
NASTURTIUM

Hardy annual

H 0.6–3m (2–10ft)

Sun

Easily grown plants in a range of varieties, including climbing and bush forms. From summer to autumn, five-petalled flowers are produced in bright colours including red, orange and yellow. Some softer shades are available, such as 'Peach Melba', a bush form with creamy-yellow, red-centred flowers. The leaves and flowers are edible and can be used for culinary purposes. Nasturtiums flower best in fairly poor, well-drained soils. Sow seed *in situ* in spring.

Tropaeolum peregrinum
CANARY CREEPER

Hardy annual

H to 3m (10ft)

Sun

Vigorous annual climber with five-lobed, light green leaves. From summer to autumn, many small, fringed, bright yellow flowers are borne in the leaf axils. Prefers a reasonably fertile soil, but tolerates most conditions. Sow seed *in situ* from early to mid-spring.

BIENNIALS

Digitalis purpurea (foxglove).

Digitalis purpurea
FOXGLOVE

H to 120cm (48in), S 30cm (12in)

Part or full shade

Woodland plant that forms a rosette of green leaves and bears tall stems clothed with tubular flowers in early summer. Purple is the most common colour, although there are white, pink and apricot forms as well. Grows in almost any soil except very wet or dry ones. Sow seed *in situ* in late spring.

Erysimum cheiri
WALLFLOWER

H 25–75cm (10–30in), S 30cm (12in)

Sun

Short-lived perennial, best grown as a biennial. Forms mounds of foliage and bears clusters of open, sweetly scented flowers in spring, in shades of yellow, orange or red. Prefers poor to moderately fertile, well drained soil, ideally alkaline. Susceptible to clubroot disease. Sow from late spring to early summer in a nursery bed and transplant to the flowering site in autumn.

Hesperis matronalis
DAME'S VIOLET, SWEET ROCKET

H to 90cm (36in), S 45cm (18in)

Sun or part shade

Tall stems bearing clusters of lilac, purple or white flowers are borne from late spring to midsummer. The flowers are fragrant, particularly in the evening. Prefers fertile, moist but well drained soil, ideally neutral to alkaline. Sow seed *in situ* in spring.

Myosotis sylvatica
FORGET-ME-NOT

H to 30cm (12in), S 15cm (6in)

Sun or part shade

Compact plant that bears dense clusters of small, saucer-shaped, yellow-eyed flowers in blue or pink, in spring and early summer. Self-seeds readily. Prefers moist, well-drained soil. Sow seed *in situ* in early summer.

TENDER PERENNIALS

Bidens ferulifolia.

Arctotis
ZULU DAISY, AFRICAN DAISY
H 45cm (18 in), S 30cm (12in)
Sun

Compact plant that bears large, exceptionally showy, brightly coloured flowers in summer, mostly in shades of red and orange, above a neat mound of divided, silver-grey or grey-green foliage. Requires well drained soil. Propagate from cuttings taken in spring or autumn.

Argyranthemum
MARGUERITE
H&S 60–90cm (24–36in)
Sun

Tall, bushy plants with finely divided foliage that is pale green or grey-green. Daisy-like flowers in many colours, including white, yellow, peach and pink, are borne on short stems from summer to autumn. Both single- and double-flowered forms are available. Requires well drained soil. Propagate from cuttings taken in summer.

Bidens ferulifolia
H 30cm (12in), S to 1.2m (4ft)
Sun

Vigorous plant which quickly forms a spreading mass of trailing stems covered with finely divided, fresh green leaves and golden yellow, single, daisy-like flowers, borne from summer to autumn. Requires well-drained soil. Sow seed at 13–18°C (55–64°F) in spring, or take cuttings in spring or autumn.

Felicia amelloides
BLUE DAISY
H&S 30cm (12in)
Sun

Rounded, bushy plant that bears many tiny blue, yellow-centred 'daisy' flowers on short stems, from summer to autumn. Requires well drained soil. Propagate from cuttings taken in late summer.

Impatiens walleriana
BUSY LIZZIE
H&S to 45cm (18in)
Sun or shade

Bushy perennial that is usually grown as an annual, with spurred flowers in a wealth of colours including white, pink, apricot, salmon, coral, orange, violet, red and white-starred forms, as well as bicolours and picotees. Prefers a fertile, moisture-retentive soil. Sow seed at 18°C (64°F) in early spring, or take cuttings from spring to early summer.

Nemesia caerulea
H&S to 60cm (24in)
Sun

Lax, bushy plant that bears masses of two-lipped flowers which are white, blue, mauve or pink, with a yellow throat. 'Confetti' is pale pink and scented. Prefers moist but well drained soil. Propagate from cuttings taken in late summer.

Pelargonium
GERANIUM
H to 60cm (24in), S 45cm (18in)
Sun

Extensive group of bushy plants that bear large clusters of flowers on short stems. Numerous varieties are available, both bush and trailing forms, with flowers in colours that include red, white, pink, salmon, and bicolours. Prefers fertile, well drained soil, ideally neutral to alkaline. Propagate from cuttings taken in spring or late summer. Do not cover the cuttings with polythene.

BULLBS

Lilium regale (regal lily).

Chionodoxa
GLORY-OF-THE-SNOW
H 10cm (4in)
Sun or part shade

Dwarf bulb that bears deep blue, white-centred, star-shaped flowers in short racemes in early spring. Grows in any well drained soil. Propagate from seed sown in a cold frame as soon as ripe.

Crocus speciosus
AUTUMN-FLOWERING CROCUS
H to 15cm (6in)
Sun or part shade

Goblet-shaped flowers in shades of blue or lilac are borne in autumn, the flowers appearing before the leaves. Self-seeds readily and is good for naturalizing in grass. Prefers well drained soil. Propagate from seed sown in a cold frame in autumn.

Crocus vernus
DUTCH CROCUS
H to 15cm (6in)
Sun or part shade

Dwarf bulb that bears colourful, goblet-shaped flowers in spring, in shades of violet and white. Requires well-drained, even gritty soil. Propagate by removing offsets from the bulbs during dormancy.

Cyclamen hederifolium
H to 15cm (6in)
Part or full shade

Dainty flowers with reflexed, swept-back petals, in shades of pale lilac-pink with dark pink markings at the mouth, are borne from mid- to late autumn. The flowers appear before the leaves, which are rounded and marbled with silver. Prefers humus-rich, well drained soil, and is best under trees and shrubs to remain dry in summer. Generally self-seeds well.

Eranthis hyemalis
WINTER ACONITE
H 8cm (3in)
Sun or shade

Dwarf bulb that is very early to flower, bearing bright yellow, cup-shaped flowers, with a 'ruff' of green leaves, in late winter and early spring. Prefers humus-rich soil that does not dry out in summer. Propagate by dividing established clumps of bulbs immediately after flowering.

Galanthus nivalis
SNOWDROP
H to 15cm (6in)
Sun or part shade

Early-flowering bulb that blooms in winter, bearing small, bell-shaped white flowers with green markings. Tolerates most soils but does best in one that is fertile and humus-rich. Establishes best if planted after flowering while in leaf ('in the green'). Propagate by dividing established clumps of bulbs immediately after flowering.

Lilium regale
REGAL LILY
H to 1.2m (4ft)
Sun or part shade

One of the easiest lilies to grow, this species produces large, trumpet-shaped white flowers, with purple markings and a yellow throat, which are exceptionally fragrant. Does best in a welldrained soil enriched with organic matter, with the roots in the shade and the 'head' in the sun. Grows in all but very alkaline soils. Propagate by seed sown as soon as ripe.

Muscari azureum
GRAPE HYACINTH
H 20cm (8in)
Sun or part shade

Vigorous bulb that bears tiny, deep blue flowers in cone-shaped clusters during spring. May self-seed freely. Prefers moist but well drained soil. Propagate from seed sown in a cold frame in autumn.

Narcissus cyclamineus varieties
DAFFODIL
H 30cm (12in)
Sun or part shade

Of the many different types of narcissi, the cyclamineus varieties, with their dainty, swept-back petals and delicate colours, are among the prettiest. They flower from early to mid-spring, and varieties include 'Jack Snipe' (white with a pale yellow trumpet) and 'Jenny' (creamy white). Narcissi tolerate a range of soils, but grow best in fertile, moisture-retentive but well drained soil. Propagate by separating bulbs from established clumps in early autumn.

Index

Page numbers in *italic* refer to the illustrations

geraniums (perennial) 49, 63, 150
Gladwyn/Gladdon iris 49, 152
Gleditsia triacanthos 67, 70, 128
globe thistle 150
glory-of-the-snow 38, 75, 157
golden elder 137
golden hop 143
golden marguerite 150
grape hyacinth 157
grass, getting rid of 17–18
grasses, ornamental 28, 36, 51, 53–4, 71, 106–7, 125, 153
greenhouses 21, 35
guelder rose 137

H

Hakonechloa marca 67, 107, 153
hanging baskets 102, 103, 104, 110, 122
heather 71, 110, 131, 133
heaths 52
Hebe 30, 53, 63, 64, 67, 69, 108, 131–2, 134
Hedera 28, 63, 64, 67, 82, 84, 98, 107, 142–3
hedges 10, 14, 23, 28, 95–8
Helichrysum italicum 30, 67, 136–7
hellebores 49, 149
herbs 30, 32
Hesperis matronalis 33, 38, 75, 155
Heuchera 50, 67, 71, *105*, 152
holly 49, 58, 108, 134
honey locust 128
honeysuckle 30, 49, 53, 82, 88, *90*, 96, 98, 135, 141
hornbeam 97
horned violet 50, 150
Hosta 28, 51, 67, 68, *105*, 106, 125, 152
Houttuynia cordata 67, 107, 152
Humulus lupulus 67, 70, 84, 88, *143*, 143
Hydrangea 48, 85, 140

I

ice plant 35, 151
Ilex 49, 58, 62, 64, 67, 108, 134
Impatiens walleriana 156
informal style 30, *31*
Ipomoea tricolor 92, 154
Iris 49, 152
Italian buckthorn 53, 55, 135
ivies 28, 33, 46–8, 82, 84, 98, 107, 142–3

J

Japanese anemone 71, 151
Japanese gardens 28
Japanese golden grass 107
Japanese maple 28, 51, 68, *135*, 135–6
jasmine 30, 67, 84, 88, 91, 98, 108, 141, 143
Judas tree 53, *126*, 128
junipers 55, 70, *147*, 147–8

K

Kaffir lily 151
Kashmir sorbus 129

L

laburnum, evergreen 141–2
lady's mantle 35, 50, 68, 69, 71
lamb's ears 36
Lathyrus latifolius 30, 63, 74, 88, 141
Lathyrus odoratus 154
laurel 28, 48, 130, 133
Laurus nobilis 62, 134
Lavandula 67, 132
Lavatera 30, 70, 74, 108, 132
lavender 28, 30, 34, 53, 132
lawns, getting rid of 17–18
layering 124
Lenten rose 49, 149
lesser periwinkle 135
Ligustrum 28, 58, 62, 64, 67, 96, 134
lilac 33, *131*, 131
lilies 74, *157*, ʼ157
lilyturf 50, 71, 106, 151
lime trees 97
Liriope muscari 50, 67, 71, 106, 151
Lonicera 49, 53, 67, 82, 88, 96, 135, 141
Lotus hirsutus 67, 132
love-in-a-mist 38, 76, *154*, 155
lungwort 49, 149

M

Macleaya cordata 64, 67, 96, *152*, 152
Mahonia 30, 64, 133
Malus 35, 94, 127, 128–9
maquis 34
marguerites 57, 77, 156
Mediterranean gardens 26, 33–4, 111
Mentha pulegium 30
Mexican orange blossom 30, 49, 134
Michaelmas daisies 35
Miscanthus sinensis 54, 153
mixed borders 64
mock orange *see Philadelphus*
Molinia caerulea 153

morning glory 92, 154
mountain ash *129*, 129
mulching *117*, 117, 120
Muscari azureum 157
Myosotis 33, 75, 155

N

Narcissus 157
nasturtiums 92, 105, 155
neighbouring plants 11, 23
Nemesia caerulea 156
Nepeta 67, 150
New Zealand flax 34, 53, 69, 80, 135
Nicotiana 105, 154–5
Nigella damascena 38, 63, 69, 76, *154*, 155
nursery area 21, 35

O

obelisks *91*, 91–2
Ophiopogon planiscapus 70, 71, 152
oriental style 26, 28–30, *29*
ornamental vine 49, 143
Osmanthus 28–9, 130
Osteospermum 34, 56, 105
overgrown gardens 21–3
overplanting 37–8

P

pampas grass 35
Papaver 35, 38
Parahebe catarractae 132
Parthenocissus 49, 82, 85, 143
Passiflora caerulea 30, 88, 98, 108, 141
paths, plants for edging 70–1
patios *18*, 21
Pelargonium 34, 156
Pennisetum orientale *153*, 153
pennyroyal mint 30
perennial pea 30, 63, 74, 88, 141
perennials
    basal cuttings 125
    in containers 105–6
    dividing 125
    drought-loving 55–6
    early-flowering 70
    herbaceous 149–52
    lifting and dividing 38
    overgrown herbaceous 22–3
    shade-tolerant 48–9, 49–50, 69
    tender 34, 77, 103, 104, 125, 156
pergolas 86–7
Persian ivy 142–3
pest control 120
Philadelphus 22, 33, 132
Phormium 34, 53, 67, 69, 80, 135

Phygelius 30, 71, *132*, 132
Physocarpus opulifolius 53, 63, 67, 137
Picea glauca 148
pinks 30–2
Pinus mugo *148*, 148
plans, drawing up 39–43
plant enthusiasts 34–5
planting 116–17
    distances 37–8
    in groups 38
    to scale 56–7
pleached hedges 96–8
plume poppy 64, 96, 152
poisonous plants 35, 36
poppies 35, 38
pot marigold 32, 38, 154
potentilla 30, *68*, 132
primroses 36
privacy 12, 93–9
privet 10, 28, 58, 62, 96, 134
pruning 120
    clematis 140
    evergreen shrubs 22
    overgrown shrubs 22
    roses 145, 146
    shrub roses 146
Prunus 58, 60, 94, 127–8
Pulmonaria 49, 67, 70, 149
purple moor grass 153
Pyracantha 28, 49, 64, 70, 74, 108, 142
Pyrus salicifolia 67, 128

Q

quince, flowering 138

R

raised beds 16, 17, 110–11, *111*
red campion 36
Rhamnus alaternus 35, 55, 96, 135
rhododendrons, dwarf 28, 51–2, 130–1
rosemary 53, 68, 132–3
roses 53, 54, 70, 144–7
    climbing 30, 54, 73, 84, 88–9, 145–6
    for containers 108
    scented 88
    for shady sites 49, 50
    cultivation 144
    diseases 144
    ground-cover 54, 146–7
    pests 144
    pruning 145–6
    rambling 30, 54, 88
    shrub roses 53, 144, 146
rowan *129*, 129
rue 137
Ruta graveolens 67, 137

ACKNOWLEDGEMENTS

Jonathan Buckley 6–7 (Designer: Penny Smith/Sycamore Mews, London), 19 Helen Yemm's Garden, London, SW17), 20 (Catalyst Television/Designer: Jean Bishop), 29 (John Tordoff's Garden, London, E8), 72 (Great Dixter, East Sussex), 117 (Catalyst Television); **John Glover** 37 (John Chamber's Garden/Design: Julie Toll), 45 (Beechcroft Rd, Oxon), 47 (Nash's Garden, Shropshire), 77 (Styling & Photography: John Glover), 131, 132, 140, 145, 146, 147 (Rushwood Close, Walsall), 153; **Jerry Harpur** 24 (Sun House, Long Melford, Suffolk), 34 (Dr Lichfield, Long Melford, Suffolk), 53 (House of Pitmuies, Forfar, Scotland), 59 (Design: Judith Sharpe, London), 69 (Park Farm, Gt Waltham, Essex), 101 (Design: Anne Alexander-Sinclair, London), 123 (Design: Christopher Masson, London), 126 (Beth Chatto), 129, 143 (Fudlers Hall, Mashbury, Essex), 147 (Keith Kirsten, South Africa), 152, 154; **Marcus Harpur** 27 (Design: Jonathan Baillie, London), 54 I Design Andy Rees, Bucks.), 57 (Design: Jonathan Baillie, London), 76 (RHS Chelsea/Design: Rupert Golby), 105 (Design: Susan Rowley), 131; **Anne Hyde** 2 (Ivan Meals & David Boyer, Great Brickhill), 9 (Lucy Sommers, 13 Queen Elizabeth's Walk, London), 15 (Helen Faulls, 35 Wincanton Rd, London), 17 (Ruth Thornton, 156 Balfour Rd, Northampton), 25 (Mr & Mrs Bennett, Lavender Hill, Enfield), 26 (Chris & Fiona Royffe, Fieldhead, Boston Spa, Yorks), 31 (Sue Hillwood-Harris, 133 Crystal Palace Rd, London), 32 (Chris Hubbard, Hitchin, Herts), 48 (Mrs John Raven, Docwras Manor, Shepreth, Cambs), 61 (Helen Faulls, 35 Wincanton Rd, London), 62 (Mr & Mrs N. Coote, 40 Osler Rd, Oxford), 66 (Ruth Thornton, 156 Balfour Rd, Northampton), 83 (Meg & Jeff Blumson, 20 St Peters Rd, Cirencester, Gloucs), 89 (Mr & Mrs Bennett, Lavender Hill, Enfield), 90 (Mrs Montgomery, Wisteria Cottage, Maidwell, Northants), 91 (Mrs Montgomery, Wisteria Cottage, Maidwell, Northants), 95 (Meg & Jeff Blumson, 20 St Peters Rd, Cirencester, Gioucs), 99 (Cecilia Gonzalez, Ellesmere Gardens, Essex), 111 (Ivan Mears & David Boyer, Great Brickhill), 113 (33 Richborough Rd, London), 116 (Mr & Mrs Nicholas Calvert, Walton Poor, Surrey), 127 (RHS Hyde Hall, Essex), 128 (Mrs M. A. Willis, Ivy Lodge, Radway, Warks), 130 (Graham & Judy Brown, Masham Manor, Surrey), 136 (Clapton Court Gardens, Somerset), 138 (Helen Faulls, 35 Wincanton Rd, London), 144 (Grallam Judy Brown, Masham Manor, Surrey), 148 (The Valley Gardens, Windsor, Surrey), 149 (Clare College Fellows' Garden, Cambridge), 151 (Mr & Mrs D. Ward, 53 Ladywood, Eastleigh, Hants), 157 (Hoare's Bank, London); **Andrew Lawson** 72, 84, 94 (Designer: Mirabel Osler), 97, 133, 135, 150, 153 (Designer: Carol Klein, Glebe Cottage Plants), 155, 156; **Clive Nichols** 13 (Designer: Anthony Noel), 14, 41 (Hilary MacPherson), 142.